Guide to
Adirondack Trails:

HIGH PEAKS
REGION

Eleventh Edition
The Forest Preserve Series, Volume I

Editor, Tony Goodwin
Series Editor, Neal S. Burdick

The Adirondack Mountain Club, Inc.

Copyright © 1985 by
The Adirondack Mountain Club, Inc.
All rights reserved.

Design by Mary Kammerer; also Lange, Collyer & Associates, Inc.

First Edition	1934
Second Edition	1941
Third Edition	1945
Fourth Edition	1947
Fifth Edition	1950
Sixth Edition	1957
Seventh Edition	1962
Reprinted with minor revisions	1966
Reprinted with minor supplement	1968
Fourth Printing	1969
Fifth Printing	1971
Eighth Edition	1972
Reprinted with minor revisions	1973
Reprinted with minor revisions	1975
Ninth Edition	1977
Reprinted with revisions	1979
Tenth Edition	1980
Reprinted with revisions	1983
Eleventh Edition	1985

Library of Congress Cataloging in Publication Data
Main entry under title:
Guide to Adirondack trails.

   (Forest preserve series ; v. 1)
   Includes index.
   1. Hiking — New York (State) — Adirondack Park — Guide-books.
2. Trails — New York (State) — Adirondack Park — Guide-books.
3. Adirondack Park (N.Y.) — Guide-books.

I. Adirondack Mountain Club.   II. Series.
GV199.42.N652A343   1985   917.47'53   85-4102
ISBN 0-935272-25-9

PRINTED IN THE
UNITED STATES OF AMERICA

DEDICATION
Orra A. Phelps

If it is possible for any one individual in her full life of achievement to personify the dual spirit and purpose of the Adirondack Mt. Club, Orra A. Phelps shines as our finest companion.

In her early seasons in the high peaks, Orra explored the mountains and the trails, then edited the first edition of this trail guide, in order to lead others to the joys and satisfaction of the wilderness experience. In subsequent years, Orra devoted her technical skills in botany and nature study to the development of our natural history program at Heart Lake, there for many years serving as Ranger-Naturalist and sharing her insights into the wondrous world around us as we climb. A whole generation of ADKers owes much of their understanding of the mountains to the educational programs presented by Orra and her associates. In the quality of her life and her service to others, Orra pioneered pathways that ever beckon others to follow, as they too explore and enjoy the many faces of the high peaks.

In that first edition, published in 1934, she proposed a series of guides to the trails throughout the Adirondacks. This eleventh edition is to be the flagship of just such a series, and thus, "better late than never," her dream is now on its way to becoming reality.

To our dear friend, Orra A. Phelps, we gratefully dedicate this eleventh edition.

E.H. KETCHLEDGE

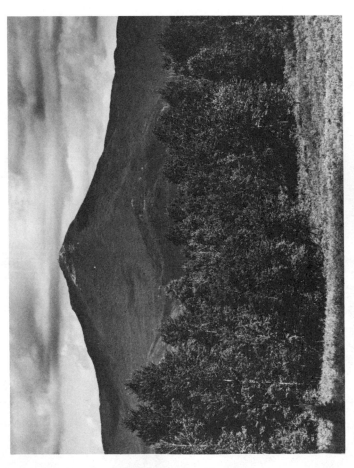

Whiteface Mt. from Rt. 73
Photo by Bob Meyer

PREFACE TO
THE ELEVENTH EDITION

Over fifty years ago, the Adirondack Mountain Club published the first edition of this guidebook under the leadership of Dr. Orra Phelps. Since then, nine further editions have been published and the book has expanded to include detailed descriptions of all the trails within the High Peaks Region. In preparing the eleventh edition, I hiked nearly 400 miles during the summer of 1984, checking and remeasuring many trails, including some not checked since the original detailed measurements were made in the mid-50s. The guide has also been thoroughly rewritten with the idea of improving readability. Unnecessary details have been eliminated in favor of emphasizing easily recognizable landmarks. Also emphasized is such information as currently legal campsites and the condition or absence of key bridges — both important for trip planning.

In previous editions, the trail descriptions were divided into ten sections plus an addendum for the Northville-Placid Trail. This edition combines several of those smaller sections such as "Saranac Lake" and "Lake Placid" into larger regions, and includes the descriptions of various sections of the Northville-Placid Trail in the appropriate region rather than as a separate section. As an aid to first-time visitors to the area, the introduction to each section now includes recommended hikes of varying degrees of difficulty within that section.

I have also done a thorough "housecleaning" of the material appended at the end of previous editions. Gone are the sections on ski centers and canoe routes, as that information is available elsewhere and does not really belong in a hiking guide. Also gone are listings of DEC campgrounds in other parts of the Adirondack

Park as well as the listing of lean-tos outside of the High Peaks Region. The ADK's Forest Preserve Series will soon cover all areas of the Adirondack Park, and this information will be available in far greater detail in the appropriate guides for the other parts of the Park.

The section entitled "Peaks Without Maintained Trails" has been continued in much the same format, with a few important revisions, such as information on the current legal approaches to Allen Mt. Other trailless areas within the High Peaks Region are at least mentioned, along with enough information on the best approaches so that interested hikers can get started on their own explorations of these seldom-visited areas.

A final and very important section that has been changed is that pertaining to wilderness camping. Since the inception of the DEC's Park Ranger Program in 1978, much information has been obtained on how to prevent the continued physical deterioration of heavily used backcountry areas. This has resulted in the promulgation and enforcement of some new regulations concerning camping. Early indications are that these regulations have successfully halted much of the deterioration, making unnecessary a cumbersome and restrictive permit system to reduce overall use. Thus each hiker has the responsibility to obey these regulations, not just out of fear of the legal consequences, but also because compliance will prevent deterioration of these beautiful wilderness lands and therefore enhance the experience of all who follow.

Finally, I would like to express heartfelt thanks to a number of people who contributed to the successful completion of this project. First, all previous editors — Orra Phelps, A.T. Shorey, L. Morgan Porter, Donald McLaughlin and Lawrence Cotter — deserve thanks for the data they have helped to compile over the years, data which made possible the rapid completion of this new edition. Second, my father, James A. Goodwin, who has had a hand in many previous editions, must be thanked for again editing the section on the trailless peaks and also for providing information on several trails I did not cover. Third, thanks is due my current employer, the Olympic Regional Development Authority of Lake Placid, which was kind enough to permit the summer's leave of absence needed to complete this project. And finally, many thanks and eternal gratitude to my wife, Bunny, who not only helped with the typing of the manuscript, but also endured my repeated absences while on the trail and my long days and nights of editing. Through it all she was supportive and understanding, even though she was fully occupied herself with the business of giving birth to and caring for a fine and healthy son named Morgan.

TONY GOODWIN
Keene, New York
May, 1985

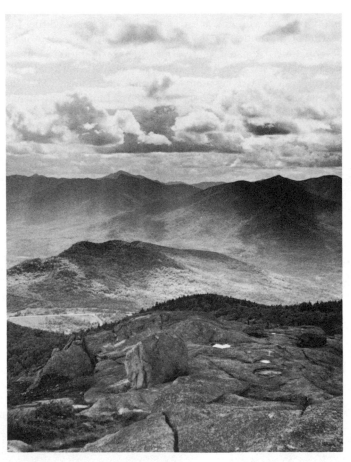

Keene Valley from Hurricane
Photo by R. Meyer

CONTENTS

PAGE MAPS

INTRODUCTION

THE ADIRONDACK MOUNTAIN CLUB
FOREST PRESERVE SERIES

The Forest Preserve Series of Guides to Adirondack Trails is the only series to cover all hiking opportunities on the more than two million acres of public Forest Preserve land located within the Adirondack Park. The Adirondack Mountain Club (ADK), published the first guidebook in this series over fifty years ago with the idea that hiking guides would eventually cover all Forest Preserve lands; it is appropriate that the completion of this series coincide with the decade-long centennial celebration of the enactment of the Forest Preserve legislation. Each guide in this series, listed below, has been written or revised within the last few years, with the most recent (or projected) date of publication provided in parentheses:

Vol. I: *Guide to Adirondack Trails: High Peaks Region* (1985)

Vol. II: *Guide to Adirondack Trails: Northern Region* (1986)

Vol. III: *Guide to Adirondack Trails: Central Region* (1986)

Vol. IV: *Guide to Adirondack Trails: Northville-Placid Trail* (1986)

Vol. V: *Guide to Adirondack Trails: Southern Region* (1987)

Vol. VI: *Guide to Adirondack Trails: West-Central Region* (1987)

Vol. VII: *Guide to Adirondack Trails: Eastern Region* (1987)

The public lands that constitute the Adirondack Forest Preserve are unique among all other wild public lands in the United States because they enjoy constitutional protection against sale or development. The story of this unique protection begins with the earliest history of the Adirondacks as recounted below, and it continues today as groups such as the Adirondack Mountain Club strive to guard this constitutional protection. The protection of many of the scenic and aesthetic resources of the Forest Preserve also rests with the individual hiker who has the responsibility not to degrade these resources in any way while enjoying their wonders. The Forest Preserve Series of trail guides seeks not only to show hikers where to hike but also to interpret the area's natural and social history and offer guidelines whereby users can minimize their impact on the land.

The Adirondacks

The Adirondack region of northern New York is unique in many ways. It contains the only mountains in the eastern U.S. that are not geologically Appalachian. In the late 1800s it was the first forested area in the nation to benefit from enlightened conservation measures. At roughly the same time it was also the most prestigious resort area in the country. In the 20th century, the Adirondacks became the only place in the Western Hemisphere to host two Winter Olympiads. In the 1970s the region was the first of significant size in the nation to experience comprehensive land use controls. The Adirondack Forest Preserve (see below) is part of the only wild lands preserve in the nation whose fate lies in the hands of the voters of the entire state in which it is located.

Geologically, the Adirondacks are part of the Canadian Shield, a vast terrane of ancient Precambrian igneous and metamorphic rock that underlies about half of Canada and constitutes the nucleus of the North American continent. In the U.S. the Shield bedrock mostly lies concealed under younger Paleozoic sedimentary rock strata, but it is well exposed in a few regions, among them the Adirondacks. The Adirondacks are visibly connected across the Thousand Islands to the Grenville Province of the eastern side of the Shield, which is around one billion years old. Upward doming of the Adirondack mass in the past few million years — a process that is still going on — is responsible for the erosional stripping of the younger rock cover and exposure of the ancient bedrock. The rocks here are mainly gneisses of a wide range of composition. One of the more interesting and geologically puzzling rocks is the enormous anorthosite mass that makes up nearly all of the High Peaks region. A nearly monomineralic rock composed of plagioclase feldspar, this peculiar rock was apparently formed at depths of up to fifteen miles below the surface. It is nearly identical to some of the rocks brought back from the moon.

The present Adirondack landscape is geologically young, a product of erosion initiated by the ongoing doming. The stream-carved topography has been extensively modified by the sculpturing of glaciers which, on at least four widely separated occasions during the Ice Age, completely covered the mountains.

Ecologically, the Adirondacks are part of a vegetation transition zone, with the northern, largely coniferous boreal forest (from the Greek god Boreas, owner of the north wind, whose name can be found on a mountain peak and series of ponds in the High Peaks region) and the southern deciduous forest, exemplified by beech/maple stands, intermingling to present a pleasing array of forest tree species. Different vegetation zones are also encountered as one ascends the higher mountains in the Adirondacks; the tops of the highest peaks are truly arctic, with mosses and lichens that are common hundreds of miles to the north.

A rugged and heavily forested region, the Adirondacks were generally not hospitable to native Americans, who used the region principally for hunting and occasionally for fighting. Remnants of ancient campgrounds have been found in some locations. The native legacy survives principally in such place names as Indian Carry, on the Raquette River-Saranac Lakes canoe route, and the Oswegatchie River in the northwest Adirondacks.

The first white man to see the Adirondacks was likely the French explorer Jacques Cartier, who on his first trip up the St. Lawrence River in 1535 stood on top of Mont Royal (now within the city of Montréal) and discerned high ground to the south. Closer looks were had by Samuel de Champlain and Henry Hudson, who came from the north and south, respectively, by coincidence within a few weeks of each other in 1609.

For the next two centuries the Champlain Valley to the east of the Adirondacks was a battleground. Iroquois, Algonquin, French, British and eventually American fighters struggled for control over the valley and with it supremacy over the continent. Settlers slowly filled the St. Lawrence Valley to the north, the Mohawk Valley to the south, and somewhat later the Black River Valley to the west. Meanwhile the vast, rolling forests of the interior slumbered in virtual anonymity, disturbed only by an occasional hunter, timber cruiser or wanderer.

With the coming of the 19th century, people discovered the Adirondacks. Virtually unknown as late as the 1830s (the source of the Nile River was located before the source of the Hudson), by 1850 the Adirondacks made New York the leading timber-producing state in the nation. This distinction did not last for long, though, as the supply of timber was quickly brought close to extinction. Meanwhile, mineral resources, particularly iron, were being exploited.

After the Civil War, people began to look toward the Adirondacks for recreation as well as for financial gain. An economic boom, increasing acceptability of leisure time, and the publication of a single book, *Adventures in the Wilderness* by the Rev. William H. H. Murray in 1869, combined to create a veritable flood of vacationers descending upon the Adirondacks. To serve them, a new industry, characterized by grand hotels and rustic guides, sprang up. Simultaneously, thanks to the pioneering work of Dr.

Edward Livingston Trudeau, the Adirondacks, particularly the Saranac Lake area, became known far and wide as a mecca for tubercular patients.

In the decades following the Civil War the idea of conservation began to take on some legitimacy, thanks in large part to the book *Man and Nature* written by George Perkins Marsh in 1864. In this remarkably influential book, which noted historian Lewis Mumford once called "the fountainhead of the American conservation movement," Marsh called for the implementation of such practices as reforestation and watershed protection, and suggested that the Adirondacks were a good laboratory for testing these ideas.

Another trend in the middle decades of the 19th century was an increasing acceptance of wilderness. This was brought about partly through the work of poets such as William Cullen Bryant, writers such as Henry David Thoreau, and artists such as Frederick Church. Also contributing to this trend was the fact that, as the frontier moved steadily westward, the wilderness was no longer seen as a physical threat, at least not in the more populous, affluent East.

Vacationers, tubercular patients, conservationists, wilderness devotees — all of these people wanted to see the resources of the Adirondacks preserved. This was partially achieved in 1885, when, after much political wrangling, the New York State legislature created the Adirondack Forest Preserve and directed that "the lands now or hereafter constituting the Forest Preserve shall be forever kept as wild forest lands." This action marked the first time a state government had set aside a significant piece of wilderness for reasons other than its scenic uniqueness.

In 1892, the legislature created the Adirondack State Park, consisting of Adirondack Forest Preserve land plus all privately owned land within a somewhat arbitrary boundary surrounding the Adirondacks, known as the "blue line" because it was drawn in blue on a large state map when it was first established. In 1894, in response to continuing abuses of the Forest Preserve law, the state's voters approved the inclusion of the "forever wild" portion of that law in the constitution of New York State, thus creating the only wild land preserve in the nation that has constitutional protection. Today the Forest Preserve consists of 2.5 million acres, being those lands owned by the people of the State of New York that are within the 6-million-acre Adirondack State Park, which is the largest park in the nation outside of Alaska.

In the first decade of the 20th century, raging fires consumed hundreds of thousands of acres of prime Adirondack forest lands; the scars from these fires can still be seen in many locations, both in exposed rock and in vegetation patterns. After World War I, tourism gradually took over as the primary industry in the Adirondacks. The arrival of the automobile, the invention of theme parks (some of the very first of which were in the Adirondacks), the development of winter sports facilities (with Lake Placid hosting the Winter Olympics in 1932), the increasing popularity of camping and hiking, and the growth of the second-home industry all brought such pressures to bear on the region that in 1968 Governor Nelson Rockefeller created a Temporary Study Commission on the Future of the Adirondacks. This commission made 181 recommendations, chief among them that a comprehensive land use plan, covering both public and private lands, be put in place and administered. This was accomplished by 1973, with the creation of the land use plans and the Adirondack Park Agency to manage them. While the plans and the Agency have remained controversial, they are indicative of the need to address the issues facing the Adirondacks boldly and innovatively.

In 1985, there are 112,000 permanent residents and 90,000 seasonal residents in the 9375-square-mile Adirondack Park, which is roughly the size of Vermont. Recreation, forestry, mining and agriculture are the principal industries in the Park.

THE HIGH PEAKS REGION

Using This Guidebook

The trails described in this book are all in the High Peaks region of the Adirondacks, which derives its name from the fact that it contains all of the Adirondack peaks with elevations over 4,000 feet, as well as numerous other mountains under 4,000 feet. The region is located in the interior of the northeastern quadrant of the Adirondack State Park (see accompanying map) and includes the villages of Lake Placid, Saranac Lake, Keene, Keene Valley and Newcomb. The principal highways in the region are NY 73 in the north and northeast, and NY 28N and Essex County Road 2B in the south; US 9 and Interstate 87, "The Adirondack Northway," establish the region's eastern boundary for the most part.

Like all the books in the Adirondack Mountain Club Forest Preserve Series of Guides to Adirondack Trails, this book is intended to be both a reference tool for planning trips and a field guide to carry on the trail. All introductory material should be read carefully, for it contains important information regarding the use of this book, as well as numerous suggestions for safe and proper travel by foot in the Adirondacks. For campers, there is an important section on the relevant rules and regulations for camping in the Adirondacks.

The introductions to each of the sections in this book will give hikers an idea of the varied opportunities available in the High Peaks region. There are many beautiful and seldom-visited places aside from the most popular hiking, climbing and camping areas; this guide will enable you to find and explore these remote spots.

Mount Marcy

Mt. Marcy, the highest peak in the Adirondacks, rises 5344 ft. above sea level. It was named in 1837 in honor of Governor William

Learned Marcy by Ebenezer Emmons, Professor of Chemistry at Williams College and Geologist-in-Chief of the second District of the Geological Survey of New York. Emmons was the leader of the party that made the first recorded ascent on August 5, 1837. An Indian name, "Tahawus," has also been applied to this peak; but in reality this name was not used by local Indians and was first used by a writer of that era in referring to the recently climbed peak. Pronounced "Ta-HA-wus," the name means "cloud-splitter."

The first trail up Marcy was cut by "Old Mountain" Phelps and other guides about 1861 from Upper Ausable Lake. This trail roughly followed the current trail from the Warden's Camp to the top of Bartlett Ridge, from which it slabbed the side of Haystack and dropped down to cross Panther Gorge NE of the present Panther Gorge Lean-to. From the bottom of Panther Gorge, the trail ascended Marcy via some slides on the SE slopes to timberline. This trail was abandoned after 1873 when men working on Verplanck Colvin's Adirondack Survey cut a trail up the valley of Marcy Brook and up to Four Corners, similar to the route of the present Elk Lake-Marcy Trail.

The last 800 ft. of its crest rises above timberline — an irregular rocky dome with alpine vegetation growing in the crevices and depressions where soil has accumulated. A copper bolt was set into the actual summit at the time of the Colvin Survey in 1875, but it has since been removed and only the drill hole now remains. A brass disk set in place in the 1940s has also regrettably been removed by souvenir hunters. On a vertical rock wall just below the summit is a bronze plaque (see below) commemorating the first recorded ascent of this "High Peak of Essex."

The view from Marcy on a clear day is of an endless wilderness of irregular mountaintops and miles of unbroken forest. Only to the N and far E are farmlands and villages visible. To the ESE near at hand is Haystack, the third highest Adirondack summit, with its

1837—MARCY—1937
Also Known by the Indian Name
TAHAWUS
Meaning "Cloud-Splitter"

ON AUGUST 5, 1837 THE FIRST RECORDED ASCENT
OF THIS MOUNTAIN WAS MADE AND ITS HEIGHT
MEASURED. IT WAS NAMED MT. MARCY IN HONOR
OF GOVERNOR WILLIAM LEARNED MARCY, WHO
HAD APPOINTED A COMMISSION TO MAKE THE FIRST
GEOLOGICAL SURVEY OF THE NORTHERN DISTRICT.

The following made the ascent:
  Prof. Ebenezer Emmons of Williams, and
  James Hall, state geologist;
  Prof. John Torrey, botanist;
  Professors Strong and Miller, geologists;
  William C. Redfield, engineer and meteorologist;
  C.C. Ingham, artist and Ebenezer Emmons, Jr.;
  Archibald McIntyre and David Henderson,
  original explorers and early owners of this region;
  Harvey Holt and John Cheney, guides;
  and three unknown woodsmen.

Erected by the Adirondack Mountain Club in conjunction
with the Conservation Department of New York State.

(Editor's note: The Conservation Department mentioned above is
presently the Department of Environmental Conservation of New
York State. Also, more recent research indicates that three of the
individuals named on the plaque — Strong, Miller and McIntyre
—did not actually make the ascent.)

long rocky crestline. Between Marcy and Haystack is the precipitous Panther Gorge. From Haystack, the Great Range runs NE toward Keene Valley. Prominent in this range, ENE from Marcy, is Gothics with its bare rock slides. Directly over Gothics is the col between Giant on the L and Rocky Peak Ridge on the R. Through this col on a clear day may be seen Camel's Hump in the Green Mountains of Vermont, about 54 mi. away. Directly to the R of Gothics is its third summit, Pyramid, beyond which a long low col leads over to Sawteeth.

To the NNE, across the Johns Brook Valley from the Great Range, the rock face of Big Slide stands out against a background of Porter and Cascade to the L. In the distance to the N the waters of Lake Placid shine below the regular cone of Whiteface, with the village of Lake Placid just to the L of Lake Placid. The large white structure in the village is the Olympic Center field house with the ski jump complex visible closer at hand and practically in line with the field house. Nearer and NNW lies little Heart Lake at the foot of Mt. Jo. Slightly W of NW, Colden, with its rock slides, stands out against the broad side of the MacIntyre Range, with Boundary Peak directly above Colden, Iroquois to the L, and Algonquin, the second highest Adirondack summit, to the R. To the R of Algonquin is Wright Peak with a prominent slide; through the col between these two peaks may be seen Street.

Due W, about 0.75 mi. away, is Gray Peak, seventh highest peak and the highest trailless summit. By walking a few yards to the SW of the summit, one can see little Lake Tear of the Clouds, the highest pond source of the Hudson River, directly below Marcy to the SW. In line with Lake Tear stands Redfield, while near at hand, SSW, is Skylight, the fourth in order of height. Between Redfield and Skylight, and about 38 mi. away, may be seen Snowy Mt., the highest peak in the southern Adirondacks, elevation 3899 ft. Slightly to the L and behind Skylight is Allen with its two summits, while almost due S the Boreas Ponds gleam in a forest setting. The Boreas Mt. fire tower may be seen to the E of the ponds, and the long, low, tree-covered ridge with many bumps SE from Marcy is the Colvin-Pinnacle Ridge. In all, the summits of 43 of the other 45 major peaks can be seen; only little Couchsachraga, hidden behind Panther Mt., is totally invisible. The highest point seen on East Dix appears to be the summit, but is actually a point 200 yds. NE of the true summit.

There are four main approaches to Marcy. These start from Keene Valley, Heart Lake, Upper Works near Tahawus, and Elk Lake. As the following summary shows, the shortest approach is from Heart Lake. The most difficult is from Elk Lake, due to the rough nature of the trail and to the extra vertical ascent caused by the presence of the Colvin Range before the start up Marcy. There are almost unlimited possibilities for backpackers to approach Marcy, including a very rugged traverse of the Great Range on the way to the summit, or a long, relatively flat approach from the W from Long Lake or Coreys.

Summary of Principal Trails to Marcy	**Miles**
Keene Valley:	
Phelps Trail via Slant Rock from Garden	9.05
Phelps Trail via Hopkins Trail from Garden	9.05
Great Range via Rooster Comb from Keene Valley	13.46
Heart Lake:	
Via Van Hoevenberg Trail	7.38
Via Avalanche Pass and Lake Colden	10.65
Via Lake Arnold	8.80
Elk Lake:	
Elk Lake-Marcy Trail	10.96
Upper Works:	
Via Calamity Brook Trail	10.31
Via Hanging Spear Falls and Flowed Lands	14.16

Maps

The maps enclosed in the back of this book are composites of U.S. Geological Survey quadrangles with updated overlays of trails, shelters and private land lines. These maps are especially valuable because of their combination of contour lines from the original base maps and recent trail information, updated with each printing of this guide. They cover most of the terrain described in this guidebook, but a few isolated trails not conveniently shown on them are shown on individual page maps within the text. Extra copies of the two-sided "High Peaks" map are available from many retailers or directly from the Adirondack Mountain Club, 172 Ridge St., Glens Falls, NY 12801.

There are now two series of USGS maps covering this area. The first is the familiar 15-minute series which was produced in the mid-1950s, while the newer series are 7.5 by 15-minute sheets with metric elevations and contours. The USGS produced this second series in the late 1970s in anticipation of the 1980 Winter Olympics, and the metric units reflect the international nature of that event. The maps enclosed with this guidebook use both of these series of base maps. The "High Peaks" map, which has been a part of this guide for years, continues to be based on the older 15-minute series maps, while the new "High Peaks — North" map is based on the newer metric maps.

For the "High Peaks" map the actual quadrangles used are the Santanoni, Mt. Marcy, and Elizabethtown (eastern half). (The corresponding metric series sheets are the Ampersand Lake,

Santanoni Peak, Keene Valley, Mt. Marcy, Elizabethtown and Witherbee sheets.) The "High Peaks — North" map is based on the Saranac Lake, Wilmington, Lake Placid and Lewis 7.5′ by 15′ metric sheets. (The corresponding 15-minute series quadrangles are Lake Placid, SE corner of Saranac Lake, and SW corner of Ausable Forks).

Trail Signs and Markers

With normal alertness to one's surroundings, trails in the Adirondacks are easy to follow. In most cases, where trails leave a highway or come to a junction there will be a sign to direct the hiker. As much as possible, descriptions in this guidebook are detailed enough so that a hiker can find the correct route even in the rare case when signs are temporarily down. The trails themselves are usually marked with metal disks bearing the insignia of the organization responsible for them. Trails maintained by the DEC are marked with blue, yellow or red disks; the particular color for each trail is indicated on the signs and in the guidebook description. Trails maintained by the ADK are marked with red and white or orange disks and more recently with paint blazes. Trails maintained by the ATIS are marked with their markers, now mostly orange, although some older blue or white markers remain.

Hikers must be aware that some trails are easier to follow than others due to the level of use. While one could practically "sleepwalk" from Adirondak Loj to Marcy Dam, for instance, considerable care is needed to follow other trails even though the pattern of marking is similar. Although this guidebook does mention particularly tricky turns in the trail descriptions, each hiker must remain alert at all times for changes of direction and group leaders have a particular responsibility not to let inexperienced members of the party travel by themselves. A trail that seems "obvious" to a more experienced person may not be that way at all to an inexperienced member of the group.

Finally, it should go without saying that one should never remove any sign or marker. Hikers noticing damaged or missing signs should report this fact to the appropriate group: Adirondack Mt. Club, 172 Ridge St., Glens Falls, NY 12801 for ADK trails; Department of Environmental Conservation, Ray Brook, NY 12977 for DEC trails; and the Adirondack Trail Improvement Society, St. Huberts, NY 12943 for ATIS trails.

All trails described in this guide are on public land or along public rights of way, but there may be "posted" signs at some points. These are usually there to remind hikers that they are on private land over which the owner has kindly granted permission for hikers to pass. In most cases, leaving the trail, camping, fishing and hunting are not permitted on these lands, and hikers should respect the owner's wishes.

Distance and Time

Except where noted, all trails in this guidebook have been measured with a professional surveyor's wheel. This makes possible readings accurate to a hundredth of a mile. Such detail may seem unnecessary, as 0.01 mi. is only 52.8 feet, but it can be useful in describing certain short sections of trail. In this edition, every effort has been made to express short distances in yards when these units would seem to be more useful to a hiker, although the number of yards has usually been derived from a wheel measurement in the field.

At the start of each section of this guide there is a list of trails in the region, the mileage unique to the trail, and the number of the page on which the trail description is located. All mileage distances given in the trail description are cumulative, the beginning of the trail being the 0 mi. point. A distance summary is given at the end of each description, with a total distance expressed in kilometers as well as in miles. If a trail has climbed significantly over its course, its total ascent in both feet and meters is provided. To the inexperienced hiker, these distances will seem longer on the trail, but he or she will quickly learn that there is a great difference between "sidewalk" miles and "trail" miles.

The distances given in this guide are often at odds with the distances given on the DEC trail signs. The DEC has used a variety of measuring methods over the years and has not always updated every sign after every change of distance caused by rerouting, etc. In all cases where there is a disagreement, the guidebook distance can be assumed to be correct; the DEC is currently in the process of revising all of its sign distances based on the wheel measurements found in this guide.

No attempt has been made to estimate times for these trails. A conservative rule to follow in estimating time is to allow an hour for every 1.5 mi., plus 1/2 hour for each 1000 ft. ascended, with experience soon indicating how close each hiker is to this standard. Most day hikers will probably hike faster than this, but backpackers will probably find they go more slowly. Some time will usually be saved on the descent, but on a rough trail the descent may take nearly as long as the ascent, especially with heavy packs.

Abbreviations and Conventions

In each of the books in the Forest Preserve Series, R and L, with periods omitted, are used for right and left. The R and L banks of a stream are determined by looking downstream. Likewise, the R fork of a stream is on the R when one faces downstream. N, S, E and W, again without periods, are used for north, south, east and west. Some compass directions are given in degrees, figuring from true N, with E as 90 degrees, etc.

The following abbreviations are used in the text and on the maps:

ADK	Adirondack Mt. Club
AMR	Adirondack Mountain Reserve
ATIS	Adirondack Trail Improvement Society
DEC	New York State Department of Environmental Conservation
JBL	Johns Brook Lodge
N-P	Northville-Placid (Trail)
PBM	Permanent Bench Mark
USGS	United States Geological Survey
ft.	Feet
mi.	Mile or miles
yds.	Yards

Wilderness Camping

It is not the purpose of this series to teach one how to camp in the woods. There are many good books available on that subject which are more comprehensive and useful than any explanation that could be given in the space available here. The information below should, however, serve to make hikers aware of the differences and peculiarities of the Adirondacks while giving strong emphasis to currently recommended procedures to reduce environmental damage — particularly in heavily used areas.

Except for Johns Brook Lodge, 3.5 mi. up the Marcy Trail from Keene Valley, there are no huts in the Adirondacks. There are, however, lean-tos at many convenient locations along the trails, and there are also many possibilities for tenting along the way. The regulations regarding tenting and the use of these shelters are simple and unrestrictive when compared to those of other popular backpacking areas in the country; but it is important that every backpacker know and obey the restrictions that do exist, since they are designed to promote the long-term enjoyment of the greatest number of people.

General Camping Guidelines:

Except for groups of ten or more (see below), no camping or fire permits are required in the Adirondacks, but campers must obey all DEC regulations regarding camping. Listed below are some of the most important regulations. Complete regulations are available from the DEC and are posted at most access points.

1) No camping within 150 ft. of a stream, other water source, or trail except at a designated campsite. Most areas near an existing lean-to are considered designated campsites; other areas are designated with the following symbol:

2) Except in an emergency, no camping is permitted above 4000 ft. in elevation. (This rule does not apply from December 1 to April 30.)

3) All washing of dishes must be done at least 150 ft. from any stream, pond, or other water source. **No soap,** even so-called "biodegradeable" soap, should ever get into the water, so use a pot to carry water at least 150 ft. away from your source and wash items and dispose of water there. One can also take a surprisingly effective bath by taking a quick dip and then using a pot for soaping and rinsing away from the stream or pond.

4) All human excrement must be buried under at least four inches of dirt at a spot at least 150 ft. away from any water source, and all toilet paper likewise buried or burned. Use established privies or latrines when available.

5) No wood except for **dead** and **down** timber may be used for fire building. Good wood is often scarce at popular campsites, so a stove is highly recommended.

6) No fire should be built near or on any flammable material. Much of the forest cover in the Adirondacks is composed of recently rotted twigs, leaves, or needles and is **highly flammable.** Build a fire at an established fireplace or on rocks or sand. Before leaving destroy all traces of any new fireplace created.

7) All refuse must be completely burned or carried out of the woods. **Do not bury** any refuse and be sure that no packaging to be burned contains metal foil — it will not burn no matter how hot the fire. Remember — if you carried it in, you can carry it out.

8) In general, leave no trace of your presence when leaving a campsite, and help by carrying out *more* than you carried in.

Lean-tos:

Lean-tos are available on a first-come, first-served basis up to the capacity of the shelter — usually about seven persons. A small party cannot therefore claim exclusive use of a shelter and *must* allow late arrivals equal use. Most lean-tos have a fireplace in front (sometimes with a primitive grill) and sanitary facilities. Most are located near some source of water, but each camper must use his own judgment as to whether or not the water supply needs purification before drinking.

It is in very poor taste to carve or write one's initials in a shelter. Please try to keep these rustic shelters in good condition and appearance.

Since reservations cannot be made for any of these shelters, it is best to carry a tent or other alternate shelter. Many shelters away from the standard routes, however, are rarely used, and a small party can often find a shelter open in the more remote areas.

The following regulations apply specifically to lean-tos, in addition to the general camping regulations listed above:

1) No plastic may be used to close off the front of a shelter.

2) No nails or other permanent fastener may be used to affix a tarp in a lean-to, but it is permissible to use rope to tie canvas or nylon tarps across the front.

3) No tent may be pitched inside a lean-to.

Groups:

Any group of ten or more persons must obtain a permit *before* camping on state land. This system is designed to prevent overuse of certain critical sites and also to encourage groups to split into smaller parties more in keeping with the natural environment. Permits can be obtained from the DEC forest ranger closest to the actual starting point of one's proposed trip. The local forest ranger can be contacted by writing to him directly; if in doubt about whom to write, send the letter to the Department of Environmental Conservation, Ray Brook, NY 12977. They will forward the letter, but allow at least a week for the letter to reach the appropriate forest ranger.

One can also make the initial contact with the forest ranger by phone, but keep in mind that rangers' schedules during the busy summer season are often unpredictable. Forest rangers are listed in the white pages of local phone books under "New York, State of; Environmental Conservation, Department of; Forest Ranger." Bear in mind when calling that most rangers operate out of their private homes, and observe the normal courtesy used when calling a private residence. Contact by letter is much preferred, and, as one

can see, camping with a large group requires careful planning
several weeks before the trip.

Drinking Water

For many years, hikers could trust practically any water source
in the Adirondacks to be pure and safe to drink. Unfortunately, as
in many other mountain areas, some Adirondack water sources
have become contaminated with a parasite known as *Giardia
lamblia.* This intestinal parasite causes a disease known as
Giardiasis—often called "Beaver Fever." It can be spread by any
warm-blooded mammal when infected feces wash into the water;
beavers are prime agents in transferring this parasite because they
spend so much of their time near water. Hikers themselves have
also become primary agents in spreading this disease since some
individuals appear to be unaffected carriers of the disease, and
other recently infected individuals may inadvertently spread the
parasite before their symptoms become apparent.

Prevention: Follow the guidelines for the disposal of human
excrement as stated in the section "Wilderness Camping" (above).
Equally important, make sure that every member of your group is
aware of the problem and follows the guidelines as well. The health
of a fellow hiker may depend on your consideration.

Choosing a Water Source: While no water source can be
guaranteed to be safe, smaller streams high in the mountains which
have no possibility of a beaver dam or temporary human presence
upstream are usually safe to drink. If, however, there is any doubt,
treat the water before drinking.

Treatment: Boil all water for 2-3 minutes, administer an iodine-
based chemical purifier (available at camping supply stores and
some drug and department stores), or use a commercial filter
designed specifically for Giardiasis prevention. If after returning

from a trip you experience recurrent intestinal problems, consult your physician and explain your potential problem.

Safety in The High Peaks

Unlike other regions of the Adirondacks, the High Peaks region presents an abundance of extremely steep terrain as well as exposed alpine environments with the potential for arctic weather conditions. On these exposed summits, one must be prepared for either a sudden loss of visibility, a rapid drop in temperature, or both, even in the summer. Hikers should therefore always carry extra clothing when traveling above timberline and should also pay close attention to their location in the event that visibility is suddenly reduced.

Summer temperatures in the High Peaks can drop below freezing at night, particularly in late August, and snow or ice, though rare, is not unknown on the summits in any month of the year. From early September through the end of May, hikers should always consider the possibility of considerable snow or freezing temperatures on the summits. True winter conditions can commence in early November and last until late April. During the winter, weather conditions in the lowlands can be relatively benign while at higher elevations, and especially above timberline, conditions may be so severe that a single miscue or a momentary lapse of concentration could prove fatal. It is imperative that persons travel in groups of not less than four and be outfitted properly when winter conditions prevail. For more information on winter travel, see the Adirondack Mountain Club publication *Winter Hiking and Camping* by John Danielsen.

Emergency Procedures

An ounce of prevention is always worth a pound of cure, but if one is in need of emergency assistance, the DEC forest rangers are the first people to contact for help. The names and phone numbers of the local rangers are often posted inside each trail register. Forest rangers are listed in the white pages of the local phone book under "New York, State of; Environmental Conservation, Department of; Forest Ranger." If this fails, one should try (during business hours) DEC headquarters in Ray Brook, NY: (518) 891-1370. The third place to call would be the New York State Police (897-2000 in Ray Brook). They will use whatever means needed to contact persons able to help. Make sure that the person going for help has the above information plus a complete *written* description of the type and exact location of the accident.

Off-Trail Hiking

In Alpine Zones:

The actual land area that is above timberline in the Adirondacks is a very small part of the Forest Preserve, but it is one of the most unique and precious natural resources in the state. The alpine vegetation of moss, grasses, lichen and rare flowers is very sensitive to human interference, and any damage done is extremely slow to heal. Hikers are therefore urged to stay on designated trails and refrain from walking on vegetation. For this plus safety reasons, camping above 4,000 feet in elevation is forbidden; and hikers camping in open areas between 3,000 and 4,000 feet are urged to camp only at established sites or on rock or gravel, which cannot be destroyed by wear.

On Peaks Without Maintained Trails:

On the "trailless peaks," as they have been called in the past, it is also imperative to stay on the beaten paths where they exist. By sticking to these "herd paths," hikers will not contribute to the erosion and unsightly conditions produced by a network of informal trails.

Whenever one travels off the marked trails, one should also be aware of private land and respect the owner's wishes. Some landowners prohibit access entirely, while others permit travel but prohibit hunting, fishing, camping or the building of fires. Other private preserves additionally prohibit dogs and other pets. The failure by hikers to recognize these restrictions on lands currently open to hiking can result in a landowner adding his lands to those already closed to public access.

THE ADIRONDACK MOUNTAIN CLUB

The Adirondack Mountain Club (or ADK, the initials AMC having been claimed by the previously formed Appalachian Mountain Club) was organized in 1922 for the purpose of bringing together in a working unit a large number of people interested in the mountains, trails, camping, and forest conservation. A permanent club headquarters was established, and with an increasing membership, club chapters were organized. The chapters are as follows: Adirondak Loj (North Elba), Albany, Algonquin (Plattsburgh), Black River (Watertown), Cold River (Long Lake), Finger Lakes (Ithaca-Elmira), Genesee Valley (Rochester), Glens Falls, Hurricane Mt. (Keene), Iroquois (Utica), Keene Valley, Knickerbocker (New York City), Lake Placid, Laurentian (Canton-Potsdam), Long Island, Mid-Hudson (Poughkeepsie), Mohican (Westchester Co.), Montreal (in formation), New York, Niagara Frontier (Buffalo), North Jersey (Bergen Co., NJ), North Woods (Saranac Lake-Tupper Lake), Onondaga (Syracuse), Penn's Woods (Harrisburg, PA), Ramapo (Pearl River), Schenectady, Seneca (Canandaigua), Shatagee Woods (Malone), and Susquehana (Oneonta). In addition, there is an extensive membership-at-large.

Most chapters do not have qualifying requirements; a note to the Executive Director, Adirondack Mountain Club, 172 Ridge St.,

Glens Falls, NY 12801, will bring you information on membership in a local chapter (e.g., names and addresses of persons to be contacted) or details on membership-at-large. Persons joining a chapter, upon payment of their chapter dues, *ipso facto* become members of the club. Membership dues include a subscription to *Adirondac,* a 10-times-yearly magazine. An application for membership is in the back of this book.

Members of the Adirondack Mountain Club have formulated the following creed, which reflects the theme of the club and its membership:

> I support the Club's work to insure that the lands of the State constituting the Forest Preserve shall be forever kept as wild forest lands in accordance with Article XIV, Section 1, of the New York State Constitution. I wish to be a part of the Club's volunteer-based conservation, education and recreation activities aimed at protecting the Forest Preserve and encouraging outdoor recreation consistent with its wild forest character.

In the 1980s the 10,000+ "ADKers" enjoy the full spectrum of outdoor activities, including hiking, backpacking, canoeing (from floating on a pond to whitewater racing), rock climbing, cross-country skiing and snowshoeing. Most chapters have an active year-round outings schedule as well as regular meetings, sometimes including a meal, and programs featuring individuals ranging from chapter members to local and state officials. Many ADKers are also active in service work ranging from participation in search-and-rescue organizations to involvement in the ongoing debate over the best use of our natural resources and forest or wilderness lands, not only in the Adirondacks but also in their immediate localities.

Adirondack Mountain Club Lodges

The Adirondack Mountain Club, Inc. owns and operates two lodges for overnight guests in the High Peaks region. Johns Brook Lodge (Keene Valley Section) is accessible only by foot, while Adirondak Loj (Heart Lake Section) can be reached by car.

Johns Brook Lodge:

Johns Brook Lodge (JBL) is on the trail to Mt. Marcy 5.12 mi. from Keene Valley and 3.52 mi. from the trailhead at the Garden. The lodge is open to all comers for meals and lodging daily from mid-June until Labor Day, during which it has a resident staff, and weekends from Memorial Day Weekend until late June and the weekend after Labor Day until Columbus Day on a caretaker basis. During the summer season, the hutmaster in charge will make every effort to accommodate transients, but only reservations in advance will guarantee space in one of the two bunkrooms. Available all year long in the immediate vicinity of JBL are other accommodations owned by the Adirondack Mountain Club, Inc.: three lean-tos, and two cabins with cooking facilities — Winter Camp, housing 12, and Grace Camp, housing six. For further details and reservation information, contact Johns Brook Lodge, c/o Adirondak Loj, P.O. Box 867, Lake Placid, NY 12946.

Adirondak Loj:

This facility, whose unusual spelling is explained in the Heart Lake Section of this guidebook, is 9 mi. by car from the village of Lake Placid. In addition to the Loj, the Adirondack Mountain Club owns the square mile of surrounding property, including all of Heart Lake and most of Mt. Jo. The Loj offers accommodations to all comers by the day or week, all year long, either in private bedrooms or in bunkrooms. Other accommodations include cabins, lean-tos with fireplaces and numerous tent sites, for which nominal charges are made. Basic camping supplies may be purchased from the Campers and Hikers Building located at the entrance to the parking lot at the Loj. A nominal parking charge is made for nonmembers not registered at the Loj or using the lean-tos and tent sites.

Several cross-country ski trails are located on the property and on nearby Forest Preserve land. This extensive network is a center of much wintertime activity. Snowshoers find much territory in which to enjoy their particular sport.

Of special interest at Adirondak Loj is a Nature Museum where one may find specimens of mosses, lichens, birds' nests, rocks and other Adirondack features. A modest library is available to help those who wish to identify their own samples.

A ranger-naturalist program is offered during the summer months. The leader conducts walks along a special nature trail and furnishes talks and slide shows on conservation and natural history topics. The latter are generally conducted in a scenic outdoor amphitheatre especially constructed for this purpose.

For full information about reservations, rates or activities, address the Manager at Adirondak Loj, P.O. Box 867, Lake Placid, NY 12946 (telephone: 518/523-3441).

NEAL S. BURDICK, Forest Preserve Series Editor
TONY GOODWIN, Editor, *Guide to Adirondack Trails: High Peaks Region*

KEENE VALLEY
SECTION

The village of Keene Valley has for many years been a favorite resort for those who love the mountains. From a multitude of trailheads, all within a few miles of each other, there is a tremendous variety of hikes available, ranging from short afternoon jaunts to rugged multi-day backpacking trips. The most popular destinations are Mt. Marcy and other peaks of the Great Range, but there are also many shorter hikes whose views are dominated by Marcy at the head of the Johns Brook Valley.

Keene Valley is located on Rt. 73, 12 mi. N of Exit 30 on the Adirondack Northway or approx. 28 mi. S of Exit 34 via Rt. 9N and 73. There is daily bus service through Keene Valley on Adirondack Trailways, starting from Albany to the S or from Massena and Ottawa to the N. In the village are a grocery store, mountaineering store, diner, and bar/restaurant. Overnight accommodations are currently very limited in Keene Valley, but there are accommodations 5 mi. to the N in Keene.

Johns Brook Lodge, 3.5 mi. up the Phelps Trail to Marcy, offers overnight accommodations from mid-June through Labor Day and is open on a caretaker basis Memorial Day Weekend until late June and the weekend after Labor Day until Columbus Day. (See section on Adirondack Mountain Club Lodges in Introduction for more information.) Staying at Johns Brook Lodge before climbing Marcy is perhaps the easiest way to ascend this peak since it is only

5.5 mi. from JBL to the summit, compared with over 7 mi. or more from any trailhead. The trails in this area are maintained by the DEC, the Trails Committee of the ADK, or various chapters of the ADK.

The following are some suggested hikes among the many excellent possibilities:

SHORT HIKES:

Baxter from Rt. 9N on Spruce Hill — 2.18 mi. round trip. Mostly easy to moderate grades lead to a series of blueberry-covered ledges with nice views of Keene Valley, the Great Range, and Marcy.

First Brother — 3.00 mi. round trip. This trail, though steep in spots, ascends via a beautiful series of ledges to a summit with good views of Keene Valley, Giant, the Great Range, and Marcy. See description for Big Slide via Brothers from Garden.

MODERATE HIKES:

Porter Mt. from Garden with return via Ridge Trail to Airport — 8.38 mi. point to point. An ascent with relatively easy grades and a nice view from Little Porter, with a return via the Ridge Trail and its many views including the ledges on aptly named Blueberry Mt. See description for Porter from Johns Brook Rd. near Garden and Porter from Keene Valley Airport via Ridge Trail.

Big Slide via Brothers with return via Slide Mt. Brook Trail and Southside Trail — 9.52 mi. round trip. An ascent over three summits with good views, culminating in the spectacular view from Big Slide. Return down pretty Slide Mt. Brook and the Southside Trail with a swim at Tenderfoot Pool. See description for Big Slide via Brothers, Big Slide via Slide Mt. Brook Trail, and Southside Trail.

HARDER HIKES:

Gothics via ADK Range Trail — 14.67 mi. round trip. A rugged loop including two peaks before Gothics' spectacular summit, followed by an even more spectacular descent of the W face. See descriptions for Johns Brook Lodge and Mt. Marcy via Phelps Trail; ADK Range Trail to Upper Wolf Jaw, Armstrong and Gothics; and Gothics via Orebed Brook Trail.

Haystack Mt. — 17.72 mi. round trip. Too many hikers come to the Adirondacks just to climb Mt. Marcy and don't realize that it is far better to sit in relative solitude on the finest summit in all of the Adirondacks and gaze *at* Marcy. See descriptions for Johns Brook Lodge and Mt. Marcy via Phelps Trail and Haystack from Range Trail.

JOHNS BROOK LODGE AND MT. MARCY
via PHELPS TRAIL

This route to Marcy was established by Ed Phelps, son of the famous Keene Valley guide "Old Mountain" Phelps. This trail is also called the Johns Brook Trail, Northside Trail, or, in its upper sections, Slant Rock Trail. This approach to Marcy leads up the Johns Brook Valley past Johns Brook Lodge, which offers the closest overnight accommodations to the summit of Marcy. This approach to Marcy is the best to use if you are traveling by public transportation, since the bus route through Keene Valley is only 1.6 mi. from the trailhead, as compared to 5 mi. or more from all other Marcy trailheads.

The start of this trail is at the Garden parking lot above Keene Valley. From the center of Keene Valley at the DEC sign, "Trail to the High Peaks," follow yellow markers along a paved road, going straight at 0.3 mi. onto Interbrook Rd. At 0.6 mi. the road turns sharp R across a bridge over Johns Brook. (Private road straight ahead is the start for Rooster Comb and an approach to the complete Range Trail.) The road now begins a steady climb, bearing L at the two junctions with other paved roads. At 1.3 mi. the road surface becomes gravel, and the Garden is reached at 1.6 mi., where there is parking for about 60 cars. On many busy weekends this parking lot can be full and hikers should be aware that parking is not permitted on the private land next to the road. Once the capacity of the lot has been reached, hikers must park in Keene Valley and walk the 1.6 mi. up to the trailhead. In winter, the road may be plowed only as far as the end of the pavement at 1.3 mi. As in the summer, parking is not permitted along the road; if one cannot make it to the Garden, one must park in Keene Valley, because even one car parked in the wrong place will prevent the large snowplows from turning around. In this instance, the threat to tow cars away is not an idle one.

Leaving the register at the far end of the Garden (0 mi.), the trail with yellow DEC disks crosses a small stream and begins a moderate climb for a few hundred yds. Easing off, it dips to cross a small stream and then continues mostly on the level to a junction at 0.51 mi. (Trail L with ADK markers is the Southside Trail, an alternate route to Johns Brook Lodge; see below.) Bearing R, the trail continues mostly on the level, crossing one brook and then crossing Bear Brook just before reaching Bear Brook Lean-to on the L at 0.88 mi. Still mostly on the level, the trail continues to Deer Brook Lean-to on the R at 1.27 mi. Just beyond, the trail dips down, crosses Deer Brook on two bridges, and climbs steeply up the far bank. Again mostly on the level, the trail passes three large boulders on the R and soon comes to a small stream at 1.50 mi.

The trail now begins a steady, moderate climb which eases at 2.00 mi. Proceeding mostly on the flat and crossing several small brooks, it comes to a junction at 2.92 mi. where a newer trail goes R to avoid some very rough, wet going on the old route. Following near the edge of a bank, the trail soon drops down to a junction at the DEC Interior Outpost at 3.10 mi. (Trail L leads 200 yds. to a suspension bridge over Johns Brook, connecting at the far side with the Southside Trail, ADK Range Trail, and the Orebed Brook Trail to Gothics and the State Range Trail; see below.)

Bearing R, the trail passes several good campsites and the Howard Memorial Lean-to on the L before crossing Slide Mt. Brook on a bridge with a junction just beyond at 3.21 mi. (Trail R with ADK markers leads 2.35 mi. to Big Slide Mt.; see below. There are also some good campsites just up this trail on the R bank of Slide Mt. Brook.) Continuing on the flat, the trail soon passes a bridge leading L across Johns Brook to the ADK Winter and Grace Camps. Crossing a bridge over Black Brook at 3.40 mi., the trail arrives at Johns Brook Lodge at 3.52 mi. Johns Brook Lodge is owned and operated by the Adirondack Mt. Club and offers overnight accommodations, meals, candy and drinks, and information to hikers. For further information, see section on Adirondack Mountain Club Lodges.

Just past JBL is a junction at a signpost. (Trail L is the State Range Trail with blue DEC markers leading to Gothics and the Upper Great Range and to the Woodsfall Trail which connects with the ADK Range Trail. Trail R is the Klondike Trail which leads to South Meadows near Lake Placid and also connects with the trail to Big Slide via Yard; see below.) Going straight at the signpost, the Phelps Trail to Marcy proceeds on the level, coming to a trail leading 30 yds. L to a lean-to at 3.64 mi. Past the lean-to, the trail continues at an easy grade near the L bank of Johns Brook to Hogback Lean-to at 4.46 mi. Crossing Hogback Brook just beyond, the trail climbs steeply up this hogback, the remnant of a lateral moraine of a valley glacier which came down the Johns Brook Valley for a short time after the last ice age. The steep climbing eases at 4.56 mi. and the trail continues at easier grades to a junction at 5.03 mi., just before reaching the first Bushnell Falls Lean-to. (Spur trail L leads 0.15 mi. very steeply down to the base of the actual falls, a favorite spot of the Rev. Horace Bushnell, and named in his honor by the Keene Valley guides, as he was a very well-liked summer resident of the valley.)

At the lean-to just past the junction with the spur trail to the falls is another junction. (The yellow markers continue to the R on the Hopkins Trail; see below.) Turning L and now with red DEC markers, the Phelps Trail descends at a moderate grade to Johns Brook at 5.15 mi. The trail crosses on the rocks to the R bank just above the confluence of Chicken Coop Brook where another lean-to is located. A third lean-to is on the R bank just below the confluence of Chicken Coop Brook. There is also a high water bridge located 125 yds. upstream of the regular crossing.

From the upper Bushnell Falls Lean-to, the trail swings away from Johns Brook at a moderate grade near the L bank of Chicken Coop Brook. Swinging R and away from Chicken Coop Brook, the grade moderates at 5.82 mi. and the trail crosses a large brook at 6.36 mi. Now mostly on the level, the trail comes to Johns Brook again with Slant Rock just beyond at 6.81 mi. This large rock which forms a natural shelter was a famous early camping spot. A lean-to now faces the natural shelter. Other camping in this area is generally limited to sites on the side of the trail away from the brook.

Swinging L just past Slant Rock, the trail follows close to the L bank of Johns Brook to a junction at 6.93 mi. (Trail L with yellow markers is the Shorey Short Cut leading 1.11 mi. to the Range Trail between Basin and Haystack; see below.) Past this junction, the climbing becomes steep in spots, with a last crossing of Johns Brook at 7.35 mi. From here, the trail is quite wet and rough as it climbs at a moderate grade with some steep pitches to a junction at the top of the pass between Marcy and Haystack at the head of Panther Gorge at 7.78 mi. (Trail L with blue markers is the State Range Trail, see below.) The Phelps Trail bears R and continues to climb steeply up a rough trail to a junction at 8.47 mi. (Trail entering from R with blue markers is the Van Hoevenberg Trail from Heart Lake; see Heart Lake Section.)

Bearing L with blue markers, the trail climbs a few yards to some bare rocks with a view of the summit and then dips down and crosses a wet area before climbing onto another rocky shoulder at 8.71 mi. From this point the trail is level for a short stretch, before beginning the final climb over open rocks. The trail is marked with cairns and yellow paint blazes and care is needed to follow it in fog or rain. The trail passes over a slightly lower eastern summit and then on the flat to the base of the summit rock with a plaque commemorating the first ascent of the peak. The actual summit is reached at 9.05 mi. (For a description of the view and history of the mountain see section on Marcy in the Introduction.) The trail continues over the summit and down the SW side toward Lake Tear and connects with the Elk Lake-Marcy Trail and the trail to Lake Colden and Upper Works near Tahawus. (See Southern Section.)

Distances: Garden parking lot to DEC Interior Outpost, 3.10 mi.; to Johns Brook Lodge, 3.52 mi.; to Bushnell Falls Lean-to and junction with Hopkins Trail, 5.05 mi.; to Slant Rock, 6.81 mi.; to junction with State Range Trail, 7.78 mi.; to junction with Van Hoevenberg Trail, 8.47 mi.; to summit of Marcy, 9.05 mi. (14.56 km.). Ascent from Garden, 3821 ft. (1165 m.). Elevation, 5344 ft. (1629 m.). Order of height, 1.

MARCY via HOPKINS TRAIL

This trail was laid out by Arthur S. Hopkins, former director of Lands and Forests for the Conservation Department, as a short cut for his survey crews during some major land acquisitions in 1920. It leads from the Phelps Trail at Bushnell Falls to the Van Hoevenberg Trail and offers a good route for those heading from the Johns Brook Valley to Heart Lake. Its grades are generally easier than those of the Phelps Trail, but it is quite wet near its junction with the Van Hoevenberg Trail.

Leaving the Phelps Trail at Bushnell Falls (0 mi.), the Hopkins Trail, with yellow markers, climbs at an easy grade to a descent across a small ravine at 0.43 mi. After a short, steep climb up the far bank, the trail levels out until it dips to cross another brook at 0.88 mi. After another steep climb, the grades are easy to moderate until the trail comes to the L bank of the L fork of Johns Brook at 1.47 mi. Now the climbing increases as the trail remains near the L bank of the brook before finally crossing it at 2.10 mi. Shortly after this crossing, the grade moderates and then levels out through some swampy terrain at 2.37 mi. After a few more short climbs and some more wet areas, the trail joins the Van Hoevenberg Trail with blue markers at 2.80 mi. (Turn R for Indian Falls, Marcy Dam and Heart Lake; see Heart Lake Section.)

Bearing L and slightly down, the trail passes the former site of the Hopkins Lean-to in 200 yds. and then climbs to the former site of Plateau Lean-to at 3.12 mi. with the summit dome of Marcy in full view. Dipping briefly across a small stream, the trail then climbs through thick scrub to the junction with the red-marked Phelps Trail, which comes in from the L at 3.42 mi. (Trail leads via Slant Rock to Johns Brook Lodge and Keene Valley; see above.)

Swinging R, the trail makes a short climb to some bare rocks and then dips across a wet area before climbing up to the first rocky shoulder of Marcy at 3.66 mi. Briefly leveling off, the trail now climbs over mostly bare rock and is marked with cairns and yellow paint blazes. Use care when following the trail, especially in poor weather. Proceeding up the bare rocks, the trail reaches the smaller E summit and flattens out for a few yards before coming to the true summit at 4.00 mi. From the summit, the yellow trail leading to Lake Colden and Elk Lake continues down the SW slope. (See Southern Section.) (See "Mt Marcy" in Introduction for information on history and view.)

Distances: Bushnell Falls to Van Hoevenberg Trail, 2.80 mi.; to junction with Phelps Trail, 3.42 mi.; to summit of Marcy, 4.00 mi. (6.44 km.). (From JBL, 5.53 mi. [8.90 km.]. From Garden parking lot, 9.05 mi. [14.56 km.]. Ascents are the same as for the Phelps Trail.)

SOUTHSIDE TRAIL TO JOHNS BROOK LODGE

This trail offers an alternate route to Johns Brook Lodge and the Range trails. It follows an old tote road along the R bank of Johns

Brook, offering many views of this characteristic mountain stream. The grades are easy throughout and some consider this a less difficult approach to Johns Brook Lodge than the Phelps or Northside Trail, but it can be very wet in spots and there is a stretch of rock-hopping next to the brook. The crossing of Johns Brook near the Garden can also be quite difficult in times of high water.

From the Garden (0 mi.), follow the Phelps Trail (see above) 0.51 mi. to the junction with the Southside Trail. Turning L and following ADK markers, the trail descends a steep hogback, turning sharp R and down off the hogback at the second flat area. From the bottom of the hogback, the trail is level to Johns Brook at 0.69 mi., which is crossed on stones. Some care is needed to find the trail on the far side. Climbing the bank, the trail comes to the old tote road at 0.75 mi., now a bulldozed tractor road to help move supplies to the DEC Interior Outpost in the winter. (Note, this turn is easy to miss coming down this trail; watch for it shortly after crossing a large tributary and climbing a short, steep grade.)

Turning R, the trail follows the bulldozed road, drops down across a large tributary, and turns L at the far side. Now at an easy grade, the trail follows the road until 1.55 mi., where the road goes up and L. Continuing straight ahead on the level, the trail descends slightly into the brook bed at 1.85 mi. and proceeds on the rocks for 175 yds. Leaving the brook bed, the trail climbs above a small flume known as the Rock Cut, swings L, and then drops down over some ledges to cross a tributary at 2.03 mi. Again mostly on the level, it rejoins the bulldozed road from the L at 2.13 mi.; 100 yds. later a side trail leads R and down to some beautiful flat rocks with good swimming holes called Tenderfoot Pools.

Continuing at easy grades and swinging away from the brook, the trail crosses several brooks and comes to a junction at 2.87 mi. (Trail L is ADK Range Trail leading to Wolf Jaws Lean-to and the Great Range.) Beyond this junction, the bulldozed road branches L shortly before the trail comes to the suspension bridge and a junction at 3.03 mi. (Trail L with blue markers is the High Water Route to the State Range Trail.) Turning R and crossing the bridge, the trail reaches the DEC Interior Outpost at 3.12 mi. Here it rejoins the Phelps Trail from the Garden. Continuing straight ahead, Johns Brook Lodge is reached at 3.54 mi.

Distances: Garden to junction with Southside Trail, 0.51 mi.; to ADK Range Trail, 2.87 mi.; to DEC Interior Outpost, 3.12 mi.; to JBL, 3.54 mi. (5.70 km.).

ADK RANGE TRAIL TO UPPER WOLF JAW, ARMSTRONG AND GOTHICS

The ADK-maintained Range Trail leads from Johns Brook over Upper Wolf Jaw, Armstrong and Gothics with a side trail leading to Lower Wolf Jaw. For the naming of Gothics and the Wolf Jaws, see the St. Huberts Section. Armstrong was named for Thomas Armstrong, a prominent lumberman in Plattsburgh, who with his partner Almon Thomas in 1866 acquired title to Township 48, Totten and Crossfield Purchase, a parcel which included much of the Great Range and Marcy. In 1887 they sold it to the Adirondack Mountain Reserve, which still owns the part near the Ausable Lakes.

Previous editions of this guidebook have described this trail as starting from Johns Brook Lodge via the Woodsfall Trail; but when approaching these peaks from the Garden, the shortest route to Upper and Lower Wolf Jaw is from the DEC Interior Outpost via this route — formerly described as the High Water Route. Those hikers starting from Johns Brook Lodge should follow the Woodsfall Trail to the ADK Range Trail at the Wolf Jaws Lean-to. Total distances for those starting at JBL are 0.02 mi. greater than those described below and the total ascents are the same.

From the DEC Interior Outpost (0 mi.), head E and down a slight grade through the open field to the suspension bridge across Johns Brook. At the far side of the bridge, turn L and follow ADK markers down the Southside Trail to a junction at 0.23 mi. (Southside Trail leads straight ahead, 2.87 mi. to the Garden; see above.) Turning R, the trail climbs at a moderate grade and comes out on the L bank of Wolf Jaws Brook at 0.45 mi. after which the grade eases and the trail swings back away from the brook and continues climbing steadily to a junction at 1.11 mi. (Trail R with ADK markers is the Woodsfall Trail to Johns Brook Lodge; see below.) Wolf Jaws Lean-to is about 50 yds. past this junction on the L.

From this junction, the trail continues at a steady, moderate climb generally along the L bank of Wolf Jaws Brook. After the second of two small tributaries at 1.67 mi., the grade steepens until the junction at the top of the pass is reached at 2.01 mi. (ADK trail L leads to Lower Wolf Jaw; see below.) Turning R, the trail begins a steep to very steep climb, switchbacking up through the many ledges on the steep slope. At 2.30 mi. there is a good view of Big Slide and Whiteface with the trail reaching the lesser summit of Upper Wolf Jaw at 2.47 mi. From here, the trail descends easily with some views through the trees to a col and then ascends, steeply at first, to a junction with a spur trail R leading 20 yds. to the summit lookout at 2.91 mi. (4.68 km.).

From the summit there are good views to the S and E. A vague trail leads NW from the summit a few yards to another ledge with good views of the Johns Brook Valley. Upper Wolf Jaw ascent from DEC Interior Outpost, 2000 ft. (610 m.). Elevation, 4185 ft. (1276 m.). Order of height, 29.

The ADK Range Trail continues straight ahead from the junction with the spur trail to the summit and drops to a col at 3.11 mi., after which it climbs over an intermediate bump before descending to the base of Armstrong at 3.41 mi. The trail has been rerouted from this point to avoid a dangerous cliff on the old route. Bearing R and descending easily for a few yards, it swings sharp L and begins climbing steeply at 3.53 mi. The climbing continues steep along the crest of a ridge with some views out through the trees to a large rock at 3.69 mi., where the grade moderates. Soon after, the trail rejoins the old route and continues on to the summit at 3.86 mi. (6.21 km.). A large ledge on the R offers views of the Johns Brook Valley and the upper Great Range. Armstrong total ascent from DEC Interior Outpost, 2500 ft. (760 m.). Elevation, 4400 ft. (1341 m.). Order of height, 22.

Continuing on, the trail descends over a few steep ledges to a col and then climbs to the S peak of Armstrong at 4.21 mi. where the trail swings R and descends to a junction at 4.31 mi. (ATIS-marked trail to the L leads to Lake Road and St. Huberts; see St. Huberts Section.) Continuing with ADK markers, the trail is level for a few yards before it climbs steeply to the summit of Gothics at 4.76 mi. (7.66 km.). The view is unobstructed with about 30 major peaks discernible. The boathouse at the Lower Ausable Lake can be seen, but to see any of the Upper Lake one must proceed past the summit 0.12 mi. to the ATIS trail over Pyramid and go L on this trail a few yards to a wide ledge with views to the S and W. Gothics total ascent from DEC Interior Outpost, 3000 ft. (914 m.). Elevation, 4736 ft. (1444 m.). Order of height, 10.

The trail continues over the summit and along the ridge to the W peak of Gothics and then down the very steep and open W face with two cables in place to aid passage. At the bottom of this face, the trail joins the Orebed Brook Trail at 5.41 mi. (see below).

Distances: DEC Interior Outpost to junction with Woodsfall Trail, 1.11 mi.; to junction with trail to Lower Wolf Jaw, 2.01 mi.; to summit of Upper Wolf Jaw, 2.91 mi.; to summit of Armstrong,

3.86 mi.; to summit of Gothics, 4.76 mi.; to Orebed Brook Trail junction, 5.41 mi. (8.70 km.).

LOWER WOLF JAW

From Wolf Jaws Notch, a branch of the ADK Range Trail leads to the summit of Lower Wolf Jaw and connects with the W.A. White Trail to St. Huberts or Keene Valley. Alexander Wyant, a well-known artist who first came to Keene Valley in 1869, is credited with conferring the name Wolf Jaws, as suggested by the deep col between the two peaks. The spot on Noonmark from which Wyant painted a view of these peaks is supposed to offer the best representation of a wolf's jaw.

From the notch (0 mi.), the trail heads E on the flat for 50 yds. to a junction with the cut-off to the Wedge Brook Trail which goes R (see St. Huberts Section). Turning L, the trail begins to climb steeply to a junction at 0.19 mi. where the Wedge Brook Trail comes in from the R (see St. Huberts Section). From this junction, the trail continues to climb to the summit at 0.49 mi. where there are good views from the lookout on the L. Trail straight ahead is the W.A. White Trail to St. Huberts with connections to Keene Valley via Hedgehog and Rooster Comb.

Distances: DEC Interior Outpost to Wolf Jaws Notch, 2.01 mi.; to summit of Lower Wolf Jaw, 2.50 mi. (4.02 km.). Ascent, 2000 ft. (610 m.). Elevation, 4175 ft. (1273 m.). Order of height, 30.

WOODSFALL TRAIL

This ADK-maintained trail offers the most direct approach from Johns Brook Lodge to the Wolf Jaws and the ADK Range Trail. For the first 0.32 mi. this route follows the blue-marked State Range Trail. From the signpost at JBL (0 mi.), the trail descends a few yards to Johns Brook, which is crossed on stones. (See below for high water routes.) Turning R and then immediately L on the far bank, the trail leads up over two small ridges to Orebed Brook at 0.24 mi. Climbing the far bank in two steep pitches with some wooden steps, the trail reaches a five-way junction at 0.32 mi. (Trail sharp R and sharp L is the blue-marked Orebed Brook Trail leading from the DEC Interior Outpost to Gothics and the upper Great Range. Trail nearly straight ahead at 110 degrees is the ADK trail to Short Job; see below.)

The Woodsfall Trail bears slightly R, heading away from this junction at 170 degrees on an easy to moderate grade. Crossing several small brooks, it reaches a height of land at 0.88 mi. and descends gradually, crossing two brooks before joining the ADK Range Trail near Wolf Jaws Lean-to at 1.13 mi. (see above). This point is 1.11 mi. from the DEC Interior Outpost, which means that all cumulative distances on the ADK Range Trail are 0.02 mi. longer if one starts from JBL.

Distances: JBL to junction with Orebed Brook Trail, 0.32 mi.; to junction with ADK Range Trail, 1.13 mi. (1.82 km.).

HIGH WATER ROUTES TO OREBED BROOK TRAIL AND ADK RANGE TRAIL FROM JBL

When high water makes it difficult to cross Johns Brook on the stones near JBL, hikers should use the suspension bridge below the DEC Interior Outpost. Follow the yellow markers on the Phelps Trail downstream to the junction at the trail register at the Interior Outpost. From here, follow the descriptions for either the ADK Range Trail or the Orebed Brook Trail. For those heading for the Wolf Jaws it is 0.47 mi. longer from JBL to Wolf Jaws Lean-to by the high water route. For those heading for Gothics it is 0.67 mi. longer from JBL to the five-way junction via the high water route.

SHORT JOB

This small knoll across the valley from JBL offers some interesting views for a short hike. From JBL (0 mi.) take the blue-marked State Range Trail (see below) to the five-way junction at 0.32 mi. From here, take the trail heading at 110 degrees, which climbs gradually at first but then up more steeply to the first lookout toward the Range at 0.69 mi. The trail continues with a slight descent to a lookout over the Johns Brook Valley at 0.74 mi.

Distances: JBL to Orebed Brook Trail at five-way junction, 0.32 mi.; to end of trail at second lookout, 0.74 mi. (1.19 km.).

GOTHICS via OREBED BROOK TRAIL

The arched peaks of this triple-crested mountain, with their great slides and bare rock, suggested Gothic architecture to Frederick Perkins and "Old Mountain" Phelps that day in 1857 when they sat on the top of Marcy and christened four mountains with characteristic names: Skylight, Basin, Saddleback and Gothics. This is the most direct route to Gothics from the Johns Brook Valley. It connects at Gothics Col with the State Range Trail to Saddleback, Basin and Haystack. Like the ADK Range Trail, the shortest approach to this trail from the Phelps Trail is from the DEC Interior Outpost, but there is also a connection from Johns Brook Lodge which joins the Orebed Brook Trail at the five-way junction. See Woodsfall Trail (above) for description of this connector.

From the DEC Interior Outpost (0 mi.), the trail goes E and down gradually through an open field a few yards to a suspension bridge over Johns Brook. On the far side of the brook at 0.07 mi. there is a junction. (ADK Trail L is the Southside Trail connecting with the ADK Range Trail; see above.) Orebed Brook Trail with blue markers leads R and up steeply and joins a bulldozed road which is followed to the R on an easy grade. At 0.14 mi. the Orebed

Brook Trail swings L away from the road (be alert as this turn is not well marked) and continues to climb on an older tote road to a five-way junction at 0.56 mi. (Trail R is a connector to Johns Brook Lodge. Trails L are the Short Job and Woodsfall Trails; see above.)

Continuing straight ahead on the old tote road at an easy grade, the Orebed Brook Trail crosses a large brook at 1.24 mi., with Orebed Lean-to just beyond to the L of the trail. There are some designated campsites down and to the R at this point as well. Continuing at an easy grade, the trail passes a huge boulder on the R at 1.54 mi. and continues on past two small brooks before descending to cross a larger brook at 1.76 mi. The trail climbs a steep bank on the far side and then continues at moderate grades along the R bank of the main branch of Orebed Brook. At 2.26 mi. the trail comes to a large new slide coming down off the small peak to the L. There is a view of Saddleback from this slide, which the trail crosses by turning L for a few yds. and then R across the slide to join the original trail at the far side.

The trail is now close to the R bank of Orebed Brook with several attractive mossy falls visible. The trail crosses the brook at 2.57 mi. and continues up the L bank around several large boulders. Some care is needed to follow the trail in this section, both going up and coming down, as the trail and brook often look remarkably alike.

The climbing soon becomes much steeper with a very steep pitch commencing at 2.73 mi. The trail climbs on bare rock for much of the time, with a steep open slide just to the R which offers some views back to the Johns Brook Valley. The grade eases slightly as the trail veers L and traverses across the side hill. The grade finally eases back to moderate at 2.96 mi. at the base of a small slide with a view of the W peak of Gothics and the summit beyond. The junction at Gothics Col is reached at 3.06 mi. (Trail R is the State Range Trail; see below.)

Turning L and now with ADK markers, the trail climbs quite

steeply up the mostly bare W ridge of Gothics. The first of two cables fastened to the rocks is reached at 3.21 mi., and above the second cable the trail continues to climb steeply to a final steep step with a small crack giving just enough of a foothold to gain the W summit at 3.36 mi. where there are good views. Crossing over this summit, the trail descends slightly and then climbs to a junction at 3.61 mi. (Trail R with ATIS markers leads to the Lower Ausable Lake via Pyramid; see St. Huberts Section.) From here, the trail continues mostly on the flat to the summit of Gothics at 3.71 mi. See ADK Range Trail for notes on views.

Distances: DEC Interior Outpost to junction with connector from JBL, 0.56 mi.; to Orebed Lean-to, 1.27 mi.; to Gothics Col and Range Trail, 3.06 mi.; to summit of Gothics, 3.71 mi. (5.97 km.). Ascent from Johns Brook, 2360 ft. (719 m.). Elevation, 4736 ft. (1444 m.). Order of height, 10.

STATE RANGE TRAIL TO SADDLEBACK, BASIN, HAYSTACK AND MARCY

This section of trail is perhaps the most spectacular of any in the Adirondacks as it goes over the bare summits of Saddleback and Basin and connects to the spur trail to Haystack that runs along its sharp, open ridge. It is also a very rugged trail and is a serious undertaking, especially with backpacks. There are many sections of steep rock, particularly on the W sides of Basin and Saddleback, which can be very uncomfortable to negotiate with a heavy pack. Day trips are suggested for those wishing to climb these peaks, and backpackers may want to consider hiking this trail in reverse direction so as to ascend the most precipitous and dangerous sections.

The trail starts at Gothics Col (0 mi.) at a junction with the Orebed Brook Trail (see above). It climbs steeply up the E side of

Saddleback with many good views back at the spectacular slides on Gothics. At 0.33 mi. the grade eases on the E peak of Saddleback, after which the trail dips to the "saddle" at 0.43 mi. with a side trail L to a good view just beyond. The trail then climbs two rock steps to the summit at 0.54 mi. (0.87 km.) where a broad ledge offers good views. Saddleback ascent from Johns Brook, 2200 ft. (670 m.). Elevation, 4515 ft. (1376 m.). Order of height, 17.

The trail turns sharp R at the summit and follows along a ledge marked with yellow paint blazes. Turning L at the end of the ledge, the trail descends precipitously over ledges where extreme caution is needed. The trail reaches the bottom of the col at 0.77 mi., after which it begins a moderate ascent through open firs with views back at Saddleback. The grade becomes progressively steeper and remains steep until it eases on a shoulder of Basin at 1.13 mi. The trail descends gradually to a col and then begins steep climbing again at 1.31 mi. At 1.42 mi., the trail crosses a spectacular narrow ledge and then turns L and up to the summit of Basin at 1.48 mi. Here in the rock is embedded the bolt placed by Verplanck Colvin during the Adirondack Survey in 1876. The view is unobstructed in all directions except to the S, but with a little walking around one can see this view as well. Gothics to the E, Marcy to the W, and Haystack to the SW are the most prominent peaks visible, with Upper Ausable Lake to the S and the valley to the SE forming an almost perfect basin from which the peak got its name. Basin total ascent from Johns Brook, 2870 ft. (875 m.). Elevation, 4827 ft. (1471 m.). Order of height, 9.

The trail goes straight over the summit, turns L at the base of the summit rocks and then descends generally easy to moderate grades along a SW shoulder to the top of a ledge at 1.85 mi. There used to be a ladder leading down this face, but now the trail detours R to get around the ledge, arriving at the bottom at 1.91 mi. The trail now descends very steeply for 75 yds. to a second ledge which still does have a ladder, but after descending this pitch the trail levels out for a few hundreds yards before descending steeply to a junction at 2.26 mi. (Yellow trail R is the Shorey Short Cut to the Phelps Trail; see below.)

The Range Trail continues its steep descent for another 100 yds. to the headwaters of Haystack Brook and then begins climbing steeply to the former site of Sno-Bird Lean-to at 2.44 mi., now a designated campsite. Just past the former lean-to site, the trail crosses a small stream with a junction on the other side. (Trail L with ATIS markers leads to Upper Ausable Lake; see St. Huberts Section.) The Range Trail now begins a very rough and eroded climb to a trail junction at 2.87 mi. (Trail L with yellow markers leads 0.55 mi. to the summit of Haystack; see below.) Turning R, the Range Trail climbs steeply to the top of a ridge at 2.97 mi. with a bare spot offering views just beyond on the R. Now the trail starts down at a moderate grade, getting progressively steeper until at 3.31 mi. it descends a near vertical pitch to the pass at the head of Panther Gorge where the Phelps Trail comes in from the R from Slant Rock and JBL at 3.40 mi. Turning L with red markers, the route from here to the summit of Marcy is the same as the Phelps Trail. (See above.)

Distances: DEC Interior Outpost at Johns Brook to Gothics Col, 3.04 mi.; to summit of Saddleback, 3.60 mi.; to summit of Basin, 4.52 mi.; to junction with Shorey Short Cut, 5.16 mi.; to former site of Sno-Bird Lean-to, 5.31 mi.; to junction with trail to Haystack, 5.76 mi.; to Phelps Trail, 6.29 mi.; to Van Hoevenberg Trail, 6.98 mi.; to summit of Marcy, 7.56 mi. (12.17 km.). Total ascent from Johns Brook via Range Trail, about 4890 ft. (1490 m.).

MT. HAYSTACK FROM THE RANGE TRAIL

This third highest peak in the Adirondacks was named by "Old Mountain" Phelps in August 1849 when he made the first recorded ascent with Almeron Oliver and George Estey. Phelps remarked to his companions that the mountain was a great stack of rock but that he would call it Haystack; and Haystack it has been ever since.

Haystack is approached from the Range Trail either over Saddleback and Basin or more directly via the Phelps Trail to the head of Panther Gorge. The distance to the junction with the Haystack Trail is 5.76 mi. from the DEC Interior Outpost via Saddleback and Basin, or 5.24 mi. (and a lot less climbing) via the Phelps Trail and Slant Rock. This trail is not as well marked as some others above timberline, and care is needed to follow it in fog or rain, but even in good weather hikers should be careful to stay on the trail to avoid trampling the fragile alpine vegetation.

From the junction with the Range Trail (0 mi.), the trail follows yellow markers for a few yards to timberline, after which it is marked with cairns. It goes over the first ledge and then R at 0.06 mi. around the R side of a ledge and up to the summit of Little Haystack at 0.18 mi. The marked trail actually passes 20 yds. to the R (W) of the summit and then swings L and descends a diagonal ledge for 150 yds. before turning sharp R and down to the few trees in the col at 0.31 mi. Ascending at an easier grade from the col, the trail sticks fairly close to the crest of the ridge, bearing slightly R as it approaches the summit to avoid the sharpest part of the ridge, and reaching the totally bald summit at 0.56 mi. The view from the summit is considered one of the finest in the mountains, with the yawning abyss of Panther Gorge and the steep cliffs on Marcy dominating the view. The trail continues over the summit and down to Bartlett Ridge, where it branches to Panther Gorge and the Upper Ausable Lake. (See St. Huberts Section.)

Distances: Range Trail to summit of Haystack, 0.56 mi. (0.90 km.). From Johns Brook Interior Outpost via Saddleback and Basin, 6.32 mi. (10.17 km.); total ascent, 4170 ft. (966 m.). From Johns Brook Interior Outpost via Phelps Trail and Slant Rock,

5.80 mi. (9.33 km.); total ascent, 2790 ft. (850 m.). Elevation, 4960 ft. (1512 m.). Order of height, 3.

SHOREY SHORT CUT FROM RANGE TRAIL
TO PHELPS TRAIL

This trail was cut by A.T. Shorey, former chairman of the ADK Guidebook Committee, when he was with the Conservation Department. It connects the Range Trail at the base of Basin with the Phelps Trail near Slant Rock and offers a shorter return from the Range Trail to the Johns Brook Valley. This trail has been much maligned by hikers over the years since it climbs well above the height of land needed to gain access to the Johns Brook Valley and it is rough going throughout. It does, however, lead past a viewpoint which is a perfectly framed "portrait" of Haystack and Little Haystack.

Leaving the Range Trail (0 mi.), the trail with yellow DEC disks climbs a moderate to steep grade to a lookout on the L at 0.19 mi., after which the grade eases a bit up past a large boulder, and finally to a height of land on the shoulder of Haystack at 0.31 mi. Now descending steep to moderate grades, the trail passes several other glimpses of the Johns Brook Valley through the trees. The descent continues to the old Slant Rock Lean-to site on the R bank of Johns Brook with the junction with the Phelps Trail on the other side of the brook at 1.11 mi. This point is 0.12 mi. above Slant Rock.

Distance: Range Trail to Phelps Trail, 1.11 mi. (1.79 km.).

MT. MARCY FROM KEENE VALLEY
via THE COMPLETE GREAT RANGE

The following table of information is included for those who wish to traverse the entire Great Range from Keene Valley to Mt.

Marcy. As the distance and vertical ascent figures indicate, this is an extremely rugged trip with very rough trail for most of the distance. Allow several days with backpacks, and be aware that there are no longer any lean-tos along this route and that there is only one designated camping area. Unless camping at this one designated campsite (at the site of the former Sno-Bird Lean-to), one must camp at least 150 ft. away from any trail or water supply. Camping is further prohibited anywhere above 4000 ft. in elevation.

The following are the applicable trail descriptions in the Keene Valley Section: Rooster Comb, Hedgehog, and Lower Wolf Jaw from Keene Valley; Lower Wolf Jaw; ADK Range Trail to Upper Wolf Jaw, Armstrong and Gothics; State Range Trail to Saddleback, Basin, Haystack and Marcy. One can return by either the Phelps or Hopkins Trail.

Summary of Distances from bridge 0.6 mi. W of Keene Valley to:

Point	Distance		Approx. Total Ascent	
	Miles	**(Kms.)**	**Feet**	**(Meters)**
Rooster Comb	1.75	(2.82)	1640	(500)
Hedgehog	3.10	(4.99)	2530	(700)
W.A. White Trail	3.50	(5.63)		
Lower Wolf Jaw	4.95	(7.96)	3670	(1120)
Wolf Jaws Notch	5.44	(8.75)		
Upper Wolf Jaw	6.44	(10.36)	4510	(1375)
Armstrong	7.24	(11.65)	5030	(1530)
ATIS Trail to St. Huberts	7.69	(12.27)		
Gothics	8.14	(13.10)	5530	(1685)
Gothics Col	8.79	(14.14)		
Saddleback	9.35	(15.04)	6130	(1870)

Basin	10.27	(16.52)	6800	(2070)
Shorey Short Cut	11.06	(17.80)		
Site of former Sno-Bird Lean-to	11.21	(18.04)		
Haystack Trail	11.66	(18.76)	7630	(2235)
Phelps Trail	12.19	(19.61)		
Van Hoevenberg Trail	12.68	(20.72)	8440	(2570)
Marcy	13.46	(21.66)	9000	(2740)

KLONDIKE NOTCH TRAIL TO SOUTH MEADOW

This route leads from Johns Brook Lodge through Klondike Notch to South Meadow, where it meets a road coming in from the Heart Lake Road providing access to Adirondak Loj. (See Heart Lake Section.) Klondike Notch between Tabletop and Yard Mts. has also been called Railroad Notch at times, but this name rightfully belongs to the lower notch between Porter and Big Slide which once was actually surveyed for a railroad.

Leaving the JBL signpost (0 mi.), the trail with red DEC disks heads across the back yard of JBL, crosses Black Brook, and climbs along the L bank of the brook at a moderate grade with occasional steeper pitches to a junction at 1.28 mi. (Trail R with ADK markers leads to Big Slide via Yard in 2.70 mi.; see below.) Continuing at a moderate grade, the trail soon descends slightly to cross a swampy area and then resumes the climb to the height of land at Klondike Notch at 1.72 mi., having gained 866 ft. (264 m.) in elevation from JBL.

Descending now at easy to moderate grades, the trail crosses Klondike Brook, turns R, and soon comes to Klondike Lean-to at 2.69 mi. Passing in front of the lean-to, the trail follows a tote road up a short climb and then continues mostly on the level to 3.70 mi.

where it starts down a moderate grade. Occasionally swinging away from the tote road to avoid eroded sections, the trail reaches the level shortly before a junction with the Mr. Van Ski Trail at 4.60 mi. (Trail R with red DEC "ski" trail markers leads to Mt. Van Hoevenberg Cross-Country Area; see Heart Lake Section.)

At 4.80 mi. the Mr. Van Trail diverges to the L (distance to Adirondak Loj, 1.90 mi., but sections of this portion of the trail can be very wet and practically impassable). Continuing on, the Klondike Trail reaches South Meadow Brook at 5.16 mi., turns upstream to a good bridge, and reaches the end of the South Meadow Road at 5.27 mi. Continuing W on this road it is slightly over a mile to the Heart Lake Road, and another mile to Adirondak Loj.

Distances: JBL to ADK Big Slide Trail, 1.28 mi.; to Klondike Lean-to, 2.69 mi.; to South Meadow Rd., 5.27 mi. (8.48 km.); to Adirondak Loj, 7.30 mi. (11.75 km.).

BIG SLIDE MT. via SLIDE MT. BROOK TRAIL

This trail starts from the Phelps Trail, 0.14 mi. above the DEC Interior Outpost and 0.31 mi. below JBL. Leaving the Phelps Trail (0 mi.) and marked with ADK markers, the trail starts at an easy grade and crosses Slide Mt. Brook at 0.22 mi., and then twice more before it comes to the base of an old slide. The trail climbs away from the brook on this slide, at the top of which, at 0.45 mi., is a good view of Gothics and some of the rest of the Great Range. Now the trail returns to the brook and follows close to it with several more crossings, finally ending up on the R bank and leaving the brook at 0.97 mi.

The climbing is now moderate through open hardwoods with some glimpses of the Range back through the trees. Gradually becoming steeper, at 1.76 mi. the trail comes to a good view of the bare rock slide which occurred in 1830 and from which the mountain takes its name. The climbing is now quite steep to a junction at 2.05 mi. (Trail R with ADK markers leads over the Brothers to the Garden in 3.55 mi.; see below.) The climbing becomes very steep with a side trail L to a view of the slide at 2.16 mi. Swinging sharp R just above this side trail, the grade eases a bit as the trail works onto the N side of the peak, swings L and climbs on past another view on the L to the summit at 2.35 mi. There are magnificent views of the Great Range, Giant and Algonquin with only the view to the N blocked by trees. The trail with ADK markers continues over the summit and down over Yard Mt. to JBL in another 3.98 mi. (see below).

Distances: Phelps Trail to trail over Brothers, 2.05 mi.; to summit of Big Slide, 2.35 mi. (3.78 km.). Ascent from Phelps Trail, 2000 ft. (610 m.). Elevation, 4240 ft. (1292 m.). Order of height, 27.

BIG SLIDE via YARD MT.

This trail starts from the Klondike Notch Trail (see above), 1.28 mi. from JBL or 0.44 mi. below the height of land coming from South Meadow. Combined with the Slide Mt. Brook Trail, it makes an interesting loop of 6.33 mi. from JBL.

Leaving the Klondike Notch Trail (0 mi.) with ADK markers, the trail climbs moderately and then more steeply until at about 0.50 mi. it swings L on a long traverse heading NW. After this traverse, the trail again climbs steeply onto the W ridge of Yard Mt. with a view of Marcy at 0.90 mi. and reaches the summit of Yard Mt. at 1.25 mi. Yard's elevation is 4018 ft., but it is not one of the 46 peaks as it is too close to Big Slide.

From the summit of Yard, the trail drops slightly and then begins a generally easy climb along the ridge with a profile view of Big Slide at 1.40 mi. Continuing the easy climb, the trail reaches the summit of Big Slide at 2.70 mi. (See above for description of the view.)

Distances: JBL to junction with Big Slide Trail, 1.28 mi.; to summit of yard Mt., 2.53 mi.; to summit of Big Slide, 3.98 mi. (6.40 km.). Ascent from JBL, 1924 ft. (586 m.). Elevation, 4240 ft. (1292 m.). Order of height, 27.

BIG SLIDE MT. via THE BROTHERS

This trail offers a spectacular approach to Big Slide Mt. from the Garden parking lot above Keene Valley over the three Brothers, all of which offer excellent views. Combined with the Slide Mt. Brook Trail and the Phelps Trail, an interesting loop of 9.53 mi. from the Garden is possible. The First and Second Brother at 1.50 mi. and 1.76 mi. are good objectives for shorter hikes. See description of Phelps Trail (above) for approach to the Garden. This trail is currently maintained by the Long Island Chapter of the ADK.

From the trail register at the end of the Garden (0 mi.), the Big Slide trail with ADK markers goes sharp R and up along the edge of the parking lot and then climbs moderately for a few hundred yards before easing off. At 0.40 mi. the trail swings L and drops down to cross Juliet Brook before beginning a steady, moderate climb to the base of a steeper pitch at 0.68 mi. Here the trail traverses to the R to avoid the steepest climbing and then switchbacks L and up to the first ledge at 0.80 mi., where there are good views of Keene Valley and the Great Range. The climbing is easier for a while over some more ledges, but it soon begins to increase as the trail goes up a series of open ledges until it moderates on a large, flat ledge at 1.16 mi. Turning R at the end of this ledge, the trail enters the woods and climbs a few steep, rocky pitches to a summit which the trail skirts on the L (W) side. Turning R just past this first summit, the trail passes a natural rock shelter and soon climbs to the bare summit of the First Brother at 1.50 mi. (2.41 km.). Elevation, 2940 ft. (896 m.). Ascent from Garden, 1437 ft. (438 m.).

Dipping slightly, the trail soon climbs steeply up open rocks to the apparent summit of Second Brother at 1.66 mi. where there are good views to the E, S, and W. Turning L, the trail is mostly level to a junction at 1.76 mi. (2.83 km.). Here a side trail R leads 20 yds. to the true summit of the Second Brother where a rock offers views to the N. Elevation, 3120 ft. (950 m.). Ascent from Garden, 1600 ft. (488 m.).

Swinging L, the trail descends an easy grade over more open ledges with a few short rises until finally dipping down to the col between the Second and Third Brother at 1.99 mi. The trail now climbs moderately with a few short dips to the summit of the Third Brother at 2.60 mi. (4.18 km.), where there is a spectacular view of Big Slide. Elevation, 3681 ft. (1122 m.). Ascent from Garden, 2160 ft. (658 m.).

From the summit of the Third Brother, the trail descends gradually, passing a rock shelter on the L at 2.73 mi. and soon flattening out in a mature spruce forest. The trail continues flat or gently down to a small stream where it swings L and up gradually and soon comes to a larger stream at 3.20 mi. Crossing the stream, the trail is wet for a few yards, and then climbs moderately to steeply to a junction at 3.71 mi. (Trail L is Slide Mt. Brook Trail, see above, leading 2.05 mi. to the Phelps Trail near JBL.)

Turning R, the trail now becomes very steep with a side trail L to a view of the slide at 3.82 mi. The trail swings sharp R just above this side trail, and the grade soon eases a bit as the trail works onto the N side of the peak, swings L, and climbs on past another view on the L to the summit at 3.91 mi. There are magnificent views of the Great Range, Giant and Algonquin with only the view to the N blocked by trees. The trail, with ADK markers, continues over the summit and down over Yard Mt. to JBL in another 3.98 mi. (See above.)

Distances: Garden to First Brother, 1.50 mi.; to Second Brother, 1.76 mi.; to Third Brother, 2.60 mi.; to junction with Slide Mt. Brook Trail, 3.71 mi.; to summit of Big Slide, 3.91 mi. (6.29 km.). Total ascent from Garden, 2800 ft. (853 m.). Elevation, 4240 ft. (1292 m.). Order of height, 27.

PORTER MT. FROM JOHNS BROOK ROAD
NEAR GARDEN

Once called West Mt., Porter is named for Dr. Noah Porter, President of Yale University from 1871 to 1886, who was a summer resident of Keene Valley and who made the first recorded ascent of the peak in 1875 with guide Ed Phelps. Although Porter does not have a bald summit, it offers 360-degree views.

This trail branches off Interbrook Rd. (also known as Johns Brook Rd.), 0.30 mi. before the Garden parking lot. See Phelps Trail (above) for approach to the Garden. Since parking is not permitted along the road to the Garden, hikers must park at the Garden and walk back down to the end of the pavement where a dirt road marked with signs goes NW. This trail is currently maintained by the Schenectady Chapter of the ADK and is marked with ADK markers.

Leaving Interbrook Rd. (0 mi.), the trail follows the dirt road, bearing R at a private driveway at 0.15 mi. and then turning sharp R and crossing Slide Brook on a bridge at 0.24 mi. The trail now climbs along an old road at easy to moderate grades to the site of an old sugar camp at 0.88 mi., where it intersects a jeep road. Turning L, the trail crosses the jeep road and climbs moderately to steeply to a level section near a private camp at 1.26 mi. The trail soon climbs again, gains the top of a ridge and comes to the end of another jeep road coming in from the R at 1.50 mi. (In descending this section, care is needed to stay on the marked trail and not end up on the jeep road.) Continuing on past the jeep road, the trail passes another private camp on the L and soon enters state land. Now going up and down on a generally open ridge, the trail reaches the summit of Little Porter at 1.76 mi., where there are excellent views.

After a short descent, the trail is level through open woods to a stream crossing at 2.10 mi. Following up the L bank, the trail begins climbing again at a moderate grade, crossing a small brook at 2.31 mi. A slight dip is followed by more climbing through an open, grassy glade until the trail enters thicker woods just before dipping to cross another larger brook at 2.85 mi. The trail now begins to slab across the side of Porter with moderate grades alternating with short descents and several small brook crossings. Much of this section of trail is through grassy glades, a legacy of the 1903 fire. The trail finally climbs to a junction with the Ridge Trail from the Keene Valley Airport at 3.40 mi. Turning L, the trail continues at easy to moderate grades to the E summit, after which it is mostly flat to the summit of Porter at 3.84 mi. A trail marked with red DEC disks continues over the summit and on to Cascade and Rt. 73 in Cascade Pass. (See Northern Section.)

Distances: Interbrook Rd. to Little Porter, 1.76 mi.; to junction with Ridge Trail, 3.40 mi.; to summit of Porter, 3.84 mi. (6.18 km.). Ascent from road, 2700 ft. (825 m.). Elevation, 4059 ft. (1237 m.). Order of height, 38.

PORTER MT. FROM KEENE VALLEY AIRPORT
via RIDGE TRAIL

This trail is the longest route to Porter and there is some steep climbing in its lower sections, but the variety of views makes it a worthwhile route. The first mile of the trail passes through some recent lumbering, but the route is now cleared and marked through this area. This trail is currently maintained by the Schenectady Chapter of the ADK and is marked with ADK markers.

From the High Peaks sign in the center of Keene Valley, proceed N on Rt. 73 for 2.0 mi. to a side road opposite the Town of Keene highway garage, marked with a small sign for Porter. Turn down this road for 150 yds. and turn R and park at the entrance to a dirt road leading to several large gravel piles. Leaving the paved road (0 mi.), the trail goes R of the gravel piles and joins the road leading up a hill. At 0.19 mi. the trail turns sharp L off this road and climbs along a side hill to the lower edge of the lumbered area at 0.33 mi. Soon after entering the lumbered area, the trail crosses a small height of land, descends slightly, and proceeds on the flat to a brook crossing at 0.60 mi. The trail now follows an eroded logging road up the R bank of the brook, bearing L at 0.72 mi. and then almost immediately turning R off the road and heading for some standing timber. Now on the edge of a bank above the brook, the trail reaches state land and the end of the lumbering at 1.08 mi. (Care is needed to follow this trail on the descent, but there are enough markers if one is careful to look for them.)

Above the lumbered area, the trail follows an old tote road until it turns sharp R and crosses the brook at 1.16 mi. The trail traverses to the R on a moderate grade but after crossing a brook bed at 1.25 mi. begins a steep climb. Reaching a view of Hurricane at 1.52 mi., the trail continues to a better view at a ledge at 1.65 mi. Now marked with both trail markers and red paint blazes, the trail climbs steeply to very steeply to a lookout at the E end of a ridge at 1.80 mi., where there are good views of Keene Valley. Now mostly on the flat, the trail comes to an open ledge on the S side of the ridge at 1.93 mi. and then drops slightly to a sag before climbing easily to the summit of Blueberry Mt. at 2.40 mi.

After descending to a col at 2.60 mi., the trail winds through a spruce forest and then climbs steeply up a ravine to a grassy summit at 3.10 mi. Now it continues along a beautiful ridge at easy grades, passing over two fine lookouts before joining the trail from Johns Brook Rd. at 4.10 mi. Continuing straight ahead along the ridge, the trail climbs at easy to moderate grades to the E summit and then is mostly flat to the summit of Porter at 4.54 mi. A trail with red DEC disks continues over the summit and on to Cascade and Rt. 73 in Cascade Pass. (See Northern Section.)

Distances: Keene Valley Airport to Blueberry Mt., 2.40 mi.; to ADK trail from Interbrook Rd., 4.10 mi.; to summit of Porter, 4.54 mi. (7.30 km.). Ascent from Airport, 3275 ft. (998 m.). Elevation, 4059 ft. (1237 m.). Order of height, 38.

ROOSTER COMB, HEDGEHOG AND LOWER WOLF JAW FROM KEENE VALLEY

This trail leads first to the rocky summit of Rooster Comb, a popular short hike, and then on over Hedgehog via a trail cut in 1953 to join the W.A. White Trail to Lower Wolf Jaw. This is the first portion of a traverse of the entire Great Range. (See above, "Mt. Marcy from Keene Valley via Great Range.")

The trail starts on Interbrook Rd. (also known as Johns Brook Rd.), 0.60 mi. W of the High Peaks sign in the center of Keene Valley on the approach to the Phelps Trail and the Garden. (See above.) Just before the bridge over Johns Brook, a narrow driveway goes straight ahead. No parking is permitted anywhere on the private driveway beyond the stone gates, so cars must be parked on the road near the bridge. This trail is currently maintained by the Glens Falls Chapter of the ADK and is marked with ADK markers.

From the stone gates (0 mi.) proceed up the driveway past one house on the R and bear L at the driveway to a second house. At 0.14 mi., bear R and up another 130 yds. to where the trail bears L and up a steep driveway. The steep grade rounds off before the trail reaches a clearing at 0.45 mi. where the Rooster Comb Trail swings sharp L onto another road and down 50 yds. to a bridge over a small stream. Just past this bridge, the Rooster Comb Trail turns sharp R and begins to ascend an eroded lumber road. The grade becomes steeper at 0.54 mi. on a very eroded section, but soon eases. At 0.79 mi. the trail turns sharp R off the lumber road and crosses a small brook. Now the trail begins to climb easily, but soon ascends at a steady, steep grade until there is a short breather at a small height of land at 1.50 mi. Turning L here, the trail resumes its steep climb to a ledge at 1.65 mi., where there are views of Porter and the Johns Brook Valley. Easier climbing leads to the summit of Rooster Comb at 1.75 mi. (2.82 km.). A side trail leads R for 75 yds. to a broad open ledge with excellent views of Marcy, the Johns Brook Valley and Chapel Pond Pass. Ascent from road, 1640 ft. (500 m.). Elevation, 2762 ft. (842 m.).

Swinging sharp L at the summit, the trail descends steeply over ledges and then down very steeply through a gully for 50 yds. to the foot of the cliff and a junction near some large boulders at 2.00 mi. (Trail straight ahead with ADK markers is the Sachs Trail, leading to Rt. 73, which connects with the trail to Snow; see below.) Turning R at this junction, the Hedgehog Trail climbs at moderate to steep grades with occasional glimpses out through the trees of the cliffs on Rooster Comb. The trail dips slightly at 2.40 mi., but soon resumes the climb to the summit of North Hedgehog at 2.70 mi. Both this and the main summit of Hedgehog are wooded, offering no views. The trail now descends, crosses a brook at 2.95 mi., and then climbs to the summit of Hedgehog at 3.10 mi. (5.00 km.). Total ascent from road, 2530 ft. (771 m.). Elevation, 3369 ft. (1027 m.).

From Hedgehog, the trail descends toward the W and SW to a brook with a junction just beyond at 3.50 mi. (Trail coming in from the L with ATIS markers is the W.A. White Trail; see St. Huberts

Section.) Turning R and now following ATIS markers, the trail continues to the crest of a ridge and climbs at moderate to easy grades to a slight sag, after which the climbing increases to the top of the Wolf's "Chin" at 4.50 mi. The trail then descends steeply to a col and soon begins an exceedingly steep climb to the summit of Lower Wolf Jaw at 4.95 mi. There are good views from the summit lookout to the N and W. The trail continues over the summit and on to connect with the ADK Range Trail in Wolf Jaws Notch (see above).

Distances: Interbrook Rd. at Johns Brook bridge to Rooster Comb, 1.75 mi.; to junction with Sachs Trail to Rt. 73, 2.00 mi.; to summit of Hedgehog, 3.10 mi.; to junction with W.A. White Trail, 3.51 mi.; to summit of Lower Wolf Jaw, 4.95 mi. (7.96 km.). Total ascent from road, 3670 ft. (1119 m.). Elevation, 4175 ft. (1273 m.). Order of height, 30.

ROOSTER COMB FROM RT. 73

Known as the Sachs Trail, this trail to Rooster Comb is slightly longer than the trail from Keene Valley but has roughly equivalent grades. The start of the trail is rather difficult to find as the land owner has requested that no signs be placed on the highway. This trail also gives access to Snow Mt.

The trail leaves Rt. 73, 0.75 mi. S of the High Peaks sign in the center of Keene Valley. There is a small, red fire hydrant just S of the private driveway with two old stone gate posts nearly hidden in the thick bushes. Park cars on the highway and proceed 0.10 mi. to a junction with a sign pointing R for Rooster Comb. The trail follows this road at easy grades past another house on the R to a sharp L turn off the road at 0.34 mi. at a point where the road swings R. The trail now climbs moderately through open hemlocks to the L bank of Rushing Brook above a small flume, and then swings R and continues the climb to a short flat area at 0.50 mi. Crossing a small stream, the trail swings R and up to another breather at 0.66 mi., after which the grade is steady to a junction at 1.24 mi. (ATIS trail L leads to Snow Mt. and St. Huberts; see St. Huberts Section.)

Continuing past this junction, the grade moderates at 1.37 mi. and continues mostly easy to a junction at 1.67 mi. (Trail L leads to Hedgehog and Lower Wolf Jaw; see above.) Continuing straight ahead, the trail passes several large boulders and begins a very steep climb up a gully for 50 yds., after which the grade eases a bit as the trail switchbacks up through small ledges to the summit at 1.92 mi. A side trail L from the junction at the summit leads 75 yds. to the broad summit ledge, where there are excellent views of Marcy, the Johns Brook Valley and Chapel Pond Pass. Trail with ADK markers continues over the summit and on down to Interbrook Rd. just W of Keene Valley (see above).

Distances: Rt. 73 to junction with ATIS trail, 1.24 mi.; to junction with Hedgehog Trail, 1.67 mi.; to summit of Rooster Comb, 1.92 mi. (3.09 km.). Ascent from Rt. 73, 1720 ft. (524 m.). Elevation, 2762 ft. (842 m.).

BAXTER MT. FROM RT. 9N ON SPRUCE HILL

There are three trails to the summit of this popular climb, of which this approach is the easiest. The many ledges on Baxter offer outstanding views of Keene Valley, the Great Range and Marcy at the head of the Johns Brook Valley. The start for this approach is on Rt. 9N, 2.0 mi. from the intersection of Rtes. 9N and 73 between Keene and Keene Valley, at the top of a long climb. The trail begins 20 yds. to the E of the junction of Hurricane Rd. and Rt. 9N. This trail is currently maintained by the Algonquin Chapter of the ADK and is marked with ADK markers.

From the road (0 mi.), the trail heads SW through some pines, crosses under a power line, and begins an easy to moderate climb to a height of land at 0.65 mi. after which it is level to a junction 40 yds. later. (Trail coming in from the L is from Beede Farm; see below.) Turning R, the trail starts a steep climb which moderates at 0.76 mi., after which there are many side trails leading L to numerous views and blueberry patches. The trail continues with alternating steep pitches and flat areas to the SE summit at 0.93 mi. The trail now descends into a col and climbs to the NW summit at 1.09 mi., where there are more views. The trail continues over this summit and down to the Upham Road near Keene Valley (see below).

Distances: Rt. 9N to junction with Beede Farm Trail, 0.67 mi.; to NW summit, 1.09 mi. (1.75 km.). Ascent from Rt. 9N, 770 ft. (235 m.). Elevation, 2440 ft. (744 m.).

BAXTER MT. FROM BEEDE FARM

This slightly longer approach to Baxter can be combined with a descent via the trail from Upham Road to make a nice loop trip; and since most hikers do this trip in this manner, the Upham Trail is included in this description going down. The use of two cars will save 0.3 mi. of road walking if one chooses to do the entire loop. This trail is currently maintained by the Algonquin Chapter of the ADK and is marked with ADK markers.

The start is at the end of Beede Rd. off Rt. 73, 0.6 mi. N of the High Peaks sign in the center of Keene Valley. Turn up Beede Rd., cross a new bridge over the Ausable River, and turn L at a junction 0.4 mi. from Rt. 73. (Approach to Spread Eagle and Hopkins goes R at this junction; see below.) Continuing up Beede Rd., the third driveway on the L at 0.6 mi. is the Upham Road, a private driveway, which is the end of the loop. Cars may be parked just beyond on the R. Now a dirt road, Beede Rd. climbs to a junction at

0.9 mi. just below the Beede Farm. Cars should be parked here and not at the farm as in the past.

From the junction (0 mi.), the trail goes L up the driveway past the Beede Farm on the L and continues up across an old pasture. There are few markers on this section, but in general the trail takes every L after the top of the pasture. At the top of the old pasture, the trail follows a grassy road and bears L at 0.32 mi. Continuing to bear L onto an older road, the trail becomes a footpath and is marked with occasional yellow paint blazes along with a few trail markers. At 1.13 mi. the trail comes to a junction. (Trail R with ADK markers comes up from Rt. 9N; see above.) Turning L, the trail starts a steep climb which moderates at 1.22 mi., after which there are many side trails leading L to numerous views and blueberry patches. The trail continues with alternating steep pitches and flat areas to the SE summit at 1.39 mi. It now descends into a col and climbs to the NW summit at 1.55 mi. (2.49 km.) where there are more views. Ascent from Beede Farm, 1150 ft. (350 m.). Elevation, 2440 ft. (744 m.).

Continuing over the summit, the trail descends to the W shoulder where there are good views to the W. Descending steeply off this shoulder, it flattens out at 1.75 mi. and comes to some more views at 1.95 mi. Swinging L off the end of the ridge, the trail descends steeply through an open forest of red pines and then into thicker trees and down to a small brook at 2.35 mi. After climbing over a small hogback on the far side of the brook, the trail swings R on an old tote road and descends gradually along a shelf above the brook valley. Bearing L where another old road diverges R, the trail takes a sharp L off the tote road at 3.00 mi. and goes over a low ridge and down to the Upham driveway at 3.05 mi., just below the house. (Hikers ascending via this route should watch for this sharp R just before the house at the end of a switchback on the driveway.) The trail now descends the driveway to Beede Rd. at 3.25 mi.

Distances: Beede Farm to junction with trail from Rt. 9N, 1.13 mi.; to summit of Baxter, 1.55 mi.; to Beede Rd. via Upham Trail, 3.25 mi. (5.23 km.).

SPREAD EAGLE AND HOPKINS

These two summits in the Giant Range just E of Keene Valley offer an opportunity for a half day's climb with rewarding views. Hopkins was named for Rev. Erastus Hopkins of Troy, New York, who later served several terms in the Massachusetts Legislature while a resident of Northampton. It was he who suggested to "Old Mountain" Phelps the name of "Resagone" meaning "the King's great saw," for the mountain we now call Sawteeth.

The direct approach to these peaks from Keene Valley was confusing to hikers for several years, because of a real estate development which the trail crosses. At the present time, this development consists mostly of a series of roads, but no houses, and the maintenance of these roads is problematical. The start as described below is therefore still recommended even though at times it might be possible to drive a little higher. This trail is now maintained by the Genesee Valley Chapter of ADK and is well marked with many new signs and ADK trail markers.

The start is off Beede Rd., which leaves Rt. 73 0.6 mi. N of the High Peaks sign in the center of Keene Valley. Proceed up Beede Rd. across a new bridge over the Ausable River and cross another smaller bridge. At 0.4 mi. turn R at a junction (road L is Beede Rd. and approach to Baxter; see above) and cross another small bridge. At 0.6 mi. the road (now quite narrow) swings sharp L and up steeply, bearing L at a private drive at 0.9 mi. (old sign pointing L) and comes to another private drive going L at 1.0 mi., where the road narrows and becomes impassable to cars. There is room to park 2-3 cars here.

From the end of the road (0 mi.), the trail climbs gradually for 0.12 mi. where it turns sharp R onto another old road and then turns sharp L and up at 0.24 mi. Climbing moderately, the trail joins a gravel road at 0.36 mi. and follows this to the L and up to another junction at 0.60 mi. Passing straight through this junction, the trail turns R 50 yds. later at the next junction. In another 80 yds. the trail turns L and up a steep, eroded road. The grade eases a bit just before a covered concrete reservoir on the L at 0.92 mi. and then reaches a junction at 1.04 mi.

This is the top of the real estate development. The trail over Spread Eagle goes straight here while the direct trail to Hopkins bears L. This direct trail is quite steep in its upper sections and is usually preferred as a return route (see below). The Spread Eagle Trail continues straight ahead and up an eroded lumber road. Above this road there is easier footing as the trail climbs through a beautiful maple forest. At 1.52 mi. there is a short side trail R to a ledge with views of the hamlet of Keene Valley. Continuing on, the trail climbs, with a few steep pitches, to another ledge at 1.69 mi. with views to the S. The trail swings L away from this ledge and ascends a series of ledges to a point just S of the actual summit of Spread Eagle. The trail now drops steeply into the col between Spread Eagle and Hopkins at 1.86 mi., then climbs steeply to the top of a ridge of Hopkins, which it ascends, passing two more lookouts on the R, and reaching the junction with the direct trail at 2.30 mi. Turning R, the trail ascends to the summit of Hopkins at 2.37 mi. There are unobstructed views in all directions except to the NE, and many blueberries in season. An ATIS trail continues over the summit and down to St. Huberts or on to Giant (see St. Huberts Section).

Distances: End of passable road to direct trail to Hopkins, 1.04 mi.; to lookout near summit of Spread Eagle, 1.69 mi.; to upper junction with direct trail, 2.30 mi.; to summit of Hopkins, 2.37 mi.

(3.81 km.). Ascent from road, 1840 ft. (561 m.). Elevation, 3183 ft. (970 m.).

HOPKINS via DIRECT TRAIL

Proceed as above to the junction at the top of the real estate development, 1.04 mi. from the end of the passable road. Turn L and follow a gravel road on the flat to a sharp R turn off the road at 1.18 mi. The trail climbs steadily along a side hill, following traces of old lumber roads. Crossing several brooks, the trail continues to climb through beautiful hardwoods until it levels out momentarily just before entering conifers. At the end of this level stretch at 1.95 mi., the trail turns R and up steeply to very steeply to the junction with the Spread Eagle Trail at 2.12 mi. Turning L, the route to the summit is the same as the Spread Eagle Trail (see above) and is reached at 2.19 mi.

Distances: End of passable road to junction with Spread Eagle Trail, 1.04 mi.; to upper junction with Spread Eagle Trail, 2.12 mi.; to summit of Hopkins, 2.19 mi. (3.52 km.). Ascents and elevation the same as the Spread Eagle Trail; see above.

HOPKINS via RANNEY TRAIL

This trail to Hopkins is rarely used, but it has moderate grades throughout and generally good footing. The trail joins the Mossy Cascade Trail to Hopkins 0.87 mi. below the summit of Hopkins. The trail starts at an iron bridge over the Ausable River, 0.5 mi. S of the High Peaks sign in the center of Keene Valley on Rt. 73. Since this is a private drive, cars should be parked on Rt. 73.

From the highway (0 mi.), follow the driveway on the flat to the far end of the clearing at 0.26 mi., where a sign pointing R marks the start of the trail. The trail enters the woods on a lumber road following along the R bank of a stream on easy to moderate grades.

Crossing the brook at 0.72 mi., it climbs steeply along an old lumber road and then turns sharp L at 0.85 mi., now climbing moderately along the L bank of the brook. The trail crosses a yellow-blazed property line at 0.96 mi. and continues at a moderate grade with a few steeper pitches to the junction with the Mossy Cascade Trail coming in from the R at 1.78 mi. Turning L, the route is the same as for the Mossy Cascade Trail (see St. Huberts Section).

Distances: Rt. 73 to Mossy Cascade Trail, 1.78 mi.; to summit of Hopkins, 2.65 mi. (4.26 km.). Ascent from Rt. 73, 2140 ft. (652 m.). Elevation, 3183 ft. (970 m.).

ST. HUBERTS SECTION

St. Huberts is located on Rt. 73, 2.5 mi. S of Keene Valley. There are over 90 mi. of trails in this area, offering a wide variety of hikes, from woodland walks along beautiful streams to ascents of Giant, Gothics and other peaks. Many of these trails are relatively un-crowded, and in the protected areas in the Adirondack Mountain Reserve wildlife is abundant and much more likely to be seen than in other hiking areas. A half mile from Rt. 73 at the top of a hill is the Ausable Club, which administers the Adirondack Mountain Reserve (AMR), a private preserve stretching over 10 mi. to the SW.

As part of the sale of higher land by the AMR to the State of New York in 1978, the state acquired permanent public easements for foot travel by the public over all of the hiking trails on AMR land with the exception of certain trails near the shores of the Upper Ausable Lake. (See Upper Ausable Lake Area, below.) These easements guarantee public access to the summits of Colvin, Blake, Dial, Nippletop, Sawteeth and the Great Range; but while still on AMR land, hikers must obey the following rules:

1) No camping, fishing or hunting.
2) No off-trail travel including rock climbing or bushwhacking along the shores of the Lower Ausable Lake.
3) No boating or swimming, including portable boats brought in

by the public; there are no boats for rent by the public.

4) NO DOGS or other pets are permitted in this game preserve.

These restrictions do not apply to approaches to Snow, Hopkins, Giant, Round, Noonmark, Dix or Lower Wolf Jaw (if approached via Deer Brook); and once past the private boundaries one may camp and fish. Hikers starting backpacking trips from St. Huberts must therefore plan an early enough start so that they can reach state land in time to set up camp. The warden of the AMR may turn backpackers away if they clearly cannot reach a legal campsite by nightfall. For the exact location of public and private land in this area, see the map that accompanies this guidebook.

The approaches to many of these hikes are on the Lake Road which runs from the clubhouse to the Lower Ausable Lake. See the description below for information on summer bus service on this road. Hikers approaching Round, Noonmark, or any of the climbs off the Lake Road, are required to park their car at the designated hikers' parking lot just off Rt. 73 opposite the parking lot for the Roaring Brook Trail. This spot is 3.0 mi. S of the High Peaks sign in Keene Valley (0.5 mi. S of the main access road to the Ausable Club) or 5.9 mi. N of the junction of Rtes. 9 and 73 in Underwood. From this parking lot it is 0.5 mi. W along the gravel road and past the golf course to the start of the Lake Road (see below).

Except for the Dix Trail from Rt. 73, all trails in this region are maintained by the Adirondack Trail Improvement Society and marked with ATIS markers. The trails in the vicinity of the Upper Ausable Lake, formerly described in a separate section in previous editions of this guidebook, are now included at the end of the St. Huberts section. See the introduction to the Upper Ausable Lake Area for information on hiking these trails.

Below are listed a few suggested hikes to help first-time visitors to the area choose among the many possibilities:

SHORT HIKES:

Snow Mt. — 3.44 mi., round trip. An easy trail along a pretty brook with a waterfall leads to an open summit with good views and plenty of blueberries. See description for Snow Mt. via Deer Brook Trail.

Giant's Nubble via the Washbowl — 3.04 mi., round trip. This rocky summit offers a spectacular view of the slides on Giant and of Chapel Pond Pass with a unique mountainside pond on the way. See descriptions for Giant via Ridge Trail and Giant's Nubble.

MODERATE HIKES:

Hopkins via Mossy Cascade — 6.34 mi., round trip. A seldom-used approach to a popular rocky summit, passing by a beautiful 50-ft.-high waterfall and several interesting lookouts.

East and West River Trails — 7.41 mi., round trip. A relatively flat walk through some beautiful forests along the banks of the Ausable River, making a loop trip to the Lower Ausable Lake and back. See descriptions for Lake Road, East River Trail and West River Trail.

HARDER HIKES:

Giant via Ridge Trail with return over Green, Hopkins and Spread Eagle — 8.55 mi., point to point. An ascent of Giant along the open rocks of the ridge trail with a descent through some lovely virgin forests and a variety of additional views enroute to Keene Valley. See descriptions for Giant via Ridge Trail, Giant via Hopkins and Green, and Spread Eagle and Hopkins from Beede Rd. (Keene Valley Section).

Gothics with return via Sawteeth "Scenic Trail" — 13.46 mi., round trip. A rugged loop but one offering unforgettable views from the summits of Gothics, Pyramid and Sawteeth, plus five more lookouts on the way down Sawteeth. Total distance would be 5.50 mi. less if the Lake Road bus is used. See descriptions for Gothics from Lake Road, Gothics from Lower Ausable Lake via Pyramid, and Sawteeth from Lower Ausable Lake via Scenic Trail.

Den from Lake Road	5.88	92
Noonmark via Stimson Trail from Ausable Club	2.06	93
Noonmark from SE via Felix Adler Trail	2.68	94
Round Mt.	3.01	96
Dix Mt. via Round Pond from Rt. 73	6.82	97
Giant via Roaring Brook Trail	3.56	99
Giant via Ridge Trail	2.94	101
Giant's Nubble	1.27	103
Giant's Washbowl from Roaring Brook Trail	1.01	104
Mossy Cascade Trail to Hopkins	3.17	105
Giant from Hopkins via Green	3.04	106
Deer Brook Trail to Snow Mt.	1.72	107
W.A. White Trail to Snow Mt. via Maghee Clearing	0.73	109
Upper Ausable Lake Area		110
Carry Trail	1.00	111
Colvin from Carry Trail	1.90	112
Blake Peak from Colvin Trail	0.55	113
Sawteeth from Warden's Camp	2.80	113
Haystack and Marcy from Warden's Camp	3.45	115
Great Range and Haystack via Haystack Brook	4.35	116
Blake Peak and Colvin via Pinnacle Ridge from Elk Lake-Marcy Trail	5.35	117

ROAD TO LOWER AUSABLE LAKE

This private road, known as the Lake Road, runs SW from the main club building to the boathouse at the foot of the Lower Ausable Lake, gaining about 700 vertical ft. in 3.5 mi. A quarter mile from the club is a locked gate, beyond which private vehicles (except those of members in the off-season) are not permitted. Bicycles are also prohibited, but foot traffic is permitted. The club operates a bus over this road in season; this service is available to the public for $1.25 one way after members have been accommodated.

From the clubhouse, the road drops down between two tennis courts and past the golf house and some private cottages. Three hundred yds. beyond the clubhouse the W.A. White Trail to Lower Wolf Jaw and the West River Trail diverge R at a small, green watchman's hut. Continuing straight ahead (the profusion of signs reminds hikers of the rules that must be obeyed while on AMR property), the gate is reached in another 90 yds. From the gate (0 mi.), the two ends of the Ladies Mile branch R at 45 yds. and 0.25 mi. At 0.30 mi., the East River Trail branches R, and at 0.73 mi. the Henry Goddard Leach Trail to Dial and Nipple Top branches L. At 0.86 mi. a bridge leads across Gill Brook to connect with the East and West River Trails. The road crosses Gill Brook at 1.10 mi., with a side trail L leading past a small flume on Gill Brook. At 1.75 mi. a trail leads R to Beaver Meadow Falls and Gothics with the Gill Brook Trail to Colvin and Nipple Top diverging L a few yards beyond. The shorter trail to Colvin and Nipple Top diverges L at 2.50 mi., and at 3.10 mi. the road reaches a height of land just above the Lower Lake. Just beyond, a side road leads R to the dam at the end of the Lower Lake and the trails to Rainbow Falls, Sawteeth and Gothics. The Lake Road now descends to the boathouse at 3.25 mi.

Distance: Gate to Lower Ausable Lake, 3.25 mi. (5.23 km.). Ascent, 700 ft. (213 m.).

EAST RIVER TRAIL

This trail follows the R bank of the Ausable River to the dam at Lower Ausable Lake. It offers some very pleasant walking and some lovely views of various falls and pools in the river as well as a few of the surrounding peaks. The trail diverges R from the Lake Road 0.30 mi. from the gate (see above). From the road (0 mi.) the trail veers away from the road and reaches the Ausable River at a bridge at 0.16 mi. Bearing L, it follows along the river bank on the level to a sign indicating a choice of "steep" or "easy" at 0.45 mi. Climbing the bank of the river, the trail quickly descends to cross Gill Brook on a bridge at 0.50 mi. and then follows up Gill Brook's L bank for a few yards before bearing R and reaching a gravel road at 0.65 mi. (Road R leads to Canyon Bridge over Ausable River and connection to West River Trail in 0.31 mi. Road L leads 0.13 mi. to Lake Road.)

Crossing the gravel road, the trail climbs to the top of a bank high above the river and levels out at 0.92 mi. After some other lesser climbs, the trail heads R and down across a steep side hill at 1.61 mi. and soon comes to a lookout over the gorge at 1.65 mi. The trail now draws slowly closer to the river, passing some other views of falls before coming to a crossing of a large plastic water line which transfers water from the Ausable to Gill Brook to supplement the Ausable Club's water supply. At 2.22 mi. the trail reaches a junction with the Beaver Meadow Falls Trail to Gothics. Bearing R and down, the two trails are together until at 2.29 mi. the Gothics Trail goes sharp R and down to a bridge. Continuing straight ahead, there is a view of Sawteeth across Beaver Meadow at 2.36 mi., and the trail continues mostly on the flat to the bridge below the dam at 3.32 mi.

Distances: Lake Road to Beaver Meadow Falls Trail to Gothics, 2.22 mi.; to bridge and dam at Lower Ausable Lake, 3.32 mi. (5.34 km.); to Lower Lake Boathouse, 3.48 mi. (3.78 mi. from the gate).

LADIES MILE

As the name implies, this is a short jaunt through the woods to the bank of the Ausable River, making about a mile round trip from the clubhouse. There are many possible variations using the East or West River Trail to return. Leaving the road (0 mi.) 45 yds. past the gate, the trail descends a short flight of steps, crosses a bridge and turns L to a tote road at 0.08 mi. Here the Ladies Mile forks, with the two branches rejoining at 0.40 mi. The R branch turns R on this tote road, and 30 yds. after turning off the tote road reaches the bank of the Ausable and follows this up to the junction with the L branch. The L branch follows a small brook up to a bridge leading L (and back to the Lake Road) at 0.25 mi. and on to the junction with the R branch at 0.40 mi.

This junction is just below the crossover bridge to the West River Trail. One may return via either the R or L branch of the Ladies Mile or make a slightly longer walk by returning via the East or West River Trail (see below).

WEST RIVER TRAIL

This trail follows up the L bank of the Ausable River to the dam at the Lower Ausable Lake. It offers pleasant walking through some virgin stands of timber, as well as some views of the pools and falls in the river and some of the surrounding peaks. Combined with either the East River Trail or the Lake Road, this provides a lovely woodland walk of about 7 mi. with relatively little climbing.

The start is on the Lake Road 300 yds. past the clubhouse at the small green watchman's hut. Leaving the road (0 mi.), the trail starts on a private driveway and descends slightly to the river, which is crossed on a bridge to a junction at the far side at 0.16 mi. (Trail R leads to Lower Wolf Jaw and the Range via the W.A. White Trail with connecting trails to Snow and Rooster Comb Mts; see below.)

Turning L, the trail proceeds along the river to another junction at a bridge at 0.62 mi. (Trail R leads to Cathedral Rocks and Bear Run; see below. Bridge L leads to East River Trail and Ladies Mile; see above.) Continuing straight, the West River Trail crosses Pyramid Brook at 1.08 mi. with the upper end of the Cathedral Rocks Trail joining the trail 25 yds. farther on. Soon climbing above the river, the trail comes to a junction with the "Direct" trail to Pyramid Brook (see below) coming in from the R and another junction 60 yds. beyond at 1.29 mi. (Trail L descends steeply and crosses the river on a bridge to connect with East River Trail and Lake Road; see above.)

Continuing straight ahead, the grade becomes easy at 1.40 mi., where there is a lookout into the gorge below. The grade soon steepens again, and there is another lookout at 1.70 mi. with views of Colvin, Nipple Top and the river, with a third lookout of Giant at 1.89 mi. Now swinging away from the river, the trail crosses Wedge Brook at 2.04 mi. and reaches a junction with the Wedge Brook Trail just beyond. (Trail R leads 2.15 mi. to Lower Wolf Jaw; see below.) Turning L and down, the trail comes to a view from the top of a new slide at 2.12 mi. and then descends to the level of the river and then on to Beaver Meadow Falls at 2.74 mi. These falls of bridal veil-like appearance are well worth the trip alone.

Crossing the brook below the falls, the trail soon comes to a junction. Beaver Meadow Falls Trail leads R to Gothics (2.80 mi.) and Lost Lookout (0.60 mi.). Trail L is to East River Trail and Lake Road (0.50 mi.). Continuing straight ahead, the West River Trail crosses the flat open area known as Beaver Meadow. Following along the base of a steep cliff at 3.20 mi., the trail continues to a junction with the other end of the Lost Lookout Trail at 3.74 mi. and reaches the bridge and dam at the Lower Lake at 3.79 mi.

The trail straight ahead leads to Rainbow Falls, Sawteeth and Gothics. Bridge L leads to East River Trail, Lake Road and the boathouse at 3.94 mi.

Distances: Lake Road to trail to Cathedral Rocks, 0.62 mi.; to Wedge Brook Trail to Lower Wolf Jaw, 2.04 mi.; to Beaver Meadow Falls and Gothics Trail, 2.74 mi.; to Lower Lake bridge and dam, 3.79 mi.; to boathouse, 3.94 mi. (6.34 km.).

CATHEDRAL ROCKS AND BEAR RUN

This interesting loop trail offers a short round trip with some interesting rock formations, two views and a pretty little waterfall. The start is on the West River Trail at the bridge at 0.62 mi.; this can also be reached via the East River Trail (see below). Leaving the West River Trail (0 mi.), the trail climbs moderately along the L bank of a small brook heading first W and then NW. The climbing steepens as the trail approaches the first rock face at 0.53 mi. Then swinging L, the trail continues along under a series of cliffs to a larger one on the R at 0.80 mi. This is Cathedral Rocks.

Just beyond Cathedral Rocks is a junction with the trail L leading 0.26 mi. across to the main trail to bypass Bear Run. Bearing R and up at this junction, the trail crosses the property line of the AMR, with the base of a large cliff reached soon after at 1.04 mi. Side trail R leads 300 yds. along the base of the cliff to a narrow slot in the cliff, which is followed up to a panoramic view ranging from Giant on the L to Sawteeth on the R. As the sign at the junction says, "don't miss."

Turning L at the base of the cliff, the trail climbs to a height of land and then descends to another lookout at 1.28 mi. Just beyond this lookout, the trail swings sharp L and descends a narrow shelf through the ledges. Now descending very steeply, it reaches the other end of the bypass trail at 1.36 mi., after which it continues descending steeply along the L bank of Pyramid Brook, past a waterfall, to flatter terrain at 1.48 mi. Now crossing to the R bank of the brook, the trail comes to a junction at 1.54 mi. (Trail R leads 0.17 mi. directly to West River Trail at crossover bridge.) Continuing L, the trail descends the R bank of Pyramid Brook to the West River Trail at 1.66 mi.

Distances: West River Trail to bypass trail above Cathedral Rocks, 0.83 mi.; to base of cliff at Bear Run, 1.04 mi.; to Pyramid Brook waterfall, 1.48 mi.; to West River Trail, 1.66 mi. (2.67 km.).

LOST LOOKOUT

This trail climbs about 500 ft. onto the side of Armstrong above Beaver Meadow to two exceptional viewpoints of Lower Ausable Lake and the surrounding mountains. The start is at Beaver Meadow Falls, which can be reached by either the East or West River Trail or directly from the Lake Road by the Beaver Meadow Falls Trail to Gothics (see above).

Leaving Beaver Meadow Falls (0 mi.), the trail coincides with the Gothics Trail, climbing a ladder and ascending steeply to a junction at 0.25 mi. Here the Lost Lookout Trail branches L and climbs steadily to the first lookout at 0.60 mi. Leveling off, the trail descends slightly to the second lookout at 0.70 mi. and then begins to descend. There is a lookout to Rainbow Falls on the R at 1.50 mi., after which the trail descends to the West River Trail at 1.65 mi. and, turning R, reaches the bridge and dam at Lower Ausable Lake at 1.70 mi.

Distances: Beaver Meadow Falls to first lookout, 0.60 mi.; to bridge and dam at Lower Ausable Lake, 1.70 mi. (2.74 km.).

RAINBOW FALLS

This nearly 150-ft.-high waterfall is a sight that should not be missed, whether one makes a trip up the Lake Road just to see the falls or as a side trip while on a longer hike in the area. From the W end of the bridge at the Lower Ausable Lake Dam, follow the Gothics Trail for 0.12 mi. and diverge R for another 0.10 mi. along, and sometimes in, the brook to the base of the falls at 0.22 mi. Distance from boathouse, 0.37 mi. (0.60 km.).

W.A. WHITE TRAIL TO LOWER WOLF JAW

This trail is named after one of the founders of the ATIS and the designer of the Range Trail from Gothics to Haystack. It is a slightly longer route to Lower Wolf Jaw than the Wedge Brook Trail, but it does offer some views on the way up and the grades are generally easier. As of 1984, lumbering operations near Maghee Clearing have necessitated some rerouting and a roughly half-mile section is now quite unattractive with the trail following some eroded skid roads through the slash. Enough markers are in place so that with care one can stay on the trail.

The start is on the Lake Road, 300 yds. from the clubhouse at the small green watchman's hut. Leaving the road (0 mi.), the trail starts down a private driveway and descends slightly to the Ausable River which it crosses on a bridge to reach a junction on the far side at 0.16 mi. (Trail L is West River Trail to Lower Ausable Lake; see above.) Bearing R, the trail climbs at an easy grade along a side hill to a junction with a recent lumber road at 0.64 mi. Turning L, the trail follows this lumber road through a freshly lumbered area up to Maghee Clearing at 0.85 mi., where there is a good view of Giant.

Shortly after this view the trail crests a small hill and descends briefly before climbing to a second crest which is where the old trail went L. Continuing on, the lumber road climbs easily for a short while and then up steeply to a junction at 1.04 mi. (Trail R leads to Snow and Rooster Comb Mts.; see below.) The trail then bears L and up steeply to the base of a cliff at 1.13 mi. Turning L, the trail follows along the base of the cliff on an easier grade and reaches the top of the lumbered area, where the old trail is rejoined at 1.30 mi. The trail now switchbacks up through a cliff band and gains the top of the ridge at 1.40 mi. Climbing the ridge at a moderate grade, the trail reaches a side trail leading 25 yds. to a lookout at 1.64 mi.

Past this junction, the trail again switchbacks to the R and continues at a moderate grade to another ledge 1.85 mi., where there are good views of the Ausable Valley as well as of the surrounding peaks. Then making a short descent, the trail climbs to a higher ledge at 2.04 mi. From here, it descends slightly and then begins an easy climb interspersed with level stretches to the junction with the Hedgehog Trail at 3.01 mi. (Trail R with ADK markers leads over Hedgehog Mt. to Rooster Comb and Keene Valley; see Keene Valley Section.)

Continuing straight ahead, the W.A. White Trail continues to the crest of a ridge and climbs at moderate to easy grades to a slight sag, after which the climbing increases to the top of the Wolf's "Chin" at 4.01 mi. The trail then descends steeply to a col and soon begins an exceedingly steep climb to the summit of Lower Wolf Jaw at 4.46 mi. There are good views from the summit lookout to the N and W.

The trail that continues over the summit leads in 0.30 mi. to the junction with the Wedge Brook Trail and further to the junction with the trail up from Johns Brook at the col between the two Wolf Jaws in 0.50 mi.

Distances: Lake Road to junction with trail to Snow Mt., 1.04 mi.; to junction with Hedgehog Trail, 3.01 mi.; to summit of Lower Wolf Jaw, 4.46 mi. (7.18 km.). Ascent from Lake Road, 2825 ft. (860 m.). Elevation, 4175 ft. (1273 m.). Order of height, 30.

WEDGE BROOK TRAIL TO WOLF JAWS

Alexander Wyant, a well-known artist who first came to Keene Valley in 1869, is credited with conferring the name Wolf Jaws, as suggested by the deep col between the two peaks. The spot on Noonmark from which Wyant painted a view of these peaks is supposed to offer the best representation of a wolf's jaw. The Wedge Brook Trail is the shortest route to either Wolf Jaw from the Ausable Club. Combined with the W.A. White Trail, it makes a nice round trip.

This trail branches off the West River Trail at the crossing of Wedge Brook, 2.04 mi. from the Lake Road (see above). Leaving the West River Trail (0 mi.), it climbs fairly steeply at first along the bank of Wedge Brook, but soon leaves the brook on an easier grade and reaches a clearing at 1.15 mi. Shortly after this clearing, the grade again becomes steep as the trail climbs the headwall of the ravine with the bare rock slides of Lower Wolf Jaw visible on the R. At 1.55 mi. the cutoff trail to Wolf Jaws Notch branches L, leading 0.30 mi. to the ADK Range Trail at the Notch.

Bearing R at this junction, the Wedge Brook Trail continues climbing to its junction with the ADK Range Trail at 1.85 mi. Turning R and now with ADK markers, the trail climbs steeply to the summit of Lower Wolf Jaw at 2.15 mi., where there are good views to the N and W. Trail straight ahead is the W.A. White Trail leading to St. Huberts (see above) and connecting with trails to Hedgehog, Rooster Comb and Keene Valley (see Keene Valley Section).

Distances: Lake Road to start of Wedge Brook Trail, 2.04 mi.; to junction with cut-off trail to Wolf Jaws Notch, 3.59 mi.; to summit of Lower Wolf Jaw, 4.19 mi. (6.74 km.). Ascent from Lake Road, 2825 ft. (860 m.). Elevation, 4175 ft. (1273 m.). Order of height, 30.

GOTHICS FROM LAKE ROAD

The arched peaks of this triple-crested mountain, with their great slides and bare rock, suggested Gothic architecture to Frederick Perkins and "Old Mountain" Phelps that day in 1857 when they sat on the top of Marcy and christened four mountains with character-istic names. They were Skylight, Basin, Saddleback and Gothics. This was the first trail to be cut up the mountain (in 1886), and it is still a popular route today.

The trail starts on the Lake Road just past the reservoir 1.75 mi. from the gate, which is 0.25 mi. from the Ausable Club. Turning R (W) from the road (0 mi.), the trail climbs at an easy grade to join the East River Trail at 0.45 mi. Swinging L and down at this junction, the trail turns sharp R and down at 0.50 mi. and crosses a bridge to a junction near the foot of Beaver Meadow Falls at 0.55 mi. Continuing straight across the West River Trail, the Gothics Trail climbs steeply up a ladder and then on at an easier grade to the junction with the trail leading L to Lost Lookout at 0.80 mi.

From this junction, the trail climbs at an easy grade, crossing the AMR boundary line at 1.00 mi. and continuing at an easy to moderate grade past two small streams to a third larger stream at 1.77 mi. Here the trail swings L and begins a steep climb which does not moderate until 2.41 mi. The trail flattens briefly; a large balanced rock on the R at 2.53 mi. could be used as an emergency shelter. After this balanced rock, the trail again climbs steeply up past the base of a rock wall to the crest of the ridge at 2.76 mi. From here, the trail begins to work its way across the steep W slope of a shoulder of Armstrong with several good views of Gothics. Some crude bridges and two ladders aid the passage across the steep rocks. Beyond this section, the trail comes to a junction with the ADK Range Trail at 2.95 mi. (Trail R leads to Armstrong, Upper Wolf Jaw and Keene Valley; see Keene Valley Section.) Turning L, the trail crosses a short flat section and then begins a steep climb to the summit of Gothics, reaching it at 3.40 mi.

The view is unobstructed with about 30 major peaks discernible. The boathouse at Lower Ausable Lake can be seen, but to see any of the Upper Lake one must proceed past the summit 0.12 mi. to the ATIS trail over Pyramid and go L on this trail a few yards to a wide ledge with views to the S and W. (The ADK Range Trail continues over the summit and on to the upper Great Range with connecting trails to Johns Brook Lodge and Keene Valley; see Keene Valley Section.)

Distances: Lake Road to Beaver Meadow Falls, 0.55 mi.; to ADK Range Trail, 2.95 mi.; to summit of Gothics, 3.40 mi. (5.47 km.). 5.15 mi. (8.29 km.) from gate to summit. Ascent from Lake Road, 3050 ft. (930 m.). Elevation, 4736 ft. (1444 m.). Order of height, 10.

GOTHICS FROM LOWER AUSABLE LAKE via PYRAMID

Known as the Alfred E. Weld Trail, this approach to Gothics was laid out and cut by Jim Goodwin in 1966. It is the shortest route to the summit and offers what may well be the single most spectacular view in the Adirondacks from the summit of Pyramid just below the summit of Gothics. The trail does have some steep climbing approaching the sharp peak of Pyramid.

The trail starts at the W end of the bridge below the dam at the Lower Ausable Lake (0 mi.). It coincides with the Sawteeth and Rainbow Falls Trails at first, but the Sawteeth Trail diverges L in 40 yds. and the Rainbow Falls Trail goes R at 0.12 mi. Now the Gothics Trail begins a steady ascent to a trail R to a lookout over Rainbow Falls at 0.28 mi. Swinging L, the trail climbs for a few yards further before easing off and crossing a brook and then continuing at a generally easy grade. A few more steep pitches are encountered before a long easy section leads to a crossing of an old slide coming down from Sawteeth at 0.92 mi.

Past this slide, the trail continues climbing and crosses a good sized brook at 1.28 mi., after which it becomes steeper and rougher as it ascends to the col between Pyramid and Sawteeth at 1.68 mi. Here there is a junction with the trail L leading 0.50 mi. to Sawteeth (see below). Turning R, the Gothics Trail starts at first at an easy grade, but soon begins climbing steeply and continues so until just short of the summit of Pyramid. Skirting the summit block to the R, the trail reaches the peak of Pyramid at 2.31 mi. The views encompass Gothics and all of the Great Range, seen at such an angle that nearly all of the considerable bare rock on the S side of these peaks is visible and serves as a spectacular foreground for the more distant view.

Turning R at the summit of Pyramid, the trail descends steeply to the bottom of the col at 2.45 mi. and then climbs equally steeply to a ledge on the S side of Gothics at 2.57 mi. A few yards on the level beyond, the trail meets the ADK Range Trail. Turning R, the trail reaches the summit of Gothics at 2.74 mi.

Distances: Bridge at Lower Ausable Lake to col between Sawteeth and Pyramid, 1.68 mi.; to summit of Pyramid, 2.31 mi.; to junction with ADK Range Trail, 2.62 mi.; to summit of Gothics, 2.74 mi. (4.41 km.). Ascent from Lower Lake, 2870 ft. (875 m.). Elevation, 4736 ft. (1444 m.). Order of height, 10.

SAWTEETH FROM LOWER AUSABLE LAKE

The striking, serrated profile of this mountain as seen from the Ausable Club suggested the obvious name of Sawteeth to the early inhabitants of the area. It was erroneously labeled "Sawtooth" on the 1953 USGS topographic maps, but that error has been corrected on the 1979 maps.

There are two trails to the summit from Lower Ausable Lake.

The older one, sometimes referred to as the "Scenic Trail," follows a wandering course up among the "teeth" and passes many interesting views. The newer trail follows the Gothics Trail to the col between Pyramid and Sawteeth and then ascends directly up the N side. Most hikers make this a loop trip with the descent of the Scenic Trail considered to be the easiest direction.

Leaving the W end of the bridge below the Lower Ausable Lake Dam (0 mi.), the trail diverges L from the Gothics Trail in 40 yds. and follows near the shore of the lake before beginning to climb away from the lake at 0.60 mi. At 1.00 mi. the trail reaches the first spectacular lookout 250 ft. above the lake, with a second lookout with a boulder on it at 1.05 mi. The trail now begins to climb steeply and comes to the base of a rock face at 1.20 mi. Some more steep climbing leads to the third lookout at 1.40 mi. After some easy going, the trail resumes its steep ascent and swings back to the R and reaches a height of land at 1.80 mi. Lookout Rock, a climb of a few feet up to the R, offers a precipitous view of Lower Ausable Lake 1600 ft. below.

Leaving Lookout Rock, the trail descends and soon begins an easy to moderate climb to a col at 2.20 mi. The trail now swings R and the climbing is very steep in spots as the trail ascends through some ledges and climbs a ladder to reach a lookout on the L at 2.45 mi. The grade moderates, and after another short steep pitch becomes easy to the SE summit at 2.60 mi. Now descending to a col called Rifle Notch, the trail again climbs steeply out of the notch and then on easier grades to a junction at 2.95 mi. (Trail L leads to Upper Ausable Lake; see below.) Just beyond this junction a boulder beside the trail indicates the NW summit with a lookout about 20 yds. to the L. There are good views of most of the Great Range from this lookout, with a view of Giant about 20 yds. to the E on the new trail.

Distances: Bridge at Lower Lake to Lookout Rock, 1.80 mi.; to NW summit, 3.00 mi. (4.83 km.). Ascent from Lower Lake, 2275 ft. (693 m.). Elevation, 4100 ft. (1250 m.). Order of height, 35.

SAWTEETH via PYRAMID-GOTHICS TRAIL

The Pyramid-Gothics Trail (see above) is followed from the bridge to the col at 1.68 mi. Turning L here, the Sawteeth Trail proceeds nearly on the level before beginning to climb at 1.82 mi. Immediately it ascends a steep cleft in the rock face with poor footing, but above this point the climbing becomes easier. It becomes nearly level at 2.06 mi., and reaches the summit at 2.18 mi. The lookout is 20 yds. to the R.

INDIAN HEAD

This rocky peak rises 750 ft. directly above Lower Ausable Lake and offers excellent views of both Ausable Lakes, Nipple Top, Colvin, Sawteeth and much of the Great Range. If one can ride the bus up the Lake Road (see above), this 1.6 mi. round trip climb from the boathouse is one of the best views for the amount of effort in the Adirondacks. Even if one must walk the Lake Road, the nearly 9 mi. round trip is still worth it. There are two approaches to this peak, which can be combined to make a nice loop trip including some very pretty walking along Gill Brook. All approaches are marked with ATIS markers.

1. From the boathouse at Lower Ausable Lake (0 mi.), start up between the main boathouse and a smaller boathouse to the L. The trail climbs via some steep switchbacks to a junction at the top of the steep bank at 0.06 mi. (Trail L leads 110 yds. to the Lake Road at the height of land above the boathouse.) Bear R and soon begin climbing a series of switchbacks to a side trail R at 0.30 mi. to a view of Gothics called the "Gothic Window." Continuing up several

more switchbacks, the trail ascends a ladder at 0.55 mi. and proceeds under a beautiful mossy cliff for a few yards before climbing steeply to a junction at the crest of the ridge at 0.76 mi. (Trail L leads to Gill Brook. Trail straight ahead leads to Fish Hawk Cliffs; see below.)

Turning R at this junction, the trail emerges on the bare ledges at 0.81 mi. Some broader ledges just below offer an even better view and some careful exploration to the R should find a view back down to the boathouse. One can also detour 0.26 mi. along the trail from the Colvin Trail (see below) for a view of Giant.

2. Another trail branches R from the Colvin Trail (see below) at a point 0.17 mi. above the junction with the Gill Brook Trail and the trail direct from the Lake Road. This is 0.65 mi. from the Lake Road via the direct trail and 1.32 mi. via the Gill Brook Trail. Leaving the Colvin Trail (0 mi.), the trail crosses a small brook and begins climbing steadily to a steep pitch at 0.30 mi. At 0.40 mi., a trail leads R to a lookout affording views of Giant and other peaks. The trail now levels off and then descends slightly to join the trail from the boathouse at 0.66 mi. with the lookout over the lakes reached at 0.71 mi.

Distances: Boathouse to Indian Head, 0.81 mi. (1.30 km.). Indian Head via Gill Brook Trail and Colvin Trail from Lake Road, 2.03 mi. (3.27 km.). Ascent from boathouse, 730 ft. (223 m.). Elevation, 2700 ft. (823 m.).

FISH HAWK CLIFFS

This slightly lower lookout just beyond Indian Head offers a spectacular view of the cliffs on Indian Head. A trail runs from Indian Head to Fish Hawk Cliffs and then on to the Colvin Trail.

Starting from the trail junction near the top of Indian Head (0 mi.), the trail descends very steeply to a col at 0.09 mi. and then climbs more gradually to the ledges on Fish Hawk Cliffs at 0.23 mi. Continuing l., the trail is pretty much on the level to the junction with the Colvin Trail at 0.68 mi. This junction is 0.64 mi. above the junction of the two trails from the Lake Road and 0.68 mi. below the junction with Elk Pass Trail to Nipple Top.

Distances: Indian Head to Fish Hawk Cliffs, 0.23 mi.; to Colvin Trail, 0.68 mi. (1.09 km.).

MT. COLVIN FROM LAKE ROAD

This mountain was named for Verplanck Colvin in 1873 by Rev. T.L. Cuyler, a member of Colvin's survey party, who thought the peak was nameless. A few years earlier, however, "Old Mountain" Phelps had named it "Sabele" for the Indian credited by some to have discovered the ore at the MacIntyre Iron Works. Colvin was superintendent of the Adirondack Survey and the single most prominent character in Adirondack Mountain history. Besides making the first positive measurement of Mt. Marcy in 1875 with level and rod, he was also largely responsible for the inauguration of the Adirondack Park and State Forest Preserve. It is therefore highly fitting that his name attached to this peak has endured.

There are two approaches to Colvin from the Lake Road. The longer approach turns L from the Lake Road at 1.75 mi., just past the Gothics Trail. This trail follows up the L bank of picturesque Gill Brook with its many waterfalls and small flumes to a junction with the shorter route at 1.15 mi. from the road. Though scenic, this trail is quite rough in spots and requires more time than its distance would indicate. It is, however, worth using this trail in at least one direction when climbing Colvin, Nipple Top or Indian Head. All of these trails are marked with ATIS markers.

The shorter route branches L from the Lake Road 2.50 mi. past the gate. Leaving the road (0 mi.), the trail climbs at an easy grade to the junction with the Gill Brook Trail at 0.48 mi. Turning R, the trail goes along the L bank of Gill Brook to a junction at 0.65 mi. (Trail R leads 0.71 mi. to Indian Head; see above.) Continuing past this junction, the trail climbs high above Gill Brook and comes to a junction at 1.12 mi. (Trail R leads 0.45 mi. to Fish Hawk Cliffs and 0.68 mi. to Indian Head; see above.)

Continuing on, the Colvin Trail climbs with a few steep pitches to a junction at 1.80 mi. (Trail L leads to Elk Pass and Nipple Top; see below.) Turning R, the Colvin Trail climbs in a series of alternating steep and flat sections to the top of the ridge and then down to a small sag on the ridge at 2.73 mi. Climbing steeply again, the trail drops into a second sag and then up very steeply to the summit at 2.85 mi. There is a lookout just to the R with splendid views of Lower Ausable Lake, Sawteeth and the Great Range. About 100 yds. S on the trail to Blake Peak there is another good view of Upper Ausable Lake, Allen Mt. and other peaks. (See below for description of trail leading to Blake, and on to the Elk Lake-Marcy Trail.)

Distances: Lake Road via shorter route to Gill Brook Trail, 0.48 mi.; to Indian Head Trail, 0.65 mi.; to Fish Hawk Cliffs Trail, 1.12 mi.; to Nipple Top Trail, 1.80 mi.; to summit of Colvin, 2.85 mi. (4.59 km.). Ascent from Lake Road, 2330 ft. (710 m.). Elevation, 4057 ft. (1237 m.). Order of height, 39.

NIPPLE TOP via ELK PASS

This peak is named for its characteristic profile when seen from Elk Lake. At one time more fastidious tourists and writers tried to eliminate the anatomical appellation used by the locals by substituting "Dial," a name probably given in 1837 by Prof. Emmons or one of his companions during their approach to climb Mt. Marcy; but with the assistance of "Old Mountain" Phelps, the current name has survived and the name "Dial" has been transferred to a lower peak to the N. The trail described here is the shortest route to the summit, but one can also ascend Nipple Top via Dial, which makes possible a loop trip.

The Elk Pass approach begins the same as for Colvin (see above) to the junction at 1.80 mi. Bearing L here, the climbing is generally moderate with two short steep sections before leveling off and then descending to a small pond on the L at 2.31 mi. The trail then crosses a small hogback and comes to a side trail leading R to a second pond at 2.38 mi. Now crossing first the outlet to the second pond and then the combined outlet, the trail circles back to the L around the first pond and crosses some wet ground before swinging R and starting up. The grade is moderate at first, but soon steepens and continues up the ridge with alternating steep and easier sections to a junction with the trail from Bear Den and Dial at the crest of the ridge at 3.27 mi. (see below).

Turning R, the grade is easy to a small knob at 3.41 mi., from which the summit is visible ahead. Dropping into a small sag, the trail soon climbs to the summit at 3.52 mi. The view of Dix and its slides is most impressive, with other good views of Colvin and the Great Range. The view of Elk Lake to the S is partially blocked by scrub growth. While not a perfect 360-degree view, the impression from the summit is one of solid and all-encompassing wilderness, which caused the Marshall brothers to rate this as having the third best view of all the high peaks.

Distances: Lake Road to departure from Colvin Trail, 1.80 mi.; to Elk Pass, 2.31 mi.; to junction with Bear Den-Dial Trail, 3.27 mi.; to summit of Nipple Top, 3.52 mi. (5.66 km.). Ascent from Lake Road, 2760 ft. (841 m.). Elevation, 4620 ft. (1408 m.). Order of height, 13.

DIAL AND NIPPLE TOP via BEAR DEN

A longer route to Nipple Top leaves the Lake Road 0.73 mi. from the gate and leads 5.88 mi. over Bear Den and Dial to the summit. Called the Henry Goddard Leach Trail, this route is 2.36 mi. longer than the route via Elk Pass, but it makes for a good loop trip.

Leaving the road (0 mi.) and marked with ATIS markers, the trail quickly begins climbing at moderate to steep grades and comes out on the W shoulder of Noonmark at 1.28 mi., having gained 1600 ft. (488 m.) from the road. There are some views to the N from this first lookout and better views from a second lookout, reached after a slight descent and gradual ascent to a side trail R at 1.64 mi. Now descending steadily, the trail switchbacks down to the col between Noonmark and Bear Den at 1.98 mi., having lost about 320 ft. (98 m.) in altitude from the shoulder of Noonmark.

The trail now climbs out of the col at a mostly moderate grade, with occasional small views back at Noonmark, to the summit of Bear Den at 2.49 mi. Total ascent from road, 2280 ft. (695 m.). Elevation, 3423 ft. (1043 m.).

Leaving Bear Den, the trail descends to a bare spot at 2.76 mi. with an obscured view of Dial and Nipple Top ahead. Continuing to descend, the trail passes through a col and ascends slightly before dropping again to the main col between Bear Den and Dial at 2.98 mi., having lost 220 ft. (67 m.) in altitude. The trail now climbs over one more small bump before beginning the final long climb to the summit of Dial, which is reached at 3.77 mi. A large rock on the R offers good views to the N and W. Total ascent, 3060 ft. (933 m.). Elevation, 4020 ft. (1225 m.).

This summit has been referred to as North Dial in previous editions of this guidebook, to distinguish it from the next peak to the S on the ridge, which is also 4020 ft. high. North Dial, however, is undoubtedly the peak "Old Mountain" Phelps had in mind when he conferred the name; and since it has the only view and is the more distinct peak, this peak should simply be called "Dial" and the other, southerly peak considered a part of the Nipple Top ridge.

Leaving Dial, the trail descends to a col at 3.97 mi., and then climbs at easy to moderate grades to a summit ("South Dial") at 4.28 mi. Leaving this summit, the trail descends to a col at 4.44 mi. and climbs again at easy to moderate grades up a fern-covered ridge, reaching a summit with a bare spot at 5.40 mi. Continuing fairly level, the trail dips slightly to the junction with the Elk Pass Trail coming in from the R at 5.63 mi. (see above). Continuing straight ahead, the trail climbs over one last bump and reaches the summit of Nipple Top at 5.88 mi.

Distances: Lake Road to S lookout on shoulder of Noonmark, 1.66 mi.; to Bear Den, 2.49 mi.; to Dial, 3.77 mi. (6.07 km.); to trail from Elk Pass, 5.63 mi.; to summit of Nipple Top, 5.88 mi. (9.46 km.). Total ascent from Lake Road, 4000 ft. (1219 m.). Elevation, 4620 ft. (1408 m.). Order of height, 13.

NOONMARK via STIMSON TRAIL

This prominent, pointed peak lies almost directly S of Keene Valley and therefore "marks noon" when the sun is directly over the summit. This trail was scouted by and named for Henry L. Stimson, Secretary of State in President Hoover's cabinet and Secretary of War under Roosevelt. The trail starts on the Ausable Club Rd. at the top of a hill at the edge of the golf course 0.40 mi. W of the hiker's parking lot on Rt. 73 (see introduction to St. Huberts Section, above). No parking is permitted on the private land at the start of this trail. The trail is marked with ATIS markers.

Leaving the road at the golf course (0 mi.), the trail follows up a private driveway. Avoiding a side road R at 0.13 mi., the trail goes straight ahead at 0.21 mi. where the road goes L to a barn. Now a footpath, the trail continues mostly on the level to a small ravine which is crossed at 0.43 mi. Now climbing moderately, the trail reaches a junction at 0.56 mi. (Trail L is the old Dix Trail, now marked with ATIS markers, which leads between Noonmark and Round Mts. to join the trail from Round Pond in another 1.65 mi.; see below.)

Bearing R at this junction, the Stimson Trail climbs moderately to steeply with only a few breathers to the base of some ledges at 1.12 mi. Swinging sharp L and up very steeply, the trail emerges on the open ledges at 1.16 mi., where there are views of Keene Valley and the Ausable Club. The climbing is now easier along a ridge to a lookout at 1.48 mi., from which the summit may be seen. From this point, the grade increases with several more open sections up to a sharp L turn at 1.89 mi. Here the trail enters the woods to avoid some steeper rocks ahead and after dropping down a few feet turns sharp R and ascends steeply back to the open rocks and then on to the summit at 2.06 mi. A trail continues on over the summit and down the SE side to the Dix Trail in 1.03 mi. (see below).

From the summit there is an unobstructed view in all directions, dominated by the Great Range to the W, the Dix Range to the S, and Giant to the NE. Both Rainbow Falls and Beaver Meadow Falls may be seen when the leaves are off the trees.

Distances: Ausable Club Road at golf course to junction with Dix Trail, 0.56 mi.; to first ledge, 1.16 mi.; to summit of Noonmark, 2.06 mi. (3.31 km.). Ascent from road, 2175 ft. (663 m.). Elevation, 3556 ft. (1084 m.).

NOONMARK FROM THE SE via FELIX ADLER TRAIL

This trail is named for Dr. Felix Adler, a philosopher and founder of the Ethical Culture Society, which sought to combine the common elements of Christian and Jewish faiths. He spent many summers at his home at the start of the Noonmark Trail and was an enthusiastic climber. This trail offers an alternate route to Noonmark; and since it is most often descended to make a loop trip when combined with the old Dix Trail, these trails are described in the direction most hikers use them.

Leaving the summit of Noonmark (0 mi.), the trail heads SE and descends steeply a few yds. to a level area and then down the partially open SE ridge of Noonmark. At 0.52 mi. the trail descends more steeply into the taller trees with the grade easing off at 0.77 mi. and the descent continuing to a junction with the Dix Trail at 1.03 mi. (Trail R leads 4.49 mi. to Dix Mt. Trail; straight ahead across the small brook it leads 2.33 mi. to Rt. 73 via Round Pond.) One can also approach Noonmark from Rt. 73 using this trail, the total distance to the summit being 3.36 mi.

Turning L, the return route to St. Huberts climbs at an easy grade along the R bank of a brook, crosses a small tributary and then crosses to the L bank at 1.38 mi. Continuing at an easy grade, the trail reaches a junction at the height of land between Noonmark and Round Mt. at 1.63 mi. (Trail R leads 0.77 mi. to the summit of Round Mt.; see below.) From here, the trail begins to descend easily and then swings R away from the old eroded tote road as the descent steepens. Swinging back to the L, the trail crosses the old tote road and soon crosses a brook at 1.95 mi. Now the trail continues a steady, moderate descent with occasional short detours to avoid the most eroded sections of the old tote road. Reaching the junction with the Stimson Trail at 2.68 mi., it is now 0.56 mi. back to the Ausable Club Road at the golf course, making a complete loop trip of 5.30 mi.

Distances: Summit of Noonmark to junction with Dix Trail, 1.03 mi.; to junction with Round Mt. Trail, 1.63 mi.; to junction with Stimson Trail to Noonmark, 2.68 mi. (4.31 km.).

ROUND MT.

As distinctively round when seen from Keene Valley as its neighbor Noonmark is pointed, this little peak offers some marvelous views of the cliffs and slides on Giant. One can also find solitude, as this peak is often ignored in favor of its larger neighbors.

The S. Burns Weston Trail ascends the NE side of the peak and continues down the W side to join the old Dix Trail, which makes possible an easy round trip. The trail starts on the Ausable Club Rd., 0.16 mi. from the hiker's parking lot just off Rt. 73. (See introduction to this section, above, for more information on parking.) Cars may not be parked at the trailhead. Leaving the road (0 mi.) and marked with ATIS markers, the trail soon becomes steep before leveling off at 0.14 mi. and proceeding along the edge of a high bank with views out through openings in the beautiful hemlock forest high above Rt. 73. At 0.43 mi. there is a good view on the L of Giant and Chapel Pond Pass, after which the trail swings R and away from the edge of the steep bank. The grades are now mostly easy with a few short dips as the trail traverses to the L on a side hill.

Crossing a brook and old mossy slide at 1.28 mi., the trail now swings R and up more steeply and comes to an open ledge at 1.40 mi., where there is a good view of Giant. The trail now climbs at a moderate to steep grade to a large ledge with good views at 1.88 mi. The trail enters thicker woods on the flat and after one more short steep pitch emerges onto open rocks at 2.08 mi. Marked with cairns, the trail is now nearly flat along open rocks to the junction with the descent route to the old Dix Trail branching R at 2.24 mi. The summit is just beyond at 2.27 mi., with views in all directions. Ascent from Ausable Club Road, 1820 ft. (555 m.). Elevation, 3100 ft. (945 m.).

The descent to the old Dix Trail heads W from the junction near the summit. The trail descends over a series of open ledges and is marked with small cairns. In general the trail heads directly for the summit of Noonmark, bearing R when there seems to be any choice. At the base of this series of ledges, the trail drops steeply into a small valley with a large cliff to the R. Bearing L at the bottom of the valley, the trail crosses a small brook at 2.82 mi., swings R to climb over one last bare spot, and descends to the junction with the old Dix Trail at 3.01 mi. Turning R, it reaches the Ausable Club Rd. at the golf course in another 1.61 mi., making a loop trip of 4.62 mi.

Distances: Ausable Club Rd. to summit of Round Mt., 2.27 mi. (3.65 km.); to old Dix Trail, 3.01 mi.; to Ausable Club Rd. at golf course via old Dix Trail, 4.62 mi. (7.43 km.).

DIX MT. FROM RT. 73

Dix Mt. was named by Ebenezer Emmons in 1837 for John A. Dix, then Secretary of State for Governor Marcy and later governor himself. He also served as a U.S. Senator, Secretary of the Treasury, and a Major General in the Civil War. The first ascent was in 1807, by a surveyor named Rykert, who had the task of running a line that now forms the southern boundary of the town of Keene and passes directly over the summit.

This trail via Round Pond is now the official approach to Dix Mt. from the N. The original route started from the Ausable Club Rd., but this route was only 0.12 mi. shorter, was considerably steeper in spots, and involved over 400 ft. more vertical climb. With the new parking arrangements at the Ausable Club, this old route is now 0.28 mi. longer in addition to its other disadvantages. It is no longer marked as a state trail and is described in this guidebook (see above) only as a return route from Noonmark via the Felix Adler Trail. The start for the current route is on Rt. 73, 1.10 mi. S of the parking area at Chapel Pond and 3.1 mi. N of the junction of Rtes. 9 and 73 in Underwood. The start is marked with a small DEC sign, and there is a small parking area just N of the trailhead. This trail is currently maintained by the Adirondack Forty-Sixers.

From the road (0 mi.) and marked with blue DEC disks, the trail climbs moderately on a traverse across a steep hillside. The grade soon eases, and the trail crosses a height of land and descends to Round Pond just beyond at 0.55 mi. There are some designated campsites to the L near the outlet. Elsewhere, camping is not permitted unless one is at least 150 ft. back from any trail or body of water. Turning R, the trail follows around the N shore of the pond and begins climbing moderately at 0.97 mi. Crossing a brook at 1.16 mi., the trail climbs steadily to a notch at 1.60 mi. Now level or slightly downhill, it crosses a brook at 1.82 mi. and continues across several wet areas to the junction with the old Dix Trail and the Felix Adler Trail at 2.33 mi. (Trail R with ATIS markers leads 2.21 mi. to Ausable Club Rd. Trail straight ahead with ATIS markers leads 1.03 mi. to summit of Noonmark.)

Turning L, the trail is practically flat to the bank of the N Fork of the Boquet River at 2.68 mi. The trail now follows near the L bank of the river on the flat to an old lumber clearing near the river at 3.12 mi. Soon swinging away from the river through thicker woods, the trail crosses a small brook and then Gravestone Brook at 3.65 mi. After the brook, the trail climbs briefly to drier ground and descends to the bank of the Boquet at 3.97 mi., where the outlet to Dial Pond comes in from the R. The trail now continues to the Boquet River Lean-to at 4.22 mi., having gained only 100 ft. since the junction with the old Dix Trail.

Crossing the river on stones, the trail swings R and follows up near the R bank on a steadily increasing grade. Reaching a fair sized tributary at 5.06 mi., the trail follows up the R bank of this brook on a steady, moderate grade and crosses it at 5.22 mi. The trail now crosses and recrosses several other brooks and arrives at the base of a large slide at 5.70 mi. Crossing the base of the slide, the trail swings L and begins the real climbing to the summit, gaining approximately 1600 ft. (500 m.) in a little over a mile. Paralleling the slide until 5.77 mi., the trail swings away and begins an unrelenting steep climb, with rough footing in spots, to a junction at the top of the ridge at 6.40 mi. (Red trail coming in from R is Hunters Pass Trail from Elk Lake; see Southern Section.)

Turning L, the climbing continues steady but not quite as steep along the ridge to the summit crest at 6.65 mi. From this point, hikers should use care to remain on the marked trail so as not to damage the fragile alpine vegetation. The going is now nearly level, past one rock on the L with a U.S. Coast and Geodetic Survey marker, and on to the summit with an old survey bolt at 6.82 mi. This bolt was placed by Verplanck Colvin in 1873 as part of his Adirondack Survey. The view is unobstructed in all directions with Elk Lake seen to the SW, Lake Champlain and the Green Mts. to the E, and the Great Range to the NW. A trail marked with yellow DEC disks continues over the summit to the Beckhorn and then on to Elk Lake (see Southern Section).

Distances: Rt. 73 to Round Pond, 0.55 mi.; to junction with old Dix Trail, 2.33 mi.; to Boquet River Lean-to, 4.22 mi.; to Hunters Pass Trail from Elk Lake, 6.42 mi.; to summit of Dix, 6.82 mi. (10.97 km.). Ascent from Rt. 73, 3200 ft. (975 m.). Elevation, 4857 ft. (1480 m.). Order of height, 6.

GIANT via ROARING BROOK TRAIL

The full name for Giant Mt., Giant of the Valley, is the name given this peak by early residents in Pleasant Valley on the E side of the mountain. From the low valley of the Boquet River, Giant does appear as a massive mountain with many ridges and subsidiary peaks towering 4000 ft. above the valley. The first ascent of Giant (and the first of any 4000-ft. peak) was in 1797, by a surveyor named Charles Brodhead, who had the task of surveying the boundaries of the Old Military Tract, which was to be divided up as compensation for soldiers who had fought in the Revolutionary War. Brodhead had to fight his way up the E face and directly down the W face, a route that has probably never been repeated since. The first trail was cut in 1866 via Hopkins, with the Roaring Brook Trail cut soon after in 1873 and later improved enough to be passable by horses to within 300 ft. of the summit. This improvement accounts for the relatively moderate grades and the long series of switchbacks leading to the crest of the ridge.

The trail begins at a small parking area on Rt. 73, 3.3 mi. S of the High Peaks sign in Keene Valley and 5.6 mi. N of the junction of Rtes. 9 and 73 in Underwood. From the end of the parking lot (0 mi.), the ATIS marked trail begins on the level to a junction at 0.09 mi. with a trail leading R to the base of Roaring Brook Falls. Bearing L, the trail begins a moderate climb to a crest at 0.27 mi., after which it dips and continues at an easier grade to a junction at 0.54 mi. (Trail R leads 80 yds. to the top of Roaring Brook Falls, where there are views of Noonmark and the lower Great Range. Approach this view with caution; there have been several unfortunate accidents at this spot in recent years.)

Bearing L, the grade soon moderates and the trail arrives at another junction just short of the R bank of Roaring Brook at 1.02 mi. Trail L leads 40 yds. to a campsite and a nearly hidden view of the slides on Giant. In 1963 there were massive slides on all sides of Giant, and the rush of water down this side widened the bed of Roaring Brook to nearly 200 yds. in spots. All the trees growing near the brook and now obscuring what was once a very spectacular view have grown up in the last 20 years. Bearing R at the junction and crossing Roaring Brook, the trail comes to a junction on the far side at 1.09 mi. (ATIS trail R leads to Washbowl and Nubble; see below.) Turning L, the trail ascends an easy to moderate grade, crosses two brooks, and comes to a short side trail leading L to some open rocks in the brook at 1.39 mi. Now the trail begins to pull away from the brook at a mostly steady, moderate grade and soon begins a series of switchbacks along the crest of a broad ridge. At 2.34 mi. a side trail R leads to a good view and a welcome chance for a breather. Continuing to climb via switchbacks, the trail reaches a junction at the top of the main SW ridge of Giant at 2.85 mi. (Trail entering from the R is the Giant Ridge Trail leading 2.22 mi. to Chapel Pond; see below.)

Turning L, the grade is more moderate to a small summit with a spectacular view of the slides just beyond at 3.02 mi., as the trail briefly slabs the L side of the ridge. Now mostly on the flat for a short way, the trail begins climbing again at 3.20 mi. and after another short flat stretch climbs steeply to the junction with East Trail from New Russia and Rocky Peak in an open area at 3.44 mi. (see Eastern Section). From here, easy grades lead to the open summit at 3.56 mi. The views range from the Ausable Club directly below to the W with the Great Range beyond, to Lake Champlain and the Green Mts. to the E. In all, 39 major peaks can be seen.

Distances: Rt. 73 to top of Roaring Brook Falls, 0.54 mi.; to junction with trail to Nubble and Washbowl, 1.09 mi.; to junction with Ridge Trail, 2.85 mi.; to junction with East Trail, 3.44 mi.; to summit of Giant, 3.56 mi. (5.73 km.). Ascent from Rt. 73, 3375 ft. (1029 m.). Elevation, 4627 ft. (1410 m.). Order of height, 12.

GIANT via RIDGE TRAIL

This slightly shorter route to Giant was completed in 1954 and offers the easiest access go the Giant's Washbowl and Nubble, as well as a route to the summit with many views from the long, open ridge. The start is on Rt. 73, 4.8 mi. S of the High Peaks sign in Keene Valley and 4.1 mi. N of the junction of Rtes. 9 and 73 in Underwood. Parking is available for several cars at the trailhead, with more available 0.2 mi. to the N at Chapel Pond. The trail is marked with ATIS markers.

From the road (0 mi.), the trail crosses a small brook and soon begins climbing. Taking a sharp L across a small stream in 150 yds., the trail recrosses the stream in another 100 yds. and climbs steeply to a short flat section. Soon after the end of this flat area, the trail turns sharp L at 0.29 mi. (trail straight ahead leads to a spring at the base of a small cliff) in the first of several switchbacks leading up a steep slope. The grade eases at 0.46 mi., but there are a few more steep sections as the trail crosses an old stream bed and climbs to an open lookout at 0.65 mi. directly above Chapel Pond. The trail now makes a slight descent to a junction at the S end of the Giant's Washbowl at 0.70 mi. (Trail L skirts the SW side of the pond and leads 1.01 mi. to the Roaring Brook Trail; see below.)

The Ridge Trail now swings sharp R away from the pond and begins a steady, moderate climb to a junction at 0.93 mi. (Trail L leads down 0.15 mi. to N side of Washbowl and then along NW shore to join trail to Roaring Brook Trail at 0.25 mi.) Continuing straight ahead, the Ridge Trail reaches another junction at 1.00 mi. (Trail L leads 0.52 mi. to the summit of Nubble; see below.)

Bearing R, the Ridge Trail climbs steadily through conifers to a sharp line of demarcation between the large conifers and smaller poplars and birches at 1.10 mi. This marks the furthest extent of the 1913 forest fire, which burned off much of the ridge above and created the views that make this trail so attractive. Here the climbing becomes steep up to the first ledge at 1.24 mi. The trail swings R to gain this ledge and then swings back L and traverses above a large boulder on the ledge to reach a gully just beyond. Now turning R and up steeply, the trail gains a higher ledge at 1.32

mi. There are good views of both Washbowl and Chapel Pond further below; and by walking 40 yds. to the R (S), one can catch a glimpse of the Giant's Dipper. Turning sharp L at two cairns, the trail leaves this ledge and continues at an easier grade over other bare ledges.

Dipping to a small col at 1.42 mi., the trail climbs a few steep pitches and emerges at the base of a long climb across a large open face. At 1.72 mi., near the top of this open area, is a junction. (Trail R goes up and over the top of a small bump with more views and is 100 yds. longer than the trail L.) Bearing L, the trail slabs across the N side of the ridge and in 110 yds. reaches the junction with the longer trail over the bump. After a short flat section in a col, the trail climbs again through another smaller bare section to easier climbing at 1.97 mi. Soon starting up again, it reaches a short side trail L to a ledge with a view to the N at 2.08 mi., after which the climbing is mostly easy to the junction with the Roaring Brook Trail at 2.22 mi. From here the description to the summit is the same as that for the Roaring Brook Trail (see above).

Distances: Rt. 73 to Washbowl, 0.70 mi.; to side trail to Nubble, 1.00 mi.; to Roaring Brook Trail, 2.22 mi.; to East Trail, 2.81 mi.; to summit of Giant Mt., 2.94 mi. (4.73 km.). Ascent from Rt. 73, 3050 ft. (930 m.). Elevation, 4627 ft. (1410 m.). Order of height, 12.

GIANT'S NUBBLE

This small, rocky knob at the end of the SW ridge of Giant offers some interesting views of St. Huberts and the slides on Giant's W face. There are two approaches, with the one branching from the Ridge Trail being the easiest. Approaching via the Roaring Brook Trail, however, one can make an interesting loop of 4.70 mi. taking in Roaring Brook Falls, the Giant's Washbowl and the Nubble.

1. From the junction 1.00 mi. up the Ridge Trail (0 mi.), the trail

crosses a small brook and climbs a short, steep pitch followed by more moderate climbing to a view of the Washbowl at 0.12 mi. Dipping across a small sag, the trail comes to better views to the S at 0.28 mi., after which the trail is flat and then climbs steeply up to a junction at 0.41 mi. (Trail R leads to Roaring Brook Trail; see below.) The trail now proceeds along a nearly flat open ridge to the summit of the Nubble at 0.52 mi.

Distances: From Chapel Pond via Ridge Trail: to junction with Nubble Trail, 1.00 mi.; to summit of Nubble, 1.52 mi. (2.45 km.). Ascent from Chapel Pond, 1150 ft. (350 m.).

2. From the junction (0 mi.) on the Roaring Brook Trail at 1.09 mi. just after crossing Roaring Brook, the trail starts on the flat, but begins climbing soon after crossing a small stream and reaches a junction at 0.15 mi. (Trail R leads to Washbowl; see below.) Turning L, the trail climbs moderately, crossing a stream at 0.32, and another at 0.55 mi., recrossing this second stream shortly before reaching a junction at 0.75 mi. (Trail L leads to Ridge Trail and Washbowl; see above.) Turning R, the trail swings R and onto a nearly flat open ridge to the summit of the Nubble at 0.86 mi.

Distances: From Rt. 73 via Roaring Brook Trail to junction with Nubble and Washbowl Trail, 1.09 mi.; to summit of Nubble, 1.95 mi. (3.13 km.). Ascent from road, 1480 ft. (451 m.). Elevation, 2760 ft. (841 m.).

GIANT'S WASHBOWL FROM ROARING BROOK TRAIL

This alternate approach to the Giant's Washbowl leaves the Roaring Brook Trail 1.09 mi. from the parking lot on Rt. 73. Turning R at the junction (0 mi.), the trail soon crosses a small stream and then climbs to a junction at 0.15 mi. (Trail L leads to Nubble; see above.) Bearing R, the trail continues to climb at a moderate grade until it eases at 0.45 mi. and reaches a height of land below the Nubble at 0.54 mi. Now descending at an easy grade, it reaches a second junction at 0.84 mi. at the NW shore of the Giant's Washbowl. (Trail L leads around N shore and then up to join the Ridge Trail in 0.25 mi.) Continuing along the shore of the pond, the trail reaches a junction with the Ridge Trail at 1.01 mi. This point is 0.70 mi. above Rt. 73 at Chapel Pond and 0.30 mi. below the turnoff of the Nubble Trail.

Distances: Parking lot on Rt. 73 to turnoff from Roaring Brook Trail, 1.09 mi.; to junction with Ridge Trail at Washbowl, 2.10 mi. (3.38 km.).

MOSSY CASCADE TRAIL TO HOPKINS

For the naming of this peak, see "Spread Eagle and Hopkins" in Keene Valley Section. The start of the trail is on Rt. 73 just S of the steel-sided bridge over the East Branch of the Ausable River 2.0 mi. S of Keene Valley. From the road (0 mi.) and marked with ATIS markers, the trail follows along above the R bank of the river to a house on the L at 0.36 mi. Swinging R onto a tote road at the house, the trail immediately swings L onto an older road and then bears R at another junction at 0.43 mi. The trail now veers around from NE to SE while remaining mostly on flat going. At 0.51 mi. the trail leaves the tote road, going L to the L bank of Mossy Cascade Brook, which is followed to a junction at 0.74 mi. (Side trail L leads to the base of Mossy Cascade in 200 yds.) Bearing R, the trail now climbs steeply to the top of a steep bank above Mossy Cascade to the edge of a recent clearing for a private camp on the R at 0.90 mi. Just past this camp the trail crosses the brook and climbs away from the brook with several steep pitches. It crosses a yellow-blazed property line at 1.18 mi. After a short moderate stretch, another steep pitch leads to a lookout on the L at 1.45 mi.

Past this lookout, the trail descends to a col, then climbs to another ledge with a view at 1.73 mi., and continues to climb through an open forest along an interesting monolithic ridge of granite. The grade moderates at 2.22 mi. and the trail comes to a junction at 2.30 mi. (Trail L is the Ranney Trail with ADK markers from Keene Valley; see Keene Valley Section.) Now the trail continues up into a ravine between Hopkins and Green and arrives at a junction in a col at 2.97 mi. (Trail R leads 3.02 mi. over a shoulder of Green Mt. to the summit of Giant; see below.) Turning L, the trail climbs very steeply for a few yards, and then eases off along bare slabs to the summit of Hopkins at 3.17 mi. There are many blueberries and the views are unobstructed in all directions except NE, with 22 major peaks discernible. (Trail with ADK markers continues over the summit to Spread Eagle and Keene Valley; see Keene Valley Section.)

Distances: Rt. 73 to Mossy Cascade, 0.74 mi.; to junction with Ranney Trail, 2.30 mi.; to junction with trail to Giant, 2.97 mi.; to summit of Hopkins, 3.17 mi. (5.10 km.). Ascent from Rt. 73, 2120 ft. (646 m.). Elevation, 3183 ft. (970 m.).

GIANT FROM HOPKINS via GREEN MT.

Due to its length and the lack of any views along the way, this is not a popular route to the summit of Giant, but it does offer pleasant walking through some virgin forests and makes for an interesting way to return from Giant to St. Huberts or Keene Valley.

Leaving the junction with the Mossy Cascade Trail in the Hopkins-Green col (0 mi.), the trail climbs a short steep pitch and then continues at moderate grades to the crest of a shoulder of Green Mt. at 0.40 mi. The trail now descends to a col at 0.53 mi., after which it slabs along a side hill on the level and enters a swampy area with lush moss at 0.69 mi. After some more flat going, the trail descends and crosses a tributary to Putnam Brook (also called Beede Brook) at 1.12 mi. After climbing out of this small valley, the trail continues the easy to moderate descent and joins an old tote road just before crossing the main branch of Putnam Brook at 1.66 mi. and coming to a junction in the col between Green Mt. and Giant at 1.70 mi. (In descending this trail, hikers should watch for the sharp R turn off the tote road 0.18 mi. below the junction in the Giant-Green col.) The trail coming in from the L is the North Trail to Giant, which leads 6.06 mi. to Rt. 9N (see Eastern Section). From here, the route is marked with red DEC disks.

Turning R at the junction, the trail begins climbing steeply out of the col and at 1.88 mi. there is a sharp switchback to the L to negotiate a small cliff band. From here the grade continues steep for a few yards, but slowly eases until it levels off at 2.47 mi. Descending slightly, the trail resumes its climb and arrives at a ledge on the R at 2.84 mi., soon after which it levels out and crosses other ledges to the summit at 3.04 mi. (ATIS trail continues over the summit and down to St. Huberts via Ridge Trail or Roaring Brook Trail; see above.)

Distances: Rt. 73 via Mossy Cascade Trail to Hopkins-Green col, 2.97 mi.; to junction with North Trail, 4.67 mi.; to summit of Giant, 6.01 mi. (9.67 km.). Ascent from Rt. 73, 3500 ft. (1067 m.). Elevation, 4627 ft. (1410 m.). Order of height, 12.

SNOW MT.

This 2360-ft. (719 m.) peak NW of St. Huberts offers some splendid views of the surrounding peaks as well as acres of good blueberries. There are two popular approaches. One is via the Deer Brook Trail from Rt. 73 and the other is from the Ausable Club via Maghee Clearing and the W.A. White Trail. A third approach is possible from the N via the Sachs Rooster Comb Trail. There are a multitude of loop trips possible, combining Snow and Rooster Comb and any of the various approaches.

1. Via Deer Brook Trail from Rt. 73: This approach starts 0.10 mi. N of the steel-sided highway bridge over the Ausable River on Rt. 73 in St. Huberts, and 1.9 mi. S of the High Peaks sign in the center of Keene Valley. This is also an approach to the W.A. White Trail to Lower Wolf Jaw and the Range (see above). The start is marked with green signs and ATIS markers.

Leaving the highway (0 mi.), the trail heads up the R bank of Deer Brook to a junction at a private driveway at 0.10 mi. (Trail straight ahead leads 0.50 mi. up the ravine of Deer Brook. It is scenic but somewhat difficult to follow, crossing Deer Brook several times before rejoining the main trail.) Turning L at the driveway, the main trail begins an easy climb, passing a house on the L and coming to a view of Noonmark on the L at 0.27 mi. Continuing up, the trail goes straight ahead into the woods on an old tote road at 0.34 mi., at a point where the gravel road followed so far goes R. The trail now follows this tote road to a four-way junction at 0.66 mi., where the trail up the Deer Brook ravine comes in from the R. (Trail L is the connection to the W.A. White Trail and leads along an orange-blazed property line to a fresh logging road and then R and up to a junction at a wider logging road, 0.18 mi. after leaving the Deer Brook Trail. Turning L, the W.A. White Trail is reached at 0.25 mi.; see above.)

Continuing straight through this junction, the Deer Brook Trail comes to another junction at the R bank of Deer Brook at 0.80 mi. (Trail L leads 90 yds. to the base of a pretty little falls.) Turning R, the trail crosses Deer Brook and follows a tote road at a moderate grade which eases off just before a junction at 1.30 mi. (Trail L is the approach from the Ausable Club; see below.) Turning R, the trail continues on the flat in a beautiful, open valley to a junction at 1.44

mi. (Trail straight ahead is the approach from the N. It leads mostly on the level for 0.36 mi. to a junction with the Sachs Rooster Comb Trail, which leads down to Keene Valley or up to Rooster Comb. See Keene Valley Section.)

Turning R, the Snow Trail proceeds across a side hill for a little over 100 yds. and then turns R and up steeply to the first ledge at 1.58 mi. with a spectacular view of the cliffs on Rooster Comb. The trail now re-enters the woods and climbs to a second ledge with views to the N of Keene Valley. The summit is just beyond at 1.72 mi. The best views are on ledges just down the SE side.

Distances: Rt. 73 to re-entry of trail up Deer Brook ravine, 0.66 mi.; to junction with trail from Ausable Club, 1.30 mi.; to junction with trail to Sachs Rooster Comb Trail, 1.44 mi.; to summit of Snow, 1.72 mi. (2.77 km.). Ascent from Rt. 73, 1360 ft. (414 m.).

2. Via Maghee Clearing and W.A. White Trail from Ausable Club: Follow the description for the W.A. White Trail (see above) to the junction at 1.04 mi. Bearing R at this junction, the grade becomes easier along the new logging road. Bearing R at the next fork in the logging roads, the trail comes to the junction with the Deer Brook Cut-off at 1.11 mi. (Trail R leads 0.18 mi. down to Deer Brook Trail; see above.) Continuing straight ahead on the level, the trail goes L and up steeply at 1.19 mi. and comes to state land and the end of the lumbered area at 1.24 mi. The walking is now more pleasant, with the trail climbing gradually to a crossing of Deer Brook at 1.33 mi. and on to a junction with the Deer Brook Trail at 1.77 mi. From here the Deer Brook Trail is followed to the summit; see above.

Distances: Lake Road to divergence from W.A. White Trail, 1.04 mi.; to Deer Brook Cut-off, 1.11 mi.; to junction with Deer Brook Trail, 1.77 mi.; to summit of Snow, 2.19 mi. (3.52 km.). Ascent from Lake Road, 1035 ft. (315 m.).

UPPER AUSABLE LAKE AREA

Following the sale of the higher land by the Adirondack Mountain Reserve (AMR) to the State of New York in 1978, most of the trails approaching the shores and along the shores of Upper Ausable Lake have been closed to the public. As before, camping, fishing and hunting on any of the private lands near this lake are prohibited, but there are several through trunk line trails which are still open to the public and offer some interesting and rugged hiking. All access to the Upper Ausable Lake area is by foot over the summits of 4000 ft. peaks, as there is no trail along the shores of Lower Ausable Lake; bushwhacking is prohibited; no boats are available for rent by the public; and portable boats brought in by the public are not permitted on Lower Ausable Lake. Hiking in this area is therefore a serious undertaking, requiring careful planning to insure that one can complete one's planned trip or arrive before nightfall at a campsite above the private land boundary.

These restrictions are designed to protect the private camp owners on the lake, who in the past have complained of illegal camping on their land, break-ins, and even some instances of burglary. Their wishes and privacy should obviously be respected. There is a Warden's Camp at the N end of Upper Ausable Lake, from which the area is patrolled. During the summer months, the Warden's Camp has radio communications with the Ausable Club in St. Huberts.

There are, however, still many interesting trips available to the public in this region, provided one is willing to do a lot of climbing and descending. Camping is allowed on state land, generally above the 2500-ft. level (see map that accompanies this guidebook for exact state/private land boundaries), although there are not yet any designated campsites on state land in this area. One must therefore be careful that in establishing new campsites the regulations regarding distances from streams and trails are obeyed and that exceptional care is taken in building fires, since much of the forest floor in this area is covered with a deep layer of "duff" which can burn as easily as wood. (See information on camping in the Introduction.)

Summary of Approaches to Upper Ausable Lake:

The "easiest" approach to this area is from St. Huberts over the summit of either Sawteeth or Colvin. A loop trip over both these summits makes an interesting but rugged day trip totaling 11.10 mi. (17.90 km.) and 4500 ft. (1370 m.) of climb and descent. (See descriptions for: Sawteeth via Pyramid-Gothics Trail, Sawteeth from Warden's Camp, Carry Trail, Mt. Colvin from the Carry, Colvin from Lake Road and Gill Brook, Fish Hawk Cliffs and Indian Head.) This round trip distance assumes one uses the bus service to the Lower Ausable Lake. Add another 7.00 mi. if the bus is not used.

A considerably more difficult approach for backpackers is a possible loop trip from Keene Valley over Marcy, down the Elk Lake-Marcy Trail, and returning to St. Huberts along Pinnacle Ridge to Colvin and down to the Lake Road. Total distance for this loop is 27.10 mi. (43.60 km.). Total ascent and descent is approximately 7200 ft. (2200 m.). See descriptions for: Mt. Marcy via Phelps Trail (Keene Valley Section), Elk Lake-Marcy Trail (Southern Section), Blake and Colvin via Pinnacle Ridge (St. Huberts Section), and Colvin from Lake Road and Gill Brook (St. Huberts Section).

Other approaches and loop trips are possible using these and other trails described in full below. ·

CARRY TRAIL

This trail runs 1.00 mi. from the boat sheds at the S end of Lower Ausable Lake to the Warden's Camp at the N end of Upper Ausable Lake. It follows close to the L bank of the Ausable River, on the flat for most of its distance. It is paralleled by a tractor trail running along further up the slope away from the river. There is a small spring beside the trail at approximately the half-way point. A few yards from the boat sheds on Lower Ausable Lake is a junction with the trail to Mt. Colvin and Blake Peak. At the Warden's Camp is a junction with the trails leading to Sawteeth, Haystack and Marcy via Bartlett Ridge.

MT. COLVIN FROM CARRY TRAIL

This trail climbs steeply up the valley between Colvin and Blake to the top of the ridge where it connects with the trail to Blake, Pinnacle and the Elk Lake-Marcy Trail. For the history of the naming of Mt. Colvin see description for Colvin from Lake Road and Gill Brook.

From the junction with the Carry Trail (0 mi.), the trail heads E on the flat on a road, but in a few yards bears R off the road and crosses the Ausable River on a bridge at 0.10 mi. The climbing starts almost immediately at the far side of the bridge, with the trail following the R bank of a small brook and then crossing it at 0.25 mi. and beginning a steep climb. The climbing soon eases a bit but remains steady. The trail climbs high above the brook and then back to brook level at 0.45 mi., where the brook forks. This area offers some possible campsites.

The trail follows but soon crosses the L fork and continues a steady grade with a few steeper pitches until the grade finally moderates shortly before the junction in the col between Colvin and Blake at 1.10 mi. (Trail R leads 0.55 mi. to summit of Blake Peak, 3.15 mi. to Pinnacle, and 4.55 mi. to Elk Lake-Marcy Trail; see below.) Turning L, the Colvin Trail climbs steeply, the grade moderating at 1.30 mi., after which the trail crosses a ridge and dips slightly before continuing at relatively easy grades up the S ridge of the mountain. There is a lookout on the L at 1.85 mi., with views of

Upper Ausable Lake, Allen and other peaks. It is only a few yards
to the actual summit at 1.90 mi., where there are good views. (Trail
continues over the summit and down to Lake Road and St.
Huberts; see above.)

Distances: Carry Trail to junction with Blake Trail, 1.10 mi.; to
summit of Colvin, 1.90 mi. (3.05 km.). Ascent from Carry Trail,
2100 ft. (640 m.). Elevation, 4057 ft. (1237 m.). Order of height, 39.

BLAKE PEAK

Blake Peak was named for Mills Blake, who was Verplanck
Colvin's chief assistant during the Adirondack Survey, and his
closest personal friend. The two worked and lived together for
forty-eight years until Colvin died in 1920, so it is therefore fitting
that the peak adjacent to Colvin bears Blake's name. Blake can be
approached from St. Huberts over Colvin following the trail from
the Lake Road and Gill Brook to Colvin's summit and then the trail
described immediately above down to the col between Colvin and
Blake.

Leaving the junction in the col (0 mi.), the trail climbs a short,
steep pitch, moderates, and then begins a very steep pitch at 0.20
mi. Reaching the crest of a ridge at 0.45 mi., the trail climbs mostly
easily to the summit at 0.55 mi., where there are views through the
trees to Elk Lake.

Distances: From Lake Road to junction at Colvin-Blake Col,
3.65 mi.; to summit of Blake, 4.20 mi. (6.75 km.). Total ascent from
Lake Road, 2800 ft. (850 m.). Elevation, 3960 ft. (1207 m.). Order of
height among the original 46 peaks, 43.

SAWTEETH FROM WARDEN'S CAMP

From the Warden's Camp at the N end of Upper Ausable Lake (0
mi.), this trail heads NW across a meadow, bearing R at a junction

with the Lake Trail (closed to the public) and coming to another junction at 0.16 mi. (Trail straight ahead leads to Haystack and Marcy via Bartlett Ridge; see below.) Turning R, the trail crosses Shanty Brook on rocks and briefly follows up the L bank, but soon swings away from the brook on an easy grade. Crossing a brook at 0.90 mi., the trail comes to a junction with the Tammy Stowe Trail at 0.96 mi. (This approximately 1 mi. loop from the Sawteeth Trail climbs, steeply at times, to the crest of a ridge where there are views of Upper Ausable Lake and some of the upper Great Range. It rejoins the Sawteeth Trail approximately 0.5 mi. above its lower end.)

Continuing straight ahead, the trail begins to climb more steeply, crossing several more small brooks and coming to the upper end of the Tammy Stowe Trail at 1.50 mi. The trail soon dips to cross a brook which is a possible campsite, being above the private land. (This is the first brook encountered on the descent from Sawteeth.) After one more short climb and a dip past this brook, the trail begins to climb steeply up the S ridge of Sawteeth with occasional views out through the trees. After several alternating steep pitches and more moderate sections, the trail reaches a small summit at 2.70 mi., and in 20 more yds. joins the trail from Lower Ausable Lake (see above). Turning L, the trail comes to the summit of Sawteeth at 2.80 mi. (Trail continues over the summit and on to Gothics or down to Lower Ausable Lake; see above.)

Distances: Warden's Camp to junction with Haystack and Marcy Trail, 0.16 mi.; to junction with Tammy Stowe Trail, 0.96 mi.; to summit of Sawteeth, 2.80 mi. (4.50 km.). Ascent from Warden's Camp, 2110 ft. (643 m.). Elevation, 4100 ft. (1250 m.). Order of height, 35.

HAYSTACK AND MARCY via BARTLETT RIDGE
FROM WARDEN'S CAMP

This trail leads to the top of Bartlett Ridge, from which one may climb Haystack or descend into Panther Gorge and ascend Marcy from there via the Elk Lake-Marcy Trail.

From the Warden's Camp (0 mi.), the trail goes NW through a field, bearing R at a junction with the Lake Trail (now closed to the public) and arriving at a junction at 0.16 mi. (Trail R leads to Sawteeth; see above.) Continuing straight ahead, the trail climbs at an easy to moderate grade, crossing several small brooks to a junction with the Sage's Folly Trail (now closed to the public) at 0.90 mi. Past this junction, the moderate grade continues to another junction at 1.50 mi. (Trail R leads via Haystack Brook to the Range Trail between Haystack and Basin; see below.)

Turning L, the trail proceeds mostly on the flat around the end of a ridge to a junction at 1.70 mi. with the Crystal Brook Trail (now closed to the public). Bearing R, the trail soon crosses Crystal Brook and begins a steep, rough climb to the crest of Bartlett Ridge at 2.40 mi. Now the grade eases and the trail crosses two brooks and many wet areas before reaching the junction with the trail to Panther Gorge and Marcy at 2.70 mi. [Trail L leads steeply down the W side of Bartlett Ridge to the Elk Lake-Marcy Trail at the Panther Gorge Lean-to, 3.45 mi. from the Warden's Camp, having lost 600 vertical ft. from the top of Bartlett Ridge. From here it is another 1.81 mi. to the summit of Marcy, making it 5.26 mi. (8.46 km.) and a total of approximately 4000 ft. (1219 m.) of climbing from the Warden's Camp to the summit of Marcy.]

Turning R, the Haystack Trail begins one of the steepest climbs in the mountains up the S side of the peak. The trail is quite eroded in spots, with almost no respite to timberline at 3.15 mi. From here, the trail is marked with cairns and care is needed to follow it as it winds up through several ledges and finally to the R (E) side of the summit ridge to surmount the final large ledge. The summit is reached at 3.45 mi. (Trail continues 0.55 mi. to the Range Trail and on to the Johns Brook Valley and Keene Valley; see Keene Valley Section.) In descending, the trail first heads W towards Skylight and then SW towards Allen.

Distances: Warden's Camp to junction with Haystack Brook Trail, 1.50 mi.; to Bartlett Ridge and junction with Marcy Trail, 2.70 mi.; to summit of Haystack, 3.45 mi. (5.55 km.). Ascent from Warden's Camp, 3070 ft. (935 m.). Elevation, 4960 ft. (1512 m.). Order of height, 3.

HAYSTACK AND GREAT RANGE via HAYSTACK BROOK TRAIL

This trail leads to the Range Trail at the former site of Sno-Bird Lean-to between Haystack and Basin. The grade is easy for much of the way, but it finishes with some very steep climbing and several ladders which can be quite difficult when backpacking. There are several possible campsites along this trail, as it is on state land from just past the junction with the Bartlett Ridge Trail.

From the Warden's Camp (0 mi.), follow the Bartlett Ridge Trail to the junction at 1.50 mi. Turning R here, the trail is mostly flat to a crossing of an old slide track and brook at 2.10 mi. Continuing at an easy grade along the lower slopes of Haystack, the trail comes near the R bank of Haystack Brook at 2.65 mi. From here the trail gets progressively steeper to the first ladder at 2.90 mi. There are several more ladders with short breathers in between before the Haystack Brook Trail reaches a junction with the Range Trail at 3.35 mi. (Trail R leads to JBL via Shorey Short Cut and Slant Rock, 4.67 mi., or to JBL via Basin and Saddleback, 5.07 mi. Trail L leads up to Haystack, 1.00 mi.; see Keene Valley Section.)

Distances: Warden's Camp to junction with Bartlett Ridge Trail,

1.50 mi.; to junction with Range Trail, 3.35 mi.; to summit of Haystack, 4.35 mi. (7.00 km.). Ascent from Warden's Camp, 3070 ft. (935 m.). Elevation, 4960 ft. (1512 m.). Order of height, 3.

BLAKE PEAK AND MT. COLVIN via PINNACLE RIDGE FROM ELK LAKE-MARCY TRAIL

The Pinnacle Ridge leading to Blake and Colvin does not offer any striking 360-degree views, but it is a beautiful series of seldom-visited peaks covered with virgin forests of spruce and balsam underlain with moss-covered rocks. The best views are from Colvin, a peak S of Blake, and the Pinnacle; but there are other narrower views including vistas of the Ausable Lakes, Elk Lake and the mountains beyond.

Since 1978, when the AMR sold its higher lands to the State of New York, this entire ridge has been public land; a short connection between the existing trails on the ridge and the Elk Lake-Marcy Trail was constructed to assist public access. Hikers should be aware, however, that the lower portions of the three trails leading to the shores of Upper Ausable Lake are closed to the public from the point where these trails reach the private land boundary. There is no water on this ridge, but there are possible campsites on the new access trail from the Elk Lake-Marcy Trail, and one could find a possible campsite by descending about 0.25 mi. from the col between Colvin and Blake. This trail is described from S to N since that is the direction in which it is hiked in the suggested loop trip in the introduction to the Upper Ausable Lake Area.

This approach to Blake and Colvin begins on the Elk Lake-Marcy Trail, 5.99 mi. from the summit of Marcy and 4.97 mi. from Elk Lake. This junction is also 0.21 mi. E of the two-log bridge over the inlet to Upper Ausable Lake. From the junction (0 mi.), the trail heads NE on the flat, crossing two brooks and following a series of shelves through a beautiful hardwood forest. After climbing a short bit, the trail winds among rocks with a view of Haystack through the trees at 0.40 mi. and continues on to a brook with a small waterfall at 0.67 mi., where there are some possible campsites. Crossing the brook, the trail climbs moderately with a few steep pitches to a junction at 1.04 mi. (Trail L is original Pinnacle Trail now closed to the public.)

Turning R, the trail climbs moderately to steeply to a junction just below the summit of the Pinnacle at 1.63 mi. (Spur trail R climbs at first steeply and then more easily to the summit of Pinnacle in 0.20 mi., where there is a spectacular view of Elk Lake and the Dix Range.) Turning L, the trail descends briefly to a col and then begins climbing over another summit and down to another col at 2.15 mi. Shortly above this col the trail comes to a junction with the Otis Ledge Trail (now closed to the public) at 2.20 mi. Climbing again past this junction, the trail goes over another summit and drops steeply to another col at 2.50 mi. Now the trail climbs quite steeply, but eases off at 2.65 mi. and soon comes to a side trail R leading to a good view of Elk Lake. Dropping steeply from this summit, the trail comes to a junction at a col at 2.90 mi. (Trail L, now closed to the public, leads to Cy Beede Ledge and Upper Lake.)

Continuing on the level for a short stretch, the trail soon begins to climb, steeply at times, to a lookout on the R at 3.20 mi. The climbing is now easier and the trail passes between two large boulders just before reaching a summit at 3.55 mi. Shortly beyond this summit, the trail passes Lookout Rock on the L, from which there are good views of Upper Ausable Lake. The trail now descends gradually to a col and begins to climb Blake, crossing a minor summit at 3.95 mi. and reaching the true summit at 4.00 mi. Total ascent from Elk Lake-Marcy Trail, approximately 2800 ft. (850 m.). Elevation, 3960 ft. (1207 m.).

See above for history of the naming of Blake as well as complete description of trail from the summit down to the col between Blake and Colvin and then up the S side of Colvin to the summit at 5.35 mi. Trail from the summit leads down to the Lake Road and St. Huberts (see St. Huberts Section).

Distances: Elk Lake-Marcy Trail to Pinnacle, 1.80 mi.; to summit of Blake, 4.00 mi.; to summit of Colvin, 5.35 mi. (8.60 km.). Total ascent, approximately 3400 ft. (1050 m.). Elevation, 4057 ft. (1237 m.). Order of height, 39.

Mt. Colden
Photo by Jim Appleyard

HEART LAKE
SECTION

This popular hiking center is reached by turning S from Rt. 73, 4 mi. SE of Lake Placid Village. There is a sign for Adirondak Loj as well as a large DEC sign, "Trails to the High Peaks."[1] The first mile of the road is open, offering views of many of the peaks that can be reached from Heart Lake. At 3.8 mi. a dirt road marked with DEC signs goes L to South Meadow. Across a bridge and up a hill, another DEC sign indicates the start of the Indian Pass Trail at 4.7 mi. (no parking permitted here), with a small entrance booth just beyond at 4.8 mi. A daily parking fee, paid here, is charged to help maintain this public facility. Past the entrance booth, turn L for the parking lot and the Campers and Hikers Building. (Road R leads to Adirondak Loj where overnight accommodations and meals are available; see Introduction.) At the Campers and Hikers Building, maps, guidebooks and information are available as well as snacks, limited camping supplies, showers and a dry area for packing up.

Heart Lake and the surrounding property are owned by the Adirondack Mountain Club and maintained for the benefit of the hiking public as well as members of the club. Heart Lake is the start

---

1. "Adirondak Loj" is spelled as it is because its builder was Melvil Dewey, champion of "simplified spelling." Dewey was founder of the Lake Placid Club, which acquired the Loj property around 1900. As noted below, the original Adirondack Lodge was built by Henry Van Hoevenberg; it was destroyed in a forest fire in 1903. Also as noted below, the Adirondack Mountain Club now owns the property and its facilities.

for the shortest approach to Marcy as well as many other trails. All of the 61 miles of trails described in this section are maintained by the DEC, except for the Mt. Jo trails.

Trying to select the best trails or loop trips in this region is difficult, since almost every destination is both attractive and popular, but below are some of the better possibilities this area offers:

SHORT HIKES:

Mt. Jo — 2.34 mi., round trip. Superior views of the High Peaks and Heart Lake for very little overall effort. See description for Mt. Jo.

Rocky Falls — 4.75 mi., round trip. An easy walk along the start of the Indian Pass Trail to an attractive little series of waterfalls and large pool for swimming. See description for Indian Pass Trail.

MODERATE

Phelps Mt. — 8.82 mi., round trip. A wonderful close-up view of Marcy and other peaks without too much steep climbing. See description for Van Hoevenberg Trail to Marcy and Phelps Mt.

Avalanche Lake — 10 mi., round trip. A relatively flat hike through Avalanche Pass and on to the S end of the lake with spectacular cliffs on both sides. See description for Van Hoevenberg Trail to Marcy and Avalanche Pass Trail.

HARDER HIKES:

Mt. Colden with return via Avalanche Pass — 13.75 mi., round trip. This loop takes in the summit of Mt. Colden with its views of Marcy, Algonquin, Avalanche Lake and Lake Colden, with a return through the spectacular Avalanche Pass. See descriptions for Van Hoevenberg Trail to Marcy, Avalanche Pass Trail, Lake Arnold Trail, L. Morgan Porter Trail to Mt. Colden, Mt. Colden from Lake Colden, and return on Avalanche Pass Trail.

Wallface Ponds — 13.71 mi., round trip. A relatively flat walk several remote and very interesting ponds with view along the way of the MacIntyre Range that is a photographer's dream. See descriptions for Indian Pass Trail and Scott and Wallface Ponds.

MT. MARCY via VAN HOEVENBERG TRAIL

This is one of the oldest and by far the most popular route to Mt. Marcy, as it is the shortest route by over 1.50 mi. It was laid out by Henry Van Hoevenberg, builder of the original Adirondack Lodge, in the 1880s. The trail has been rerouted several times over the years as heavy use caused erosion, but the reroutes generally follow the original line which manages to ascend to the summit at a relatively easy grade. Marcy is the only major peak (save Whiteface via the highway) that can be skied, and sections of the Van Hoevenberg Trail were widened in the 1930s to make skiing easier.

In the past few years, ADK and DEC trail crews have done extensive work on this trail to try to stem the steady deterioration caused by erosion and increasing numbers of muddy areas. While much work still needs to be done, the trail is in better overall shape than it was five years ago. Log and board bridges now cross many of the mud "wallows" referred to in earlier editions of this guidebook; and in many cases unattractive wide muddy sections have recovered to become grassy areas with only a narrow path through the center. The hope is that this level of trail maintenance will continue on these trails and spread to other badly deteriorated trails.

The trail begins at the end of the parking lot at the Adirondak Loj Campers and Hikers Building. Leaving the trail register (0 mi.), it proceeds on the level, crossing the Mr. Van Ski Trail in 175 yds. Continuing on the level, an alternate ski route diverges R at 0.12 mi. just before the trail starts down a short, moderate descent. Swinging L at the bottom of this hill, the trail passes through a stand of red pines and comes to a bridge over Algonquin Brook at 0.39 mi. At the far side of the bridge, the trail turns sharp R while a ski route continues straight ahead. The trail now climbs away from the brook and proceeds with short rises and falls to a junction at 0.98 mi., where the Algonquin Peak Trail (yellow markers) goes straight ahead and the original route of the Van Hoevenberg Trail comes in from the R.

Turning L, the trail proceeds mostly on the flat, with a few short climbs, to the L bank of Marcy Brook at 1.88 mi. Swinging R, it climbs two short pitches, levels off, and then drops slightly to Marcy Dam at 2.28 mi. The trail crosses the dam, from which there are views of Phelps, Colden and Algonquin, and comes to the trail register at the far end. (Yellow trail L is the South Meadow Truck Road leading 2.60 mi. to South Meadow; see below.) The Marcy Dam Interior Outpost is 50 yds. straight ahead from the trail register.

There are seven lean-tos and numerous designated campsites at this popular camping area. Three lean-tos are located on the E side of the small pond (also referred to as Marcy Dam), two more are located at the S or upper end, and two more are on the W side. A trail circles Marcy Dam giving access to these lean-tos and campsites. Be aware that in this area camping is permitted only at designated areas. Also realize that firewood is very scarce in this area, which makes a camping stove highly advisable.

Turning R at the trail register, the Van Hoevenberg Trail comes, in just over 100 yds., to a junction with the Avalanche Pass Trail, which leads R with yellow markers (see below). Bearing L at this junction, the trail climbs gradually to the L bank of Phelps Brook at 2.48 mi. (Bridge on L crossing the brook is the high water route. Turn R at far end of bridge to rejoin main trail in 125 yds.) Bearing R, the trail continues up the L bank of Phelps Brook to a crossing at 2.56 mi., with the high water route rejoining the trail at the far side. Now climbing at a steady, easy to moderate grade along the R bank of the brook, the trail comes to a short side trail R to Phelps Lean-to at 2.98 mi. Continuing at an easy grade, the trail reaches a junction at 3.24 mi. (Red trail L leads 1.17 mi. to summit of Phelps; see below.)

Bearing R, the trail continues at the same easy grade to the wide ski bridge over Phelps Brook at 3.48 mi. after which the trail climbs steeply to a four-way junction at 3.61 mi. The trails going straight ahead and L at this point are two variations of the ski route which take a slightly longer course from here to Indian Falls. The Van Hoevenberg Trail turns sharp R and climbs at a steady, moderate grade with some steeper pitches until finally easing off at 4.09 mi. Now crossing several wet areas, the trail climbs again at an easy grade to the junction at the upper end of the ski route at 4.35 mi., where it turns R and quickly arrives at a height of land just before Indian Falls. From this point there is a view of Marcy straight ahead. The only designated camping areas in the Indian Falls vicinity are just L of this height of land.

Just past this height of land, the trail comes to the R bank of Marcy Brook, which it crosses (no bridge) at 4.44 mi. Fifty yds. to the R and down from this point is the top of Indian Falls, with a spectacular view of the MacIntyre Range from the flat, open rocks.

Just beyond the brook crossing, the trail come[s to]
the yellow trail leading R in 0.81 mi. to the Lake[; see]
below). Turning L at this junction, the trail clin[bs at a]
moderate grade to a level spot at 5.00 mi. just befor[e a]
recently abandoned alternate trail. Dropping down s[lightly, the]
trail begins climbing moderately and then steeply at 5.23 mi. At
5.43 mi. the grade begins to ease off as the trail approaches the top
of a ridge where there are views of Marcy. Continuing along the
ridge with only a few short rises, the trail comes to a junction at 6.18
mi. (Yellow trail L is the Hopkins Trail to Keene Valley; see Keene
Valley Section.)

Bearing R and slightly down, the trail passes the former site of
the Hopkins Lean-to in 200 yds. and then climbs to the former site
of Plateau Lean-to at 6.50 mi., with the summit dome of Marcy in
full view. Dipping briefly across a small stream, the trail then
climbs through thick scrub to the junction with the red-marked
Phelps Trail which comes in from the L at 6.80 mi. (Trail leads via
Slant Rock to Johns Brook Lodge and Keene Valley; see Keene
Valley Section.)

Swinging R, the trail makes a short climb to some bare rocks and
then dips across a wet area before climbing up to the first rocky
shoulder of Marcy at 7.04 mi. Briefly leveling off, the trail now
climbs over mostly bare rock and is marked with cairns and yellow
paint blazes. Use care when following the trail, especially in poor
weather. Proceeding up the bare rocks, the trail reaches the smaller
E summit and flattens out for a few yards before coming to the true
summit at 7.38 mi. From the summit, the yellow trail leading to
Lake Colden and Elk Lake continues down the SW slope. (See
Southern Section.) (See "Mt. Marcy" in Introduction for information on history and view.)

Distances: Adirondak Loj to Marcy Dam, 2.28 mi.; to Indian
Falls, 4.44 mi.; to Hopkins Trail, 6.18 mi.; to Phelps Trail, 6.80 mi.;

mmit of Marcy, 7.38 mi. (11.87 km.). Ascent, 3166 ft. (965 m.). Elevation, 5344 ft. (1628 m.). Order of height, 1.

PHELPS MT.

Phelps is named for Orson Schofield Phelps, better known as "Old Mountain" Phelps, who cut the first trail up Marcy and over the years guided many parties to its summit. It is thus fitting that this peak whose view is so dominated by Mt. Marcy is named after Phelps, even though he probably never climbed the peak himself. Phelps is the easiest high peak to climb from the Marcy Dam area, and is thus a good alternative for Marcy-bound parties which find themselves short of time.

The red-marked trail turns L from the Van Hoevenberg Trail to Marcy (see above) at a point 0.96 mi. from Marcy Dam or 3.24 mi. from Adirondak Loj. The trail immediately climbs away from the Van Hoevenberg Trail on a moderate grade and continues with occasional steeper pitches to the first open rock at 1.05 mi. The red markers are now supplemented by yellow paint blazes as the trail soon comes to a second rocky outcrop with views of Marcy Dam. From here, the trail is mostly flat to large open ledges at the summit at 1.17 mi.

Distance: Adirondak Loj to start of Phelps Trail, 3.24 mi.; to summit of Phelps, 4.41 mi. (7.10 km.). Ascent from Adirondak Loj, 1982 ft. (604 m.). Elevation, 4161 ft. (1268 m.). Order of height, 32.

INDIAN FALLS-LAKE ARNOLD CROSSOVER

From the Van Hoevenberg Trail to Marcy at Indian Falls, 4.45 mi. from Adirondak Loj (see above), a trail with yellow markers branches R and connects with the blue trail to Lake Arnold and ᵈdspar Brook from Avalanche Camp (see below). This trail is extremely rough and wet and is not recommended, although it does provide a useful route between the popular camping areas at Lake Colden and Indian Falls without a traverse of Marcy or a descent all the way to Marcy Dam.

Leaving the junction (0 mi.) just above the brook crossing at Indian Falls, the trail descends for 75 yds. to a good view of Indian Falls from below. In another few yards, the trail swings L and away from the original route of the Van Hoevenberg Trail, climbs briefly, and then begins a rough descent to a sharp L turn at 0.57 mi. Now more of a stream than a trail, it climbs gradually, crosses an extensive wet area, and reaches the R bank of a stream. Following the R bank for a few yards, the trail crosses on the rocks to the junction with the Lake Arnold Trail at 0.81 mi. (Turn R for Avalanche Camp, 1.04 mi.; L for Lake Arnold 0.50 mi.)

Distance: Indian Falls to Lake Arnold Trail, 0.81 mi. (1.30 km.).

THE MACINTYRE RANGE[1]

The series of peaks known as the MacIntyre Mts., or the MacIntyre Range, rises loftily against the sky S of Heart Lake. Named in honor of Archibald McIntyre, the dominating figure in the Tahawus Iron Works enterprise that bore his name, this is one of the noblest groups of peaks in the Adirondacks. Standing apart from all surrounding peaks, the range extends for about 8 miles, running NE and SW. Its steep NW slopes form one side of Indian Pass and the SE spur helps to form the spectacular cliffs of Avalanche Pass.

The most northerly major peak is Wright Peak, 4580 ft., named after Governor Silas Wright. A lesser peak NE of Wright is called

1. The spelling of MacIntyre conforms to the USGS topographic map spelling which has been approved by the U.S. Board of Geographic Names. It is used throughout this guidebook to be consistent, but the man for whom the range is named spelled his name McIntyre.

Whale's Tail because of its shape when viewed from Marcy Dam. The NE shoulder of Wright, adjacent to Whale's Tail, is sometimes referred to as the "Whale" and offers some interesting views for those willing to make the short bushwhack up to this point from the ski trail in Whale's Tail Notch. See below for description of Whale's Tail Notch Ski Trail.

To the SW of Wright is Algonquin Peak, 5114 ft., the highest peak in the range and the second highest in the Adirondacks. Algonquin has also been called Mt. MacIntyre and is still referred to as such on a few DEC trail signs. SW of Algonquin stands Boundary Peak, so named because it is supposed to have marked the boundary between the Algonquin and Iroquois Indian tribes. In reality, it stands on the southern boundary of the Old Military Tract which was originally surveyed in 1797 by a Charles Brodhead, who thus lays claim to the first ascent in the MacIntyre Range —forty years before Ebenezer Emmons first climbed Algonquin in 1837. Although high enough to count as one of the 46 high peaks, Boundary is considered to be merely a prominence on the ridge to Iroquois.

At 4840 ft., Iroquois is the second highest peak in the range and the eighth highest in the Adirondacks. Its rocky summit offers many fine views, particularly the view of Wallface Mt. in Indian Pass. Farther to the SW and separated from Iroquois by a deep valley is Mt. Marshall. For the history of the naming of this peak as well as information on approaches to its summit, see "Peaks Without Maintained Trails."

ALGONQUIN PEAK FROM HEART LAKE

From the Adirondak Loj Campers and Hikers Building, take the Van Hoevenberg Trail (see above) to the trail junction at 0.98 mi. Here the trail to Algonquin continues straight ahead. (Trail L leads to Marcy Dam.) Continuing at a generally easy grade with a few steeper pitches, the trail reaches the junction with the Whale's Tail Notch Ski Trail at 1.42 mi. Bearing R and up at this junction, the trail climbs at a steady, moderate grade along the lower portion of the old Wright Peak Ski Trail. Crossing several small streams as it climbs, the trail veers R from the old ski trail at 2.30 mi. and in 50 yds. joins the original trail from Heart Lake which comes in from the R. The trail soon climbs a steep rock step, after which markers point L and up to a designated campsite. The trail then comes to a beautiful cascade on the L at 2.40 mi.

After this waterfall, the trail climbs a short, steep pitch, levels out for a bit, and then climbs again steeply to a flat area at 2.90 mi. with a small rock cobble on the R. Turning L and up, it climbs over one steep rock step, after which the grade eases a bit across a side hill before the trail reaches the junction with the spur trail to Wright at 3.10 mi. (Trail L leads 0.43 mi. to summit of Wright; see below.)

Bearing R at this junction, the Algonquin Trail begins to climb steeply, going up over several sections of smooth rock and leveling out just before reaching timberline at 3.57 mi. From timberline the trail is marked with cairns and yellow paint blazes. Hikers should use care and stay on the marked trail so as to avoid damaging the fragile alpine vegetation.

In the past few years several groups, most notably the Adirondack 46ers, have done much to restore the areas near Algonquin's summit which had become denuded of their natural vegetation. The techniques for sowing grass seed in this harsh climate were developed by Dr. E.H. Ketchledge of Syracuse, and they have proven successful enough to warrant their use on other summits as well. These restoration efforts have improved the summit's appearance noticeably, but this fine effort can easily be negated by the carelessness of individual hikers.

On the summit, the trail meets the Lake Colden Trail coming up the SW slope and similarly marked with cairns and yellow paint blazes. The view from the summit is spectacular and expansive, being highlighted by the view of Mt. Colden with its many slides and famous dike, or cleft, as well as by the view of Lake Colden and Flowed Lands at the foot of the mountain. The further view encompasses most of the high peaks to the E and S, with many lakes visible to the W and N. On the descent, hikers should pay close attention to the markers, especially in poor weather. The route down generally traverses slightly to the R across the fall line to reach the trail at timberline.

Distances: Adirondak Loj via blue trail to junction with yellow trail for Algonquin, 0.98 mi.; to blue trail to Wright Peak, 3.10 mi.; to summit of Algonquin, 3.98 mi. (6.40 km.) Ascent, 2936 ft. (895 m.). Elevation, 5114 ft. (1559 m.). Order of height, 2.

WRIGHT PEAK

The blue-marked trail to Wright Peak diverges L from the yellow trail to Algonquin 3.10 m. from Adirondak Loj. Leaving the trail junction (0 mi.), the trail climbs steadily to timberline at 0.21 mi., after which the route is marked with cairns up the bare rock ridge. Soon after timberline the grade eases, with the summit reached at 0.43 mi.

A bronze plaque on a large vertical rock face just N of the summit memorializes four airmen who lost their lives in the crash of a B-47 bomber at that spot in 1962. Some parts of the ill-fated aircraft are still scattered around the area close to the top of the mountain.

Distances: Adirondak Loj to blue trail for Wright Peak, 3.10 mi.; to summit of Wright Peak, 3.53 mi. (5.68 km.). Ascent from Adirondak Loj, 2400 ft. (732 m.). Elevation, 4580 ft. (1396 m.). Order of height, 16.

BOUNDARY AND IROQUOIS PEAKS

Although not an official trail, there is a reasonably well-defined route from the col between Algonquin and Boundary along the mostly open ridge to Iroquois. The trail is marked with cairns in the open areas, but there are no other signs or markers. In 1975, the Adirondack 46ers improved this trail somewhat, mainly to establish a route around a unique alpine bog on Boundary, in order to prevent the bog from being trampled. No significant maintenance has been done since.

The trail leaves the Lake Colden Trail to Algonquin 0.38 mi. below the Algonquin summit, at a large cairn at timberline. The "herd path" for Iroquois goes straight ahead, while the marked trail for Lake Colden swings L and down.

Leaving the col (0 mi.), the route climbs quickly to the first summit of Boundary, dips down and bypasses the above-mentioned bog on the R, and comes to the summit of Boundary at 0.22 mi. The route now descends over open rock, enters the woods for a few hundred yards, and finally climbs steeply up and slightly L to the summit of Iroquois at 0.65 mi. from the Algonquin Trail.

Distances: Algonquin summit to start of "herd path," 0.38 mi.; to summit of Iroquois, 1.03 mi. (1.66 km.). Elevation, 4840 ft. (1475 m.). Order of height, 8.

WHALE'S TAIL NOTCH SKI TRAIL

This trail leads from Marcy Dam over a notch NE of Wright to a point on the Algonquin Trail. The trail is quite rough and is not maintained for summer travel. It does offer a 0.45 mi. shorter approach to the Algonquin Trail for those camped at Marcy Dam, but this saving in distance is not great when compared to the rough footing and 380 ft. vertical climb through Whale's Tail Notch. The trail is thus described from Marcy Dam to the Algonquin Trail instead of as an alternate approach to Marcy Dam, as in earlier editions of this guidebook.

The start of the Whale's Tail Notch Ski Trail is at the top of a slight rise a few yards from the W end of Marcy Dam on the Van Hoevenberg Trail (no sign). Leaving this junction (0 mi.), proceed past the first lean-to to a trail R at approximately 100 yds. from the Van Hoevenberg Trail. (Trail straight ahead leads around Marcy Dam to other lean-tos and campsites.) Turning R, the trail proceeds mostly on the level through an open forest before starting to climb at 0.25 mi. The climb is steady and becomes steeper near the height of land. Easing off at 0.64 mi., the trail reaches the actual top of the pass at 0.82 mi., having gained approximately 380 ft. from Marcy Dam. Now starting down a slightly easier grade than that just ascended and going in and out of a small brook, the trail reaches the Algonquin Trail at 1.28 mi.

Distance: Marcy Dam to Algonquin Trail, 1.28 mi. (2.06 km.).

AVALANCHE PASS TO LAKE COLDEN OUTLET

The trail through Avalanche Pass is probably the most spectacular route in the Adirondacks. Sheer rock walls rise directly out of the water on both sides of Avalanche Lake, and the trail is forced to wind among large boulders, and even cross two catwalks set into the rock face, in order to negotiate this impressive piece of terrain. This is the most popular approach to Lake Colden and is much used. Backpackers should be aware, however, that this is a very rough trail in spots, and should allow plenty of time so as not to have to rush. Many parties, for instance, find that it takes an hour to cover the one-mile section from the top of the pass to the lower end of Avalanche Lake.

The Avalanche Pass Trail diverges R from the Van Hoevenberg

Trail to Marcy at Marcy Dam (see above) just over 100 yds. past the trail register and right in front of a lean-to. Marked with yellow DEC disks, the trail proceeds along the flat for 200 yds. where a trail leads R and over a bridge to additional lean-tos and campsites. Bearing L and still on the flat, the trail soon comes to the R bank of Marcy Brook, which it now follows. At 0.35 mi. the trail swings away from the brook and soon crosses two small bridges. At the second bridge, an obscure trail leads R to Kagel Lean-to. Continuing up a gradual climb, the trail passes another lean-to on the R at 0.78 mi. and then crosses the brook on a bridge just before the two lean-tos at Avalanche Camp at 1.08 mi. At the second lean-to there is a trail junction. (Blue trail L leads to Lake Arnold and Feldspar Brook; see below.)

Continuing R, the Avalanche Pass Trail crosses a wet area and begins to climb steeply with several log stairs. At 1.24 mi. the trail swings sharp L, and continues climbing as it comes to a junction where the ski trail crosses at 1.34 mi. (This ski trail follows a slightly longer route down from the top of the pass and eventually joins the Lake Arnold Trail just above Avalanche Camp. It is extremely rough and not suited for summer travel.) Continuing straight ahead, the trail swings R at 1.42 mi., where the ski trail again crosses, and then continues on to the top of the pass at 1.60 mi. Here, at the height of land, a small waterfall descends a cliff during wet seasons and splits, with one part flowing N to the St. Lawrence River and the other flowing S to the Hudson.

The trail now descends toward Avalanche Lake, which it reaches at 2.10 mi. The precipitous slopes of Mt. Colden rise on the left, while the even steeper slopes of Avalanche (Caribou) Mt. rise on the R. The trail proceeds along the R side and is quite rugged but interesting — passing over ledges, around huge boulders, and across crevices aided by ladders and bridges. At two places the cliffs rise directly out of the water, and only bridges bolted into the cliff make the passage possible. These structures are known as "Hitch-up Matildas" after a young lady of that name who was carried across this section on the back of her guide. As the water became deeper, her sister on the shore exhorted her to "hitch-up," and the whole scene was recorded by an artist for *Harper's* magazine, whose drawing of the scene made this spot famous.

From the second such bridge at 2.47 mi., there is an impressive view directly up the slide of Colden, with the Trap Dike just to the left. The largest slides date from 1869 and 1942. The deep cleft of the Trap Dike was caused by the differential erosion of the gabbro dike intruded into the native anorthosite granite.

The trail reaches the foot of the lake at 2.63 mi., crosses the outlet, and follows down the L bank. There is a trail L 200 yds. past the outlet, which leads in 125 yds. to a designated campsite. Continuing down, the trail reaches a junction near the former site of Caribou Lean-to at 2.94 mi. (Blue trail R leads around NW shore of Lake Colden to the Interior Outpost and then on to the dam at the outlet; see below.) Bearing L, the yellow trail leads to the E shore of Lake Colden and then along the shore to the junction with the red trail leading L to Mt. Colden at 3.43 mi. Continuing on, the trail reaches the register at the junction with the red trail to Marcy at 3.83 mi. Trail L leads to Marcy. Trail R leads 200 yds. to a bridge and dam at the outlet, from which the red trail continues on to Flowed Lands and Lake Sanford (see Southern Section). The far side of the dam is also the end of the blue trail around the NW shore of Lake Colden.

There are now six lean-tos at Lake Colden, but there were once as many as thirteen. This reduction in numbers is an attempt to reduce the physical deterioration of this popular camping area by offering fewer attractions for campers. There are, however, many designated tenting sites in the area. Two of the lean-tos are visible from the junction of the Avalanche Pass Trail and the red trail to Marcy.

Two others are located on the L bank of the Opalescent River 0.10 mi. and 0.15 mi. below the Lake Colden outlet. These can be reached by crossing the Opalescent (use suspension bridge just upstream on the Marcy Trail in high water) and following the trail down the L bank. The other two lean-tos are located on a point on the S shore of Lake Colden and are reached by crossing the dam and turning R for 0.10 mi. There are designated camping areas at many spots along both banks of the Opalescent River. In general, they are back away from the river on the opposite side of the trail running along the river.

Distances: Marcy Dam to Avalanche Camps, 1.08 mi.; to Avalanche Lake, 2.10 mi.; to trail around NW shore of Lake Colden, 2.94 mi.; to junction with Marcy Trail at Lake Colden, 3.83 mi. (6.16 km.). (6.13 mi. from Heart Lake.)

TRAIL AROUND NORTHWEST SHORE OF LAKE COLDEN

Starting at the trail junction 0.31 mi. from the foot of Avalanche Lake or 2.94 mi. from Marcy Dam, this trail connects with the Algonquin Trail, Lake Colden Interior Outpost, and the Algonquin Pass Trail to Indian Pass. Leaving the junction (0 mi.), follow blue markers across a brook and past a trail L leading to the former site of Caribou Lean-to. Bearing R, the trail continues on the level to the L bank of a stream and the junction with the blue trail leading R 2.09 mi. to the summit of Algonquin (see below). Continuing L across the bridge, the trail reaches a trail register at 0.56 mi. (Side trail L leads 150 yds. to the Lake Colden Interior Outpost.) Continuing R, the trail immediately comes to the junction with the yellow trail leading straight ahead 3.31 mi. to the Indian Pass Trail (see below). The blue trail turns sharp L, crosses Cold Brook, and swings L and back to Lake Colden. Rounding the S end of the lake, the trail passes Beaver Point Lean-to on the L at 0.89 mi. and West

Lean-to (named in honor of Clinton West, a ranger at Lake Colden for many years) at 0.92 mi. (This lean-to has also been called Cedar Point.) Now the trail swings R and comes to the dam at the outlet at 1.04 mi, ending the blue markers. Red trail straight ahead leads to Flowed Lands and Upper Works (see Southern Section). Trail L crosses the dam and leads to Marcy and the other lean-tos and campsites described above.

Distances: Junction with yellow trail to Interior Outpost, 0.58 mi.; to dam at outlet, 1.04 mi. (1.67 km.). (6.28 mi. from Heart Lake.)

MT. COLDEN FROM LAKE COLDEN

Though seemingly dwarfed by its neighbors Marcy and Algonquin, Mt. Colden is perhaps even more interesting with the extensive slides and unique large dike on its W side. Forming the SE rampart of Avalanche Pass, Colden offers an unforgettable view practically straight down from its summit to the inky depths of Avalanche Lake. Colden was named for David C. Colden, one of the proprietors of the McIntyre Iron Works. Professor Ebenezer Emmons later tried to name it Mt. McMartin in honor of another leader in the McIntyre Iron Works, but the first name has endured. The trail from Lake Colden is very rough and steep with the approach from Lake Arnold generally preferred. Ascending from Lake Arnold with a descent via this trail and a return via Avalanche Pass, however, makes for one of the most spectacular and interesting circuits in the mountains.

The trail starts on the E side of Lake Colden, 0.44 mi. NE from Lake Colden Outlet on the yellow trail and 5.82 mi. from Adirondak Loj. Leaving the yellow trail (0 mi.), the red trail immediately climbs several steep log steps but then eases off as it continues at a steady grade through a thick spruce forest. At 0.60

mi. the trail swings L and up a ladder and begins a nearly unrelenting steep climb — much of it over trail washed right down to bare rock. Finally moderating at 1.25 mi., the trail passes under two huge boulders and soon comes to a ladder leading up a small cliff to a flat area above. Veering L, the trail emerges onto open rock and then veers back R and up a bare rock step to the top of the ridge just below the summit. When descending this section, follow the markers very carefully, as it is easy to lose the trail and there is only one possible route to the ladder that makes it possible to get past the cliffs.

After a short level stretch on the ridge, the trail climbs a final rock step and arrives at a large open area just S of the actual summit. Here is the best view of Lake Colden and Flowed Lands, but just beyond at a large balanced boulder on the L is a view of Avalanche Lake and the "Hitch-up Matildas" (see above) with the actual summit just beyond at 1.62 mi. Here the Lake Colden Trail meets the L. Morgan Porter Trail which leads 1.37 mi. to Lake Arnold (see below).

Distances: Lake Colden to summit of Mt. Colden, 1.62 mi. (2.61 km.). Ascent from Lake Colden, 1950 ft. (594 m.). Elevation, 4714 ft. (1437 m.). Order of height, 11.

ALGONQUIN PEAK FROM LAKE COLDEN

This trail leads 2.09 mi. from the trail on the NW shore of Lake Colden to the summit of Algonquin. (See above for additional information on Algonquin and the MacIntyre Range.) The trail climbs 2350 ft. from Lake Colden to the summit, which makes this one of the most continuously steep climbs in the mountains. Although actually a slightly shorter route between Lake Colden and Heart Lake, this trail up and over Algonquin is not recommended for backpackers in either direction.

The trail begins 0.18 mi. NE of the Lake Colden Interior Outpost and 0.40 mi. from the junction with the Avalanche Pass Trail near the former site of Caribou Lean-to. The actual junction is at a bridge over a stream. Leaving this junction (0 mi.), the yellow-marked trail climbs moderately at first along the L bank of the stream. Reaching the top of a cataract at 0.19 mi., the grade soon eases and the first stream crossing is reached at 0.27 mi. The trail crosses and recrosses the brook several times, finally returning to the L bank at 0.48 mi. Shortly after, the grade again steepens, and the trail reaches the foot of a waterfall at 0.60 mi. Jogging R to get around the falls, the trail then enters the stream bed and climbs the sloping ledges next to the stream where there are some fine views of the slides on Mt. Colden.

The trail leaves the brook at 0.70 mi. and continues steeply up the L bank, with only occasional slight breathers. At 0.90 mi. the trail again crosses the brook and winds among the boulders on the R bank, returning to the L bank just before it reaches a big pool at 0.99 mi. The trail now climbs away from the brook on a very rough section, on a steady, steep grade. Coming back to the stream a few hundred yards later, it again leaves the stream before finally crossing to the R bank for the last time. There is a very steep pitch up over some large roots before the trail settles down to being merely steep to timberline, just above the col between Boundary and Algonquin, which is reached at 1.71 mi. An unmarked trail leads L to Boundary and Iroquois Peaks (see above). Following cairns and yellow paint blazes, the trail reaches the summit of Algonquin at 2.09 mi., where it meets the trail from Heart Lake. (See above for description of trail from Heart Lake as well as cautions on staying on marked trail to preserve the alpine vegetation.)

Distances: Trail junction with blue trail around NW shore of Lake Colden to waterfall, 0.60 mi.; to trail to Boundary and

Iroquois, 1.71 mi.; to summit of Algonquin, 2.09 mi. (3.36 km.).
Ascent from Lake Colden, 2350 ft. (716 m.). Elevation, 5114 ft.
(1559 m.). Order of height, 2.

TRAIL FROM LAKE COLDEN TO INDIAN PASS TRAIL

Cut in 1965, this trail leads from the trail on the NW shore of
Lake Colden near the Interior Outpost, through Algonquin Pass
between Iroquois and Marshall, to a point on the Indian Pass Trail
0.90 mi. from Scott Clearing and 1.10 mi. from Summit Rock in
Indian Pass. This trail is quite steep and rough in spots, which
makes for slow going — especially with backpacks — but it is a
useful connection for those wishing to combine a trip through
Indian Pass with a stay at Lake Colden.

Marked with yellow markers, the trail starts just NE of the bridge
over Cold Brook on the blue trail around the NW shore of Lake
Colden. This point is 0.62 mi. from the Avalanche Pass Trail
junction and 0.42 mi. from Lake Colden's outlet. Leaving the
junction (0 mi.), the trail begins at an easy grade along the L bank of
Cold Brook. Crossing two small tributaries as it begins to climb, the
trail then crosses Cold Brook at 0.28 mi., just below the junction of
the two branches of Cold Brook. Climbing more steeply, the trail
soon enters the bed of the S branch of Cold Brook for easier going.
Leaving and again entering the brook several more times, the trail
finally climbs onto the R bank at the bottom of a short steep pitch.
At 0.65 mi., the trail crosses the S branch of Cold Brook for the last
time and climbs away from the brook onto a shoulder of Iroquois.
Several more steep pitches lead to easier grades, if not smoother
footing, at 1.03 mi, as the trail begins to slab across the shoulder of
Iroquois. Crossing a small height of land at 1.43 mi., the trail drops
slightly and then climbs gradually to the top of Algonquin Pass at
1.50 mi., having gained approximately 1100 ft. from Lake Colden.

The trail is now level through the grassy col, but soon begins to

descend easy to moderate grades as it crosses a brook and follows
down its L bank through an open forest. At 2.16 mi. the trail
descends steeply and crosses two branches of a large brook coming
in from the L. Now veering away from the brook into an adjacent
valley, the trail descends to the R bank of another large brook at
2.47 mi. Turning R, the trail joins an old tote road, veers away from
the brook, and then returns to cross it at 2.72 mi.

Passing a very steep falls in the brook, the trail crosses to the R
bank at 2.84 mi. and recrosses at 2.98 mi. Now veering away from
the brook, the trail climbs briefly before dropping down and
joining the red-marked Indian Pass Trail at 3.31 mi. Trail L leads
1.10 mi. to Summit Rock in Indian Pass. Trail R leads 1.12 mi. to
Scott Clearing Lean-to.

Distances: Start of trail at Lake Colden to Algonquin Pass, 1.50
mi.; to Indian Pass Trail, 3.31 mi. (5.33 km).

AVALANCHE CAMP TO LAKE ARNOLD AND
FELDSPAR BROOK

Characterized by a very rough ascent from Avalanche Camp to
Lake Arnold and by an equally undesirable swampy finish to
Feldspar Brook, this trail has seen little use in recent years. It has,
however, received a good deal of attention from both ADK and
DEC trail crews in recent years, whose efforts may make this direct
route to the upper Opalescent River valley more appealing.

The Lake Arnold Trail begins at Avalanche Camp, 1.08 mi. from
Marcy Dam on the yellow-marked Avalanche Pass Trail. Marked
with blue markers, the Lake Arnold Trail diverges L at a signpost (0
mi.) next to the upper lean-to. For the first few hundred yards it is
also the ski route through Avalanche Pass. Beginning on a gradual
grade, the ski route goes R at 0.16 mi. just before the Lake Arnold
Trail turns sharp L and crosses a small brook on a bridge. The trail

now beings climbing along an old tote road high above Marcy Brook. At 1.04 mi. the trail reaches a junction near a small stream. (Trail L with yellow markers leads 0.81 mi. to Indian Falls.)

From this junction, the trail bears R, crosses a stream in 75 yds., and comes to the former junction with the Van Hoevenberg Bypass Trail. Swinging R after the brook, the trail continues to climb along the R bank of the brook. At 1.44 mi. the trail forks, with the L fork staying on the old tote road and bypassing the former Lake Arnold Lean-to site. This route, however, is only 50 yds. shorter than the R fork, which is now the most used. Bearing R, the trail comes to Lake Arnold and the former lean-to site at 1.54 mi. (Yellow trail R leads 1.37 mi. to Mt. Colden.) Although the lean-to has been removed, this remains a designated campsite.

Crossing the outlet to Lake Arnold, the trail soon joins the direct route and swings R towards Lake Arnold Pass, which is reached at 1.79 mi., 1200 ft. above Avalanche Camp. The trail now descends steeply along a small brook before easing off at 2.05 mi. Continuing a moderate descent, the trail reaches the R bank of the Opalescent River at 2.76 mi. Crossing the river on stones, the trail veers away from the L bank through some very marshy going and returns to the bank of the Opalescent River opposite Feldspar Lean-to at 3.13 mi. In another 60 yds. the trail crosses Feldspar Brook and comes to a junction with the yellow-marked Marcy Trail from Lake Colden at 3.17 mi. (Turn L for Marcy, 2.36 mi.; R for Lake Colden Dam, 2.23 mi.; see Southern Section.)

Distances: Avalanche Camp to Indian Falls Crossover Trail, 1.04 mi.; to Lake Arnold, 1.54 mi.; to junction with Marcy Trail, 3.17 mi. (5.10 km.)

MT. COLDEN FROM LAKE ARNOLD via
L. MORGAN PORTER TRAIL

This approach to Mt. Colden from Lake Arnold replaces the now abandoned trail which formerly turned off 0.67 mi. S of Lake Arnold on the trail to Feldspar Brook. Rudy Strobel laid this trail out in 1966, and it was cut by ADK with the approval of DEC, which now maintains it. It has officially been named the L. Morgan Porter Trail in memory of the man who produced the sixth and seventh editions of this guidebook.

The trail starts at Lake Arnold at the former lean-to site (0 mi.). Marked with yellow markers, the trail bears R and soon begins climbing. The climbing is not steady, with steep pitches alternating with nearly flat areas. At 0.65 mi., the climbing becomes steeper, and at 0.97 mi. the trail emerges on the bare N summit of Colden, from which there are some interesting views. The trail veers L and quickly descends back into the timber. (This spot is not well marked and should be noted for the return trip.) Dropping into a small sag, the trail climbs over another small bump and then drops to the col at the base of the main peak at 1.11 mi., where the abandoned trail enters on the L. From here the trail climbs steadily to the summit at 1.37 mi., where it meets the route from Lake Colden. (See above for trail description and notes on the view.)

Distances: Lake Arnold to summit of Colden, 1.37 mi. (2.20 km.); from Heart Lake, 6.33 mi. (10.18 km.). Ascent from Heart Lake, 2535 ft. (772 m.). Elevation, 4714 ft. (1437 m.). Order of height, 11.

INDIAN PASS FROM HEART LAKE

Indian Pass is a stupendous gorge between Wallface Mt. and the MacIntyre Range. The pass is over a mile in length, and its sheer NW wall rises nearly 1000 ft., which makes it one of the highest cliffs in the East, rivaled only by Cannon Cliff in Franconia Notch in the White Mountains. At places, the bottom of the gorge is an almost impossible tangle of boulders that have fallen off the cliff over the ages. There are several places where ice and snow remain throughout the year deep in caves that never see the light of day. The trail passes above this rock jumble on the SE side of the pass, but nevertheless the going is often difficult.

The trail begins on the W side of the Heart Lake Road just before the parking lot at the Campers and Hikers Building. Since parking on the road is prohibited, hikers must park in the lot, return to the road and turn R, going a few yards on the road to get to the start. Leaving the road (0 mi.) and marked by red markers, the trail proceeds on the level, swinging slightly L, and joins a campground road next to Heart Lake at 0.10 mi. The trail turns sharp R, passing the trail R to Mt. Jo 50 yds. later. Continuing straight ahead along the lake, the trail comes to a register at 0.35 mi., where all hikers should register.

At 0.45 mi. the Old Nye Ski Trail diverges R, but the Indian Pass Trail bears L and down past the end of Heart Lake and then up to the property line and Westside Ski Trail at 0.59 mi. The trail now goes gently up and down through a mature open forest, crossing a brook on a bridge at 1.63 mi. and then a second larger brook without a bridge at 2.11 mi. Just beyond this second brook is a junction with the first of two trails leading to Rocky Falls. (Trail R leads 100 yds. to the bank of Indian Pass Brook and then up R bank to crossing to lean-to above the upper part of Rocky Falls at approximately 300 yds. from the Indian Pass Trail. The falls are not high, but there is a good swimming hole below the lower falls. The side trail then continues steeply up to rejoin the Indian Pass Trail in another 150 yds.)

Bearing L at this junction, the Indian Pass Trail soon begins a steep climb of 150 yds., easing off just before the second junction of the side trail to Rocky Falls at 2.35 mi. Now mostly on the flat and with some extensive wet areas, the trail crosses a large stream at 2.56 mi., climbs for a few yards, and then continues with short rises and falls to another stream at 3.58 mi. Crossing this stream and another one shortly after, the trail comes to Scott Clearing Lean-to at 3.81 mi. From the lean-to bear R, cross another small stream, and climb gradually to Scott's Dam at 4.06 mi. and the junction with the Wallface Ponds Trail. (Trail R leads 2.80 mi. to Scott and Wallface Ponds; see below.) Scott Clearing is the former site of a lumber camp, and the high rock dam was used to control the flow of water in Indian Pass Brook for driving logs. Turning L at the junction, there are two choices. One is to use the old low water route which runs up the gravel bars next to Indian Pass Brook. Beaver dams or recent rains may make this route impractical, but it does save quite a bit of climbing on the high water route. Continuing on the marked trail (high water route), follow up the L bank of a large brook before veering up and R to a height of land at 4.17 mi. Descending gradually, the trail reaches a view of Scott's Dam at 4.31 mi., where it climbs again briefly before rejoining the low water route at 4.48 mi.

Turning L and crossing two brooks, the trail comes to a junction with the trail over Algonquin Pass from Lake Colden at 4.90 mi. (Trail L leads 3.31 mi. to Lake Colden; see above.) At 5.02 mi. the trail crosses Indian Pass Brook diagonally and shortly after recrosses it to the R bank. Now beginning a very steep, rough climb, the trail ascends into the pass. There is a short level stretch at 5.47 mi. where the first views of the cliff are possible. The actual height of land is at 5.54 mi. where there is a sign, but most hikers continue on to Summit Rock at 6.00 mi. where there is the most spectacular view of the cliff. From Summit Rock it is 4.42 mi. to the Upper Works. (See Southern Section.)

Distances: Adirondak Loj to Rocky Falls, 2.11 mi.; to Scott

Clearing Lean-to, 3.81 mi.; to trail to Scott and Wallface Ponds, 4.06 mi.; to trail to Lake Colden, 4.90 mi.; to Summit Rock, 6.00 mi. (9.65 km.).

SCOTT AND WALLFACE PONDS

Starting at Scott's Dam on the Indian Pass Trail, this trail climbs W to a series of remote and seldom-visited ponds. There are possible campsites at both Scott and Wallface Ponds as well as a spectacularly framed view of the MacIntyre Range from one of the upper Scott Ponds. This area offers unexcelled opportunities for solitude in a very pretty setting, and is thus highly recommended as a place to camp for a night or more. The only thing lacking from these ponds is fish, as because of their altitude, they were apparently among the first ponds to be affected by acid precipitation.

Leaving the Indian Pass Trail (see above) at the stone dam (0 mi.), the trail goes R (W) and crosses Indian Pass Brook just below the old spillway. Climbing the steep bank on the far side, the trail joins an old tote road and begins a steady, moderate climb to a flat area at 0.54 mi. Dropping slightly, the trail crosses a small stream and climbs again to a height of land at 1.14 mi. The trail now drops slightly, flattens out, and then drops more steeply to a trail sign at 1.50 mi. with Scott Pond visible beyond. Just past this sign, a side trail goes R and steeply down 30 yds. to a possible campsite at the inlet. The trail now drops down to the old dam at the outlet and bears L and down the L bank a few yards to a crossing at 1.61 mi. The trail now goes steeply up the R bank and swings back R to the other side of the old dam. (It may be possible to cross the dam itself in low water.)

The trail now skirts the shore but quickly veers away to the L. (There are more possible campsites on this shore beyond the point where the trail leaves the shore.) Climbing to an open area, the trail crosses it, skirts a second open swampy area on the L and then climbs, steeply at times, to a ridge at 2.17 mi. Dropping now, the trail passes a small pond on the L at 2.29 mi., and then swings R and down to a large open area with a small pond at one end at 2.43 mi. Here is an outstanding view of the MacIntyre Range perfectly framed by the valley at the end of the pond. Bearing L, the trail enters the woods and climbs to an extremely wet area. There are now (thanks to volunteers from the Adirondack 46ers) just enough logs and bridges to make this section passable to Wallface Pond at 2.80 mi. From the shore of this attractive large pond there are views of MacNaughton. A vague trail leads L 150 yds. from this spot to an attractive campsite on a point.

Distances: Scott's Dam to Scott Pond, 1.50 mi.; to Wallface Pond, 2.80 mi. (4.50 km.). (6.86 mi. from Heart Lake.)

MT. JO

On the N shore of Heart Lake is Mt. Jo, a small but steep and rocky peak rising 710 ft. above the lake. It was named in 1877 by Henry Van Hoevenberg in honor of his fiancee, Josephine Schofield. There are two routes to its summit, both of which begin from the Indian Pass Trail 0.13 mi. from the Heart Lake Road. From the parking lot at the Campers and Hikers Building at the end of the Heart Lake Road, return to the road and turn R 100 yds. to the trail signs at the start of the Indian Pass Trail. (Note: parking is not permitted on this section of the road.)

Leaving the road (0 mi.), the trail proceeds on the flat to the road through the Adirondak Loj Campground at 0.11. Turn R 30 yds. and find the sign for Mt. Jo. Turn R and climb moderately up to a junction where the Long Trail and Short Trail split at 0.27 mi. The Long Trail goes L and is 0.28 mi. longer but less strenuous. Taking the Long Trail, proceed along a side hill practically on the level before turning R and up at 0.57 mi. Climbing over some rocks, the trail turns sharp L and then starts swinging back to the R to a trail junction at 0.70 mi. (Trail L with blue paint blazes leads to the W property line which can be followed back down to the Old Nye Ski Trail and thence back to Heart Lake.)

The Mt. Jo Trail bears R and climbs to a lookout on the R at 0.92 mi., and at 0.99 mi. the Short Trail enters on the R. Just after this junction, a side trail leads L and up a rock step to the W summit. Continuing to the R on the flat to the base of the summit rocks, the trail reaches the summit at 1.14 mi. From the summit the views are impressive, reaching from Cascade to Marcy to Algonquin to Indian Pass, making this one of the best views for the least effort in the Adirondacks.

The Short Trail which diverges R at the junction at 0.27 mi. climbs through some boulders and then up a gully to a sharp L turn at 0.55 mi. The trail ascends to a good view at 0.66 mi. and then joins the Long Trail at 0.71 mi. Turn R to reach the summit at 0.86 mi.

Distances: Heart Lake Road to junction of Short and Long Trails, 0.27 mi.; to summit via Long Trail, 1.14 mi. (1.63 km.); to summit via Short Trail, 0.86 mi. (1.38 km.). Elevation, 2876 ft.

SOUTH MEADOW

South Meadow is a clearing that can be reached by auto from Heart Lake Road. There are several primitive but attractive campsites at the end of the road, which is also the start for the Klondike Notch Trail and the South Meadow Truck Trail to Marcy Dam. The dirt road, which is marked with DEC trail signs, starts 3.8 mi. S of Rt. 73 on the Heart Lake Road and 1.0 mi. N of Adirondak Loj. It leads 0.85 mi. to a fork, with the R fork leading to the Truck Trail and the L fork leading to the best camping areas and the start of the Klondike Notch Trail.

SOUTH MEADOW TO MARCY DAM

This fire truck trail is a graded gravel road offering an alternate route to Marcy Dam that is only about 0.30 mi. longer than the approach from Heart Lake. It was constructed by the Civilian Conservation Corps in the 1930s. Since this area is now classified as wilderness, even DEC vehicles are prohibited from using this road except in the event of an emergency. This route can be especially recommended during the raspberry season.

From the junction 0.85 mi. from the Heart Lake Road (see above), bear R and down to a small parking area at a bar gate and trail register. Leaving the gate (0 mi.), the road crosses South Meadow Brook and proceeds along the flat to a junction with the Mr. Van Ski Trail at 0.33 mi. (Trail R leads 1.33 mi. to Heart Lake, L 4.63 mi. to Mt. Van Hoevenberg Cross-Country Area; see below.) The road now begins a short climb, and after several more ascents and descents crosses a large brook at 1.60 mi. At 1.95 mi. the road dips down to the R, crosses another large brook, and climbs back before dropping down two pitches to the R bank of Marcy Brook at 2.31 mi. The road now continues straight up a gradual grade along the brook to the Van Hoevenberg Trail at Marcy Dam at 2.60 mi.

Distance: Parking area at trail register to Marcy Dam, 2.60 mi. (4.18 km.).

KLONDIKE NOTCH TRAIL TO JOHNS BROOK LODGE

This route leads from South Meadow through Klondike Notch to Johns Brook Lodge where it meets the Johns Brook Trail to Marcy. Klondike Notch between Tabletop and Yard Mts. has also been called Railroad Notch at times, but this name rightfully belongs to the lower notch between Porter and Big Slide which once was actually surveyed for a railroad.

The trail, marked with red markers, starts at the signpost (0 mi.) at the end of the South Meadow Road. It immediately crosses South Meadow Brook on a good bridge just above an old dam and then swings R to join an old tote road, which it follows all the way to Klondike Lean-to. At 0.25 mi. the Mr. Van Ski Trail comes in from the R and then diverges L at 0.45 mi. (Marked with red "ski" trail markers, the Mr. Van Trail leads L 3.85 mi. to the Mt. Van Hoevenberg Cross-Country Area and R 1.57 mi. to Adirondak Loj.) After the second junction, the Klondike Trail begins a steady, gradual to moderate climb, which continues to a level area at 1.57 mi. Continuing on the level, the trail crosses one fair sized brook and finally dips slightly to Klondike Lean-to at 2.58 mi.

The trail now follows up the L bank of the brook for 125 yds. before crossing it and continuing on with mostly gradual grades to the height of land at 3.55 mi., having gained 1127 ft. (344 m.) from South Meadow. Now descending at a moderate grade, the trail crosses one wet level stretch and then continues down to a junction at 3.99 mi. (Trail L with ADK markers leads over Yard to Big Slide in 2.70 mi.; see Keene Valley Section.) From this junction, the trail continues down at moderate grades, coming to the L bank of Black Brook at 4.90 mi. and then crossing the brook just before reaching Johns Brook Lodge at 5.27 mi.

Distances: South Meadow to Klondike Lean-to, 2.58 mi.; to ADK Big Slide Trail, 3.99 mi.; to Johns Brook Lodge, 5.27 mi. (8.48 km.).

MT. VAN HOEVENBERG FROM SOUTH MEADOW ROAD

Mt. Van Hoevenberg is a low mountain rising above South

Meadow and offering a spectacular view of the high peaks and Lake Placid. Originally called South Mt., its name was changed in 1932 when the Olympic Bobsled Run was built on its north side. Hiking over the mountain and down the N side offers the unique opportunity to see the Olympic Bobsled and Luge runs as well as enjoy the fine view.

The trail starts from the South Meadow Road 0.25 mi. from the Heart Lake Road and is marked with blue DEC disks. Starting on an old road blocked by a bar gate, the trail proceeds on the level until it dips down to cross a wet area at 0.93 mi. After climbing a bit and dipping again to cross a small stream, the trail begins climbing steadily, first L across the slope and then R and under some small cliffs before arriving at a height of land at 1.58 mi.

From here, the trail climbs the W ridge of Mt. Van Hoevenberg to the first open ledges at 2.06 mi., where there are views of Marcy, Algonquin and Lake Placid. These first ledges offer perhaps the best views, but the trail continues on to the summit ledge at 2.15 mi., with a view further to the E including Porter and Giant.

To continue down the N side, turn sharp L at the summit ledge. The trail soon begins descending through thick woods and joins the upper end of an old road at 2.32 mi. This point was the original start of the Bobsled Run when it was 1.5 mi. long. The run was shortened to the present 1 mi. length in 1936 because greater speeds by technically superior sleds had made the longer run unsafe. There are occasional traces of the old run on the L. Passing through a small clearing at the end of a newer gravel road, the trail comes to the upper end of the Bobsled Run at 2.81 mi.

Turning L, the trail follows the spectator walkway down the R side of the Bobsled Run, coming to the famous Shady Curve at 3.31 mi. and a small grandstand at Zig-Zag Curves at 3.58 mi., with the Luge Run visible to the R. The trail reaches the foot of the run at 3.78 mi. The parking lot on the other side of the gate is at the end of the access road that branches off from Rt. 73 3.00 mi. E of the Heart Lake Road. One could start the climb from the Bobsled Run side of Mt. Van Hoevenberg, but there is a fee charged ($1.00 to $2.50 in 1984 depending on the services offered that day) to enter through the gate at the base of the run.

Distances: South Meadow Road to summit of Mt. Van Hoevenberg, 2.15 mi. (3.45 km.). To foot of Bobsled Run, 3.78 mi. (6.08 km.). Ascent, 740 ft. (225 m.). Elevation, 2860 ft. (872 m.).

THE MR. VAN SKI TRAIL

The Mr. Van Ski Trail was named after Henry Van Hoevenberg, builder of the original Adirondack Lodge. It provides a useful connection between the ski trails around Adirondak Loj and the cross-country center at Mt. Van Hoevenberg. It is used mostly by skiers, since the first section of the trail between Adirondak Loj and the South Meadow Truck Trail crosses several beaver flows that make the trail wet at any time, and nearly impassable after heavy rains. It is described from Adirondak Loj to Mt. Van Hoevenberg because that is the easiest direction in which to ski it. Those who follow this trail in reverse direction should be aware that finding one's way through the complex of cross-country trails to Hi-Notch can be confusing. (See notes at the end of this description.)

Starting at the parking lot at the Campers and Hikers Building at Adirondak Loj, the Mr. Van Trail proceeds along the Marcy Trail for 175 yds. to a junction where the Mr. Van Trail goes sharp L. Proceeding through a thick spruce forest on the level, the trail passes a junction with the "Easy Side" ski trail and begins to descend gradually to Marcy Brook, which it reaches at 0.74 mi. Crossing the brook on a bridge, the trail continues across the generally open alder swamp, with views of Colden and Algonquin, to the first of two beaver dams at 1.04 mi. Crossing these dams, the trail reaches the South Meadow Truck Trail at 1.32 mi. (see above).

Crossing the truck trail, the Mr. Van Trail continues mostly on the flat to a point near the base of a new (1979) slide coming down off a shoulder of Phelps at 1.86 mi. Just beyond this point, the trail reaches the Klondike Trail and turns R for approximately 250 yds. along the Klondike Trail. Diverging L at 2.10 mi., the trail soon crosses Klondike Brook (no bridge as of 1984) and continues with short ups and downs along a side hill to the Mr. Van Lean-to at 3.64 mi. Immediately crossing South Meadow Brook (no bridge as of 1984), the trail crosses some flat, swampy ground before beginning a steady, moderate climb to Hi-Notch, which it reaches at 4.71 mi.

Hi-Notch is the edge of the Mt. Van Hoevenberg Cross-Country Area, and the Mr. Van Trail now follows wide, graded ski trails. Bearing L, the trail descends to a sharp L turn, passes straight through the first junction, continues to descend to a second junction (#35), and then descends gradually to junction #36 at 5.32 mi. Here skiers should follow the "Stadium" signs to the L to maintain one-way traffic, but hikers can save some distance by bearing R and down. Continue straight through the next junction (#4) and finally arrive at the bottom of the descent at 5.75 mi. at a small open area. From here, bear L on a very wide trail leading to the Cross-Country Stadium. The parking lot is at the far end of the stadium at 5.95 mi. This parking lot is 200 yds. from the entrance to the Bobsled Run and the end of the access road which leaves Rt. 73 3.00 mi. E of the Heart Lake Road.

For those persons following this trail from the Mt. Van Hoevenberg end, the marked route is slightly different from the descent route described above. Signs for "The Mr. Van Trail" lead from the stadium via the best route for skiing to Hi-Notch (so as to maintain one-way traffic).

Distances: Adirondak Loj to South Meadow Truck Trail, 1.32 mi.; to Mr. Van Lean-to, 3.64 mi.; to Mt. Van Hoevenberg Cross-Country Area, 5.95 mi. (9.57 km.).

NORTHERN SECTION

This section includes those trails formerly included in the Saranac Lake and Lake Placid sections of previous editions of this guidebook, plus those trails W of the East Branch of the Ausable River formerly included in the Cascade-Keene-Hurricane section. There is also a description of the Northville-Lake Placid Trail from Averyville Rd. to Duck Hole which was formerly included in a separate section on the N-P Trail. This region is dominated by Whiteface Mt., but there are many other excellent summits and ponds, most of them relatively uncrowded.

Both Saranac Lake and Lake Placid have been popular resort areas for many years, and little needs to be added here about Lake Placid's role in hosting the 1932 and 1980 Winter Olympics. To provide hiking opportunities for the early visitors to the Lake Placid area, the Adirondack Camp and Trail Club, initiated by Henry Van Hoevenberg in 1910, began to construct a system of formally marked and regularly maintained trails with shelters available along them. This system allowed far greater numbers of people to hike in the mountains, since getting lost was less of a problem and an overnight pack could be considerably lighter. Although no one can claim that Henry Van Hoevenberg "invented" such facilities for hikers, in this area at least he is the one who deserves the credit for starting the current system of trails and shelters (now maintained by the DEC) that most hikers take for granted.

This northern region offers a great variety of hikes, particularly easy to moderate ones, and many of them should be more popular than they are. Below are a few recommended hikes:

SHORT HIKES:

Owls Head — 1.10 mi. round trip. A near-perfect little hike for children with views starting almost immediately, plenty of blueberries, and a great view from the summit.

Baker Mt. — 1.74 mi. round trip. The same could be said about Baker as about Owls Head, except that one must wait a little longer for the first view.

MODERATE HIKES:

Pitchoff Mt. — 4.90 mi. point to point. A wonderful hike along a long, rocky ridge with two possible shorter destinations.

Ampersand Mt. — 5.42 mi. round trip. The truly commanding view from this bald summit is good enough to make one forget the very steep spots on the way up.

HARDER HIKE:

Whiteface via Whiteface Landing and Connery Pond Trail — 7.04 mi. round trip hiking distance plus 6 mi. round trip paddling. Surely the most civilized way to do this very civilized peak is to paddle from the boat launching site at the S end of Lake Placid to Whiteface Landing and then ascend the peak. Great views from both the lake and summit. See general description of Whiteface for paddling information and Whiteface Mt. from Connery Pond Trail for hiking description.

Northville-Lake Placid Trail		
to Duck Hole	12.2	182
Scarface Mt.	3.35	185
Baker Mt.	0.87	186
Ampersand Mt.	2.71	187

WHITEFACE MT.

Standing alone over 10 mi. to the N of any other 4000 ft. peak, Whiteface and its lower companion, Esther, are an impressive sight from any viewpoint. Equally impressive are the views from the summit. Lake Placid and its heavily wooded islands are directly below, with the rest of the high peaks arrayed beyond, while to the N and E Lake Champlain and Mount Royal in Canada are visible. Even with the intrusions of the summit buildings and the accompanying throngs of tourists, it is still a magnificent wilderness view from this summit.

Geologically, Whiteface is unique in that its anorthosite granite welled up from the earth from a separate source from the rest of the high peaks. More recently, geologically, mountain glaciers clung to its higher slopes long enough in the aftermath of the last ice age to create the most distinct alpine features to be found on any Adirondack peak. On the N, W, and E faces of Whiteface are well-defined bowl-shaped cirque valleys with sharp aretes separating the cirques. The walkway from the top of the highway ascends the sharpest of these aretes, while the Wilmington Trail ascends another.

Whiteface has also seen more development than any other high peak; it now has a paved two-lane highway, a major ski area, and a complete summit weather observatory. Beginning in Wilmington, the Memorial Highway is a toll road leading to within 300 vertical feet of the summit. From here there is an elevator to the summit as well as an improved stone walkway up the spectacular NW arete. The summit observatory provides weather information for local and national forecasters as well as providing a base for atmospheric research on such phenomena as acid precipitation.

Opened in 1956, the present Whiteface Mt. Ski Center replaced the original, smaller development on Marble Mt. Expanded several times since 1956, the ski center was the site for the alpine events at the 1980 Winter Olympics.

There are two hiking trails to the summit of Whiteface. One ascends steeply from Connery Pond and Lake Placid, with another coming from Wilmington. The easiest route is from Wilmington, using the old Marble Mt. Ski Area approach. An only slightly harder, and in many ways more scenic approach, is via boat to Whiteface Landing on Lake Placid and then up the peak via the Connery Pond Trail. There is a boat launching site at the S end of Lake Placid located on Mirror Lake Dr., 0.6 mi. N from the Hilton Hotel at the end of Main St. The adjacent marina does not rent canoes or small power boats, but one can arrange for a boat trip to Whiteface Landing. (As of 1984, the prices charged were probably economical only for a larger group and even then only for one-way transportation.)

WHITEFACE MT. via CONNERY POND AND WHITEFACE LANDING

This trail starts on Rt. 86, 3.1 mi. E from its junction with Rt. 73 in Lake Placid and 0.2 mi. W of the bridge over the West Branch of the Ausable River. From the small DEC sign on the highway, turn down a narrow dirt road marked with red DEC disks. Drive down the road and bear L at 0.5 mi. to a parking area marked with signs about 70 yds. farther. From the parking lot (0 mi.) continue on the road, bearing L after 130 yds. to avoid a private residence. The trail now skirts the NW shore of Connery Pond on an old road, avoiding a trail L at 0.30 mi. Bearing away from the pond, the old road climbs to a junction with another road at 0.43 mi., where the Connery Pond Trail bears L and down to a bar gate at the start of an old truck trail used to salvage timber in the aftermath of the 1950 hurricane.

From the gate the road is at first on the level, but slowly begins climbing to a height of land at 1.40 mi., after which it gently descends to a junction at 2.49 mi. (Trail L leads 110 yds. to Whiteface Landing on Lake Placid. Trail straight ahead is a Shore Owners Association trail around N side of Lake Placid; see below.) Turning R, the trail climbs gently to a straight section of old road at 3.10 mi., with Whiteface in view directly ahead. The trail now drops down to the L to cross Whiteface Brook, which it recrosses three times before arriving at Whiteface Lean-to above the L bank of the brook at 3.55 mi.

Turning L here, the grade steepens as the trail climbs along above the L bank. At 3.95 mi. a cascade is visible to the L, and at 4.52 mi. the trail turns sharp R away from the brook and the old phone line which the trail has followed to this point. The grades are now easy to moderate for a short stretch, but soon the trail joins and then leaves a small brook and the grade becomes mostly steep to a short breather where there is a view to the S at 5.59 mi. Reaching timberline at 5.76 mi., the trail is now marked with yellow paint blazes and climbs steeply over numerous ledges to the S summit at 5.98 mi. The actual summit is a few yards farther at 6.02 mi.

Distances: Parking area at Connery Pond to junction at Whiteface Landing, 2.49 mi.; to Whiteface Lean-to, 3.55 mi.; to summit of Whiteface, 6.02 mi. (9.67 km.). Ascent from Connery Pond, 3232 ft. (985 m.). Elevation, 4867 ft. (1483 m.). Order of height, 5.

WHITEFACE MT. via WILMINGTON TRAIL

This trail branches L from the Whiteface Memorial Highway 0.6 mi. from Rt. 86 in Wilmington on a dirt road marked with a small DEC sign. At the Town of Wilmington Reservoir 0.2 mi. up this road there is a parking area on the R, just before a sign that promises any car parked beyond will be towed. From the parking area (0 mi.), bear L and cross the brook below the dam on a good bridge and then turn R and up the R bank of the brook. The trail slowly veers away from the brook, crossing an old road at 0.32 mi. Continuing to veer L, the trail soon heads S along a side hill practically on the level through an open maple and oak forest.

Finally reaching the S side of a ridge, the trail turns R at 1.44 mi. and begins a steady, steep climb which continues to the summit of Marble Mt. at 2.17 mi. Here the route from the base of the old Marble Mt. Ski Area comes in from the R. The summit rocks on Marble Mt. can be reached by an overgrown trail which branches R from this side trail a few feet from the junction. It is 150 yds. to the top of the former T-bar lift, where there are views to the S and E.

Turning L on the level with a view of Esther straight ahead, the trail soon begins to climb and comes to a steep stretch of bare rock at 2.43 mi. The trail bears L a few feet up this rock, but there are good views of Esther, the Wilmington Range and to the N and E, by continuing straight ahead on the rock for 75 yds. Climbing now through small alders and birches, the trail enters thicker woods at 2.63 mi. and then climbs in several stages to the top of the ridge at 3.14 mi. Continuing to climb a few more short, steep pitches along the top of the ridge, the trail finally levels off at 3.35 mi. where there is an old toboggan shelter on the L with a good view of Whiteface straight ahead.

The entire plateau ahead was once covered with a network of ski trails, including one to the summit of Esther, and there are many old signs along this next section of trail marking the former (and now indiscernible) junctions with these trails. At the upper end of this plateau there was a series of two small rope tows leading up to the Wilmington Turn on the Memorial Highway. In the days before snowmaking was common at ski areas, these rope tows were a high altitude back-up in the event that the snow was insufficient at lower Marble Mt. — an occurrence much more frequent than the Lake Placid Chamber of Commerce would have cared to admit. Skiers were trucked up the road and at the end of the day had the option of skiing back down the highway or descending via a ski trail that followed very closely the route of the current hiking trail.

From this first view of Whiteface, the trail drops gently to the junction with the unmarked trail leading R to Esther at 3.44 mi. (See "Peaks Without Maintained Trails".) The trail now continues generally down until it crosses a wet area on several log bridges at 3.96 mi., after which it is flat for a short ways before climbing again to a lean-to on the R at 4.53 mi. Now the trail goes steeply up an old ski tow line before diverging L and coming to the base of the wall of Wilmington Turn, which is skirted on the L over large boulders to the Memorial Highway at 4.76 mi. The trail now climbs the steep ledge to the L and proceeds through small trees to timberline at 4.90 mi. The final climb along the arete is spectacular, with fresh slides visible down to the L and the top of the Whiteface Ski Center chairlift further to the L. Veering L of the summit buildings, the trail arrives at the summit at 5.16 mi.

Distances: Parking area at Wilmington reservoir to summit of Marble Mt., 2.19 mi.; to unmarked trail to Esther Mt., 3.44 mi.; to lean-to, 4.53 mi.; to summit of Whiteface, 5.16 mi. (8.30 km.). Ascent from parking area, 3620 ft. (1103 m.). Elevation, 4867 ft. (1483 m.). Order of height, 5.

OLD MARBLE MT. SKI AREA APPROACH TO
WILMINGTON TRAIL

Many hikers prefer to shorten their climb of the Wilmington Trail by driving to the Atmospheric Sciences Research Center, which is reached by a road off the Memorial Highway 2.4 mi. from Rt. 86 in Wilmington. There is a large paved parking lot at the Research Center, which is housed in what used to be the Marble Mt. Ski Lodge. There are no signs or markers for the start of this approach, but the route is used enough to be fairly plain.

From the parking lot (0 mi.), bear L and down across a mowed lawn past a weather instrument station and then go steeply down a straight cut in the alders. At the bottom of the hill at 0.11 mi., the route goes R past a radio tower, with the old T-bar lift line visible straight ahead. Go straight up through a veritable tunnel in the alders along the eroded lift line. At 0.78 mi., near the top of Marble Mt., a small white sign points R to the main trail, which is reached at 0.84 mi. Distance saved using this approach is 1.36 mi. Vertical climb saved is 570 ft.

COOPER KILN POND TRAIL

This is an interesting walk through a notch between the Stephenson and Wilmington Ranges to a seldom visited pond with a lean-to. This pond has also been called Cooper "Kill" Pond on the USGS maps, but the name on the DEC signs is used here. The route is probably more often skied than hiked because it offers an exceptional downhill run of nearly 2000 ft. and a net drop of over 1000 ft.

The start is on the Franklin Falls Road, found by driving 2.8 mi. up the Whiteface Memorial Highway from Rt. 86 in Wilmington and then turning R just before the toll house. There is a DEC sign on the R 0.7 mi. from the Memorial Highway. Leaving the road (0 mi.), the trail climbs briefly, turns L and proceeds on the flat on a good road. At 0.20 mi. the trail bears R and begins a gentle climb to an open area at 0.30 mi. The climbing continues easy to moderate with some eroded sections to a bridge over a small brook at 1.55 mi. Here the climbing steepens a bit before easing off near a height of land at 1.79 mi.

Beginning to descend at 2.22 mi., the trail reaches the outlet to Cooper Kiln Pond at 2.69 mi., with the lean-to (mis-located on the 1978 USGS map) just beyond the outlet. The pond itself is approximately 1/4 mi. long with some large rocks which make nice picnic spots near the E shore. Swimming is possible but hardly ideal from these rocks, and fishing is problematical, given the size and altitude of the pond; but this is a picturesque spot far from the populated trade routes, and solitude is just about guaranteed.

To continue past the pond, turn sharp R at the lean-to and descend to a crossing of the outlet at 2.80 mi. The trail ascends a short, steep bank and turns L onto an overgrown tote road which has been marked as a snowmobile trail. Following this old road, the trail crosses the outlet again at 3.25 mi. and two additional times, ending up on the L bank at 3.73 mi. where it veers L away from the brook and comes to a good jeep trail at 3.88 mi. Joining another jeep trail coming in from the L at 4.18 mi., the route (still marked with snowmobile trail markers) turns R and down. Passing several other side roads, the grade slowly flattens out as the trail crosses a large stream at 5.39 mi. and levels out shortly thereafter. The trail reaches Bonnieview Rd. in Wilmington at 5.93 mi. This point is 3.2 mi. N of Rt. 86 in the center of Wilmington and 2.9 mi. S of the Silver Lake Road leading W from Ausable Forks.

Distances: Franklin Falls Rd. to Cooper Kiln Pond Lean-to, 2.73 mi. (4.39 km.); to Bonnieview Rd., 5.93 mi. (9.54 km.).

CATAMOUNT MT.

Catamount is one of the most spectacular small peaks in the Adirondacks. Much of the mountain's steep S side is bare as a result of first cutting for charcoal and later burning. The trail is not marked or maintained, but it remains relatively easy to follow. Be careful, however, on the many open ledges, as the old paint blazes are fading and the cairns are few.

The start is now a few hundred yards N of the original tote road start in order to keep this route entirely on state land. From Rt. 86 in the center of Wilmington, go up the Whiteface Memorial Highway for 2.8 mi. and turn R on the Franklin Falls Rd., which is followed for 3.3 mi. to another R turn. Follow this road 0.8 mi. and turn R again onto Forestdale Rd., from which the mountain is soon visible. At 2.2 mi. down this road, on a short straight stretch at the bottom of a small hill, there is a vague path marked by some old orange surveyor's tape. This is the start of the trail. (This point is also 6.2 mi. S of the Silver Lake Rd. running W from Ausable Forks.)

Leaving the road (0 mi.), the narrow trail is level to a well-marked property corner post at 0.26 mi. After this corner the trail follows an orange painted property line straight across an old field. At the far end of the old field, at 0.56 mi., do not follow the orange property line, but instead turn R and enter the woods at the far corner of the field. The trail soon begins to climb steeply before dipping briefly to cross a small brook at 0.80 mi. The trail now climbs at moderate to steep grades over several ledges to a balanced boulder at 1.26 mi. Soon thereafter, a steep rock scramble up the S summit begins, ending with a nearly vertical chimney in the rock. Reaching the S summit at 1.45 mi., the trail dips slightly through thick trees to the col and then climbs to the summit at 1.80 mi. The views from the summit are expansive and dominated by Whiteface

Mt., Taylor Pond and Silver Lake. In season, the blueberries are almost as good as the views.

Distance: Road to summit of Catamount, 1.80 mi. (2.90 km.). Ascent from road, 1542 ft. (466 m.). Elevation, 3168 ft. (966 m.).

SILVER LAKE MT.

This peak is located about 10 mi. N of Whiteface on the road running from Ausable Forks to Silver Lake and Clayburg. The attractions of this peak are the rocky ledges on the summit, which offer wonderful views of Whiteface, Silver Lake and Taylor Pond, as well as the many blueberries in season.

The start is 0.8 mi. E of Silver Lake at a point where the power and telephone lines cross the road. There is an old signpost with a tin can lid trail marker on it at the entrance to a grassy road. Leaving the road (0 mi.), the trail is level for a few yards before climbing moderately to an open area at 0.3 mi., where the grade eases a bit. From here there are frequent red DEC markers. Soon after this open area, the grade again becomes moderate, with a lookout on the L at 0.52 mi. and another at 0.70 mi. where the trail turns sharp R just before reaching two angular boulders on the ledge. From here, the trail climbs steeply up a ridge with ever-expanding views to the summit at 0.92 mi. A vague trail continues over the summit, but this fades out within 0.25 mi. before reaching the first col on the ridge. For the adventurous, however, there are many more ledges on this more than 2 mi. ridge.

Distance: Road to summit of Silver Lake Mt., 0.92 mi. (1.48 km.). Ascent from road, 900 ft. (275 m.). Elevation, 2374 ft. (724 m.).

Silver Lake Mt.
Base map is Redford quadrangle, 7.5 min. series, 1968.

OWEN, COPPERAS AND WINCH PONDS

This scenic trio of ponds offers some very pleasant walking with little climbing, good views, and ample opportunities for swimming, picnicking, and camping in one of the two lean-tos on Copperas Pond. Their easy accessibility makes these ponds some of the most popular destinations in the Lake Placid area. There are two starts from Rt. 86 in Wilmington Notch, approximately 1 mi. apart. Both approaches are marked with small DEC signs.

The easier approach is the southerly one, located 5 mi. from the junction with Rt. 73 in Lake Placid and 3.9 mi. S of the entrance to Whiteface Mt. Ski Center. Leaving the road (0 mi.), the blue-marked trail leads gradually up near the R bank of Owen Pond Brook and comes to the NW corner of Owen Pond at 0.55 mi. The trail follows the shore to the NE corner at 0.72 mi., where it veers away to the L as it climbs a few easy grades and then a steeper one at 1.00 mi. Swinging R at the top of this grade, the trail soon descends and reaches a lean-to on the shore of Copperas Pond at 1.28 mi. From here there is an excellent view of Whiteface Mt.

Passing behind the lean-to, the trail immediately crosses the outlet and continues along the shore to a junction at 1.44 mi., where the yellow-marked trail to Winch Pond turns R. (This trail climbs a short steep pitch, after which there are several gradual ups and downs to Winch Pond at 1.88 mi.) Continuing straight ahead, the blue trail follows the shore to a junction at 1.56 mi. (Trail straight ahead leads 0.10 mi. along the shoreline to the Copperas No. 2 Lean-to.) The blue trail now turns R and climbs to a height of land, and descends to a junction at 1.79 mi. (Red trail R leads 0.51 mi. to Winch Pond. Using this approach to Winch Pond from the N end of the blue trail, it is 0.73 mi. from the highway to the pond.) The blue trail now continues down, becoming rocky and eroded in spots, and reaches the highway at 2.01 mi.

Distances: Highway at S approach to Owen Pond, 0.55 mi.; to Copperas Pond (S shore), 1.28 mi. (2.06 km.); to Winch Pond, 1.88 mi. Highway at N approach to Copperas Pond (N shore), 0.45 mi.; to Winch Pond, 0.73 mi.

THE SENTINEL RANGE

Running for nearly 10 miles NE and SW between the valleys of the East and West Branches of the Ausable River, the Sentinel Range is the major feature of the 23,000-acre Sentinel Wilderness Area. The three major peaks, Stewart, Kilburn and Sentinel, lack significant views and thus have seen little hiker traffic over the years. The best views are from 3893-ft. Mt. Kilburn, which can best be approached from the North Notch Trail. Stewart and Sentinel offer some views in the winter when the snow pack raises hikers above the level of the smaller balsams and permits some interesting views out through the numerous blowdown areas. The only real rocky peak with a view is a 2080-ft. eastern shoulder of Sentinel called Cobble Mt., which offers views of the valley of the E Branch of the Ausable as well as of Cascade and other peaks. Cobble Mt. has no trail, but can be approached from Bartlett Rd. running between Keene and Upper Jay.

For those wishing to explore the central part of the Sentinel Range, there are two trails that penetrate from the western edge of the area. These trails are all that is left of the ski trail system constructed for the 1932 Olympics, which once went through North Notch and South Notch and connected near Keene to form a long loop. The maintained portions of both these trails are still skiable, and recently a ski route has been marked through North Notch to connect with some old roads leading up the E side of the range.

NORTH NOTCH

The North Notch Trail is currently maintained for 2.70 mi., stopping approximately 0.5 mi. below the top of the notch. The grades are easy to moderate throughout. The start is on River Rd. near Lake Placid, 1.0 mi. S of Rt. 86 and 3.0 mi. N of Rt. 73. There is a sizeable turnout on the E side of the road at a small iron bridge over a small brook. Leaving the road (0 mi.) and marked with red DEC disks, the trail follows an old tote road along the R bank of the brook. At 0.06 mi. the trail turns sharp L and up away from the tote road to avoid a large swampy area. Gaining higher ground, the trail swings sharp R and parallels the brook before dipping to cross it on a bridge at 0.41 mi. Soon climbing to higher ground again, the trail swings L and rejoins the tote road beyond the swamp at 0.84 mi., just after recrossing the stream.

Turning R the trail begins to climb at an easy grade. Crossing a small stream at 1.42 mi., it encounters a short flat, wet area before resuming a steady gradual to moderate climb which eases off at 2.31 mi. Shortly afterwards, the trail crosses another small stream and climbs in gradual stages to the sign announcing the end of the maintained trail at 2.70 mi., at the R bank of a sizeable brook. A square blue marker is visible from this point, indicating the ski route to the top of North Notch.

Distance: River Rd. to end of maintained trail, 2.70 mi. (4.34 km.). Ascent from River Rd., 1200 ft. (365 m.).

SOUTH NOTCH

The South Notch Trail leads 2.75 mi. to an old and barely serviceable lean-to located approximately 0.5 mi. below the top of South Notch. The grades are easy to moderate throughout, and this trail offers some very pleasant walking, particularly the 0.75 mi. section next to a pretty brook with moss-covered rocks.

The trail starts on River Rd. near Lake Placid, 2.0 mi. N of Rt. 73 and 2.0 mi. S of Rt. 86. The start is also 1.0 mi. S of the North Notch Trail and just N of the entrance to Camelot, a Catholic-run boys' home. There is a sign marking the chained-off road. Marked with red DEC disks, the trail leaves River Rd. (0 mi.) on a flat, grassy road in an open field and passes two bridges on the R. At the second bridge, the trail swings L and up and climbs to a private lean-to on the L at 0.26 mi. Now nearly on the flat, the trail enters state land at 0.41 mi. and soon reaches the R bank of a brook, which it follows closely for over 0.75 mi., crossing the brook three times on bridges in varying states of disrepair.

After the third crossing at 1.38 mi., the trail climbs away from the brook and swings sharp R approximately 150 ft. after leaving the brook. The trail now climbs at a steady, moderate grade until another sharp R at 2.25 mi. Now on the level on a side hill, the trail crosses a height of land at 2.36 mi. and drops slightly before resuming a gradual climb to the South Notch Lean-to at 2.75 mi. There is no apparent trace of the trail beyond this point, but the open woods make it an easy hike or ski for the final 0.5 mi. to the top of the notch.

Distance: River Rd. to South Notch Lean-to, 2.75 mi. (4.42 km.). Ascent from River Rd., 1100 ft. (335 m.).

CASCADE MT. FROM CASCADE LAKES

As the easiest of all the 4000-ft. peaks to ascend, this bald summit attracts many hikers in all seasons to enjoy its marvelous views of the other high peaks and the Champlain Valley. Once called Long Pond Mt., Cascade is named for the steep falls which tumbles down between the two Cascade Lakes. The current trail follows a route laid out in 1974 by the Algonquin Chapter of ADK to replace the old trail which was steep and badly eroded. It follows the SW ridge on generally moderate grades with only a few steeper pitches, making this a very enjoyable hike.

The trail starts on Rt. 73, 6.80 mi. from Keene and 4.50 mi. from Adirondak Loj Road, and is marked with red DEC disks. Leaving the highway (0 mi.), the trail descends for 30 yds. and then begins an easy climb. Swinging R and leveling out, the trail crosses a small brook at 0.35 mi. and resumes an easy climb until it steepens at 0.70 mi. It continues steep to moderate to the top of the ridge at 1.17 mi. Now on the crest of the ridge, there are several moderate climbs alternating with flatter sections until a short, steep climb brings the trail to a ledge with a good view at 1.82 mi. Now the grade eases, and the trail reaches a junction with the trail to Porter Mt. at 2.10 mi. (see below). Bearing L, the trail soon reaches the base of the open rocks and ascends along the R side of the open rocks to the summit at 2.35 mi.

Distances: Highway to Porter Trail junction, 2.10 mi.; to summit of Cascade, 2.35 mi. (3.78 km.). Ascent, 1940 ft. (591 m.). Elevation, 4098 ft. (1249 m.). Order of height, 36.

PORTER MT.

Once called West Mt., Porter is named for Dr. Noah Porter, President of Yale University from 1871 to 1886, who was a summer resident of Keene Valley and who made the first recorded ascent of the peak in 1875 with guide Ed Phelps. Although Porter does not have a bald summit, it offers 360-degree views and is a worthwhile side trip from Cascade. Two other trails ascend the peak from the Keene Valley side.

Leaving the junction near the summit of Cascade (0 mi.), the trail descends to the col at 0.20 mi. and then climbs moderately to steeply to a large boulder at 0.55 mi. and then at easy grades along the ridge to the summit at 0.70 mi. (Trail with ADK markers continues straight ahead, leading either to the Keene Valley Airport at 4.54 mi. or to the Garden at 3.84 mi.; see Keene Valley Section.)

Distances: Highway to trail junction, 2.10 mi.; to summit of Porter, 2.80 mi. (4.50 km.). Ascent from highway, 1960 ft. (597 m.). Elevation, 4059 ft. (1237 m.). Order of height, 38.

PITCHOFF MT.

This bare ridge N of the Cascade Lakes offers exceptional views and as described below is a nice traverse. There are also several worthwhile intermediate destinations which make excellent up-and-back trips. The two ends of this trail are separated by 2.70 mi. on Rt. 73, so two cars are advisable, but one can also hike just to the broad ledge with the balanced boulders at 1.55 mi. or to the summit at 1.97 mi. In season there are blueberries on all the ledges along this ridge.

The W end of the trail starts just down and across the road from the Cascade trailhead (see above). Leaving the highway (0 mi.) and marked with red DEC disks, it climbs some steps to the R of a retaining wall and enters the woods on a moderate climb. Soon swinging R, the trail levels off and after some short ups and downs comes to a lookout on the R at 0.84 mi. About 70 yds. farther there is a better lookout with views of the Cascade Lakes directly below, as well as of Marcy and other peaks.

Descending to a small saddle, the trail now climbs several steep pitches before angling L across a steep hillside below the base of some cliffs and then swings R and up to a junction at the top of the ridge at 1.41 mi. (Trail R leads 0.14 mi. on the level to the broad ledge with the balanced rocks.) Continuing L, the trail climbs at first easily and then encounters a few steep pitches before reaching the summit of Pitchoff at 1.97 mi. (3.17 km.). Elevation, 3600 ft. (1097 m.). Ascent from highway, 1440 ft. (439 m.).

From this first summit, the trail continues along the crest of the ridge, passing over three lesser summits at 2.15 mi., 2.58 mi., and 3.01 mi. From the fourth summit the trail makes a longer descent to a lower col at 3.55 mi., after which it climbs steeply up rocks to the fifth and final summit at 3.64 mi.

Straight ahead, the trail begins to descend steeply to the woods, where it doubles back to the R under the fifth peak and soon begins a steep descent, which lessens as the trail beings to follow down the L bank of a brook. Crossing the brook at 4.57 mi., the trail recrosses the brook 60 yds. later and continues an easy descent to the highway at 4.90 mi. This point is just below a small bridge 4.10 mi. from Keene and 2.70 mi. from the starting point.

Distances: Highway to balanced rocks, 1.55 mi.; to summit of Pitchoff, 1.97 mi.; to fifth summit, 3.64 mi.; to end of trail at highway, 4.90 mi. (7.88 km.).

OWLS HEAD

This little rocky peak has long been a popular climb and has probably been the first climb for many, many junior hikers. The start has changed considerably in recent years, but it is now easy and access is seemingly assured; but remember that this is private land practically all the way to the summit.

The start is on Rt. 73, 3.2 mi. above Keene and 3.6 mi. from the Cascade Mt. trailhead. Turn off Rt. 73 at a sign for Owls Head Acres and follow the gravel road for 0.2 mi. up to a turnout on the L where the road makes a sharp R. There is a small green sign marking the start of the trail. There are no other markers on this trail.

From the parking area (0 mi.), the trail climbs moderately through open woods to the crest of a ridge where it joins the original route at 0.12 mi. Turning L, the trail quickly reaches the first ledge and continues on to a second and larger ledge at 0.28 mi. Flattening out above the second ledge, the trail soon resumes the climb and reaches a third ledge at 0.34 mi. Above this ledge, the trail flattens again before scrambling up the L side of the summit rocks and reaching the summit at 0.55 mi. There are views of Cascade, Pitchoff, Giant and Hurricane, with views to the N and E found by walking around the summit.

Distance: Parking area to summit of Owls Head, 0.55 mi. (0.88 km.). Ascent from parking area, 460 ft. (410 m.). Elevation, 2120 ft. (646 m.).

NOTCH NORTHWEST OF PITCHOFF MT.

This unmarked trail follows the route of the original road from Keene to Lake Placid through a wild and rugged notch with high cliffs rising to the E and many signs of beaver activity along the way. The trail has become overgrown in places and some of the beaver ponds necessitate short detours, but it is maintained for skiing, which means that at least the major blowdowns are cleared. Most hikers choose to traverse this route from the Lake Placid end since there is a net drop of 360 vertical feet in this direction.

The start is at the end of a dirt road called the Old Mountain Rd. which leaves Rt. 73 2.3 mi. E of Adirondak Loj Road and 0.7 mi. W of the entrance to the Mt. Van Hoevenberg Recreation Area. This road is passable for 1.0 mi., where there is parking for a few cars. From the parking area (0 mi.) the trail is mostly level, passing some large boulders on the L and then coming to a large sloping rock on the R at 0.65 mi. One can scramble to the top of this "summit in a valley" for a view of the cliffs and the notch ahead.

At 0.74 mi. the trail comes to a beaver dam and pond with a vague trail skirting the L shore until the original road is rejoined and the summit of the pass reached at 0.97 mi. Now descending, the trail crosses a side hill at 1.08 mi. with a view through the trees down the valley and then goes past an old beaver pond on the L to a large beaver pond on the R. Now the trail descends a short, steep pitch to a beaver pond blocking the road at 1.41 mi. Bushwhack R around this pond and continue the descent, crossing several small brooks before arriving at two large beaver ponds at the bottom of the hill at 2.52 mi. Fortunately, there is a dam running between these ponds which acts as a natural causeway over 70 yds. long to the road on the far side. The descent is now easy to the end of Alstead Hill Rd. at 3.50 mi. This point is 3.9 mi. above Keene.

Distance: Parking area to end of Alstead Hill Rd., 3.50 mi. (5.63 km.).

COBBLE HILL

This small, rocky knob rising directly above the village of Lake Placid offers interesting views of the village as well as of the high peaks farther away. The trail is not marked and the start is not easy to find, but it is worth the effort required to find one's way through a developed section of Lake Placid to the start. From the stoplight at the junction of Rtes. 73 and 86, proceed NE on Rt. 86 past the golf course to the second L at 1.1 mi. This is Cobble Hill Rd., which is followed up the hill for 0.3 mi. to a gravel drive leading R. Go down this drive for 0.1 mi. to a grassy area on the L. At the upper edge of this grassy area (where cars may be parked) there are several large white pines with small orange paint spots on them. In this obviously suburban setting it should go without saying that this is private land. Hikers are now welcome to pass through, but this permission is contingent upon each hiker respecting the owner's property to the utmost.

Leaving the parking area (0 mi.), the trail goes up through the large pines and past a private home on the L. At 0.10 mi. the trail beings climbing steeply, with one trail soon coming in from the L and another at 0.22 mi. Bearing R at this second junction, the trail reaches the base of a steep open ledge at 0.28 mi., with the easiest route of ascent on the R. At the top of the ledge is an excellent view of Lake Placid (village and lake) as well as Mirror Lake. Just past the top of the ledge, there are some concrete foundations which are the remains of an old chairlift that was part of an attempt to develop this peak as a ski area 20 years ago. Bearing R at another junction, the trail reaches the summit at 0.44 mi. Just beyond the summit are ledges with good views to the S and E with glimpses of Whiteface possible to the N. On the descent, there are no signs or markers, but bearing L at every turn will reverse the route back to the parking area.

Distance: Parking area to summit of Cobble Hill, 0.44 mi. (0.71 km.). Ascent, 460 ft. (140 m.). Elevation, 2343 ft. (714 m.).

McKENZIE MT. FROM WHITEFACE INN

This is the shortest approach to this 3861-ft. peak which rises impressively above the W shore of Lake Placid. Though mostly wooded, the summit has two ledges which combine to offer a complete 360-degree view with Lake Placid, Algonquin, the Seward Range and the Saranac Lakes being most prominent. One can make this a loop trip by descending the old Shore Owners Association trail, which returns past Bartlett Pond to the W shore of Lake Placid approximately 0.5 mi. up the lake from the starting point. The Shore Owners Association trail is recommended as a descent route only, as it is very difficult to find going up, for it is no longer maintained and the markers are left from 20 years ago when it was last cared for.

The start is on the Whiteface Inn Rd., which begins 1.3 mi. W of the Village of Lake Placid on Rt. 86. Turn N on this road. The unmarked trailhead is a dirt road on the L, 1.4 mi. from Rt. 86 just past the Olympic Resort condominiums. Leaving the road (0 mi.), the trail heads up past a bar gate (apparently frequently bypassed by vehicular traffic) and begins a steady, gradual climb with occasional yellow DEC markers visible on the trees. At 0.75 mi. a road diverges R along with most of the vehicular traffic, but the trail bears L and continues mostly on the level to a brook crossing and lean-to at 1.50 mi.

Past the lean-to, the trail descends gently to a junction at 1.92 mi., with the trail from Rt. 86 near Ray Brook coming in from the L. (Road straight ahead leads to McKenzie Pond near Saranac Lake, but there is no access at that end due to private property.) Turning sharp R at this junction, the trail is now marked with red DEC disks and an occasional ADK marker. The trail climbs moderately at first and even levels off for a brief stretch, but it soon begins a steep to very steep climb, gaining over 1000 ft. in just over half a mile. The steep climbing ends at a side trail R to a view to the S at 2.61 mi.

Soon crossing the first summit, the trail descends and then climbs to pass just below the second summit at 2.84 mi. Dipping and climbing again, the trail arrives at the third summit at 3.04 mi., with views to the N and W from a ledge just L of the trail. The trail continues to the fourth summit at 3.17 mi., and then descends steeply before beginning the final climb to the true summit. Climbing over a ledge at 3.50 mi., the trail levels out near the summit, with a trail L a few yards farther leading to a spectacular "balcony" over the NW Adirondacks, with views as far E as Marcy as well. This is the best and most unique view from McKenzie, but just beyond at the true summit at 3.55 mi. there is a good 180-degree view encompassing Whiteface, Lake Placid and many of the high peaks. This is the end of the red DEC markers and the officially maintained trail.

For those wishing to make a loop trip, it is possible to descend via the old Shore Owners Association trail. Continuing on over the summit, the trail descends steeply to a junction at 3.72 mi. with the former trail along the ridge to Moose Mt. (no trace of the trail exists beyond 0.25 mi. on the 2 mi. ridge). Turning R and descending steeply, the trail comes to Bartlett Pond at 4.33 mi. Because the pond is now enlarged by beavers, the trail must detour L through some thick terrain, but it turns R after crossing the outlet and joins the original route at 4.43 mi. Now following basically down the R bank of the outlet, the trail is at times on a shelf high above the brook, but returns to the R bank of the brook and comes to signs marking a junction with the now non-existent Twin Brook Trail to Moose Mt. at 5.58 mi.

Continuing along the brook, the trail passes an old dam at 5.89 mi. and soon reaches a road and turns R. Approaching the shore of Lake Placid, the trail turns sharp R at a junction with the Lake Trail at 6.25 mi. and follows this trail on the level past several private camps. As the signs indicate, hikers "pass at their own risk and at the owner's pleasure," and courtesy dictates that one refrain from leaving the trail even to see the view from the end of a dock. The Lake Trail reaches Whiteface Inn at 6.91 mi., from which it is a short climb up through the buildings to the paved road leading back to the starting point.

Distances: Whiteface Inn Rd. to junction with trail from Rt. 86 near Ray Brook, 1.92 mi.; to summit of McKenzie, 3.55 mi. (5.71 km.). Ascent, 1940 ft. (591 m.). Elevation, 3861 ft. (1177 m.).

SHORE OWNERS ASSOCIATION TRAILS

At one time the Lake Placid Shore Owners Association maintained an extensive system of trails along the shores of Lake Placid and on to the mountains above. Maintenance continued long enough to clear away much of the damage left by the 1950 hurricane, but since then no trail save the Lake Trail has seen much maintenance. The three approaches to Moose Mt. have completely vanished except for a few signs and markers, although these trails seem to continue to show up on maps, includng the 1978 USGS maps. Of the routes to the summit of Moose Mt., the one up Twin Brook from the SE is now the best route to this nearly 4000-ft. peak which offers views in all directions from various lookouts.

The Lake Trail is easily followable along the W shore as far as Undercliff, but beyond that is obscure in spots as it circles the N side of the lake to Whiteface Landing. The Lake Trail on the E side is plain at Whiteface Landing, but access at the McLenathan Bay end is blocked by many new camps. The trail up Eagle Eyrie from the N end of the lake was improved a few years ago and is now followable, but the view from the top, while interesting, includes only the E portion of Lake Placid and a few of the high peaks.

HAYSTACK MT. FROM RT. 86 NEAR RAY BROOK

This approach to Haystack and McKenzie Mts. formerly started behind the DEC Headquarters in Ray Brook, but recent access problems over a piece of private land have necessitated the cutting of a new approach, which was finished in the fall of 1984. The new approach is approximately 0.9 mi. longer than the previous route, but it follows easy grades throughout and even takes in an additional view. Like the old route, this trail is also skiable and can be part of an enjoyable through-trip from Whiteface Inn. Even with the additional distance of this new approach, Haystack (not to be confused with the 4960-ft. peak of the same name) still offers a very rewarding view for relatively little effort.

The new trail begins at a turnout on Rt. 86, 1.6 mi. E of DEC Headquarters in Ray Brook and 1.4 mi. W of the junction with Old Military Rd. The trail is marked with a DEC sign and blue DEC markers. From the highway (0 mi.) the trail crosses a small knoll and dips to cross a small wet area after 100 yds., before swinging L and beginning a gradual climb to a crest at 0.30 mi. in an open hardwood forest. Dipping slightly, the trail climbs gradually to a second crest and soon crosses a stream at 0.52 mi. Swinging L after crossing the stream, the trail slabs gently upward along the base of some low ledges until it begins an equally gentle descent at 1.10 mi. Following down a small ridge, the trail comes to a small open area at 1.52 mi., with some views to the SW. After a short, moderate descent, the trail swings to the R and continues to descend gently to a small brook at 1.82 mi., where the old route comes in from the L.

Now following an old road, the trail is practically level for a few hundred yards before beginning a gradual to moderate climb along the L bank of Little Ray Brook. Passing some old foundations on the R at 2.18 mi., the trail reaches a junction at 2.40 mi. (Red-marked trail to the R continues on the old road and leads to McKenzie Mt.; see below.) Bearing L and still with blue markers, the Haystack Trail crosses a small brook in 25 yds. and then Little Ray Brook just below an old dam in another 50 yds. From this dam the trail begins to climb a series of steep pitches interspersed with short stretches of easier going. At 3.03 mi. the trail begins the final pitch, going up a steep gully to the L of some cliffs to emerge on the first ledge at 3.20 mi. After a slight dip, the trail continues to the summit at 3.32 mi., where there are good views from Whiteface to Marcy, Algonquin, the Seward Range and many of the larger lakes to the W.

Distances: Rt. 86 to junction with trail to McKenzie Mt., 2.40 mi.; to summit of Haystack Mt., 3.32 mi. (5.34 km.). Ascent, 1240 ft. (377 m.). Elevation, 2878 ft. (877 m.).

MCKENZIE MT. FROM RT. 86 NEAR RAY BROOK

Though not the shortest approach to McKenzie, this trail is an excellent ski tour when combined with the road from Whiteface Inn. This route follows the Haystack Mt. Trail to the junction at 2.40 mi. (see above). Bearing R at the junction the McKenzie Trail, with red markers, continues to follow the old road at gradual to moderate grades. Crossing a brook near the foundations of an old camp at 2.63 mi., the trail continues to climb until it crosses the headwaters of Little Ray Brook at 3.38 mi. From this brook, the grade moderates but the trail becomes quite wet to the junction with the yellow-marked trail from Whiteface Inn at 3.61 mi. Continuing straight ahead with red markers, the trail leads to the summit in another 1.63 mi. (See above for description of route from Whiteface Inn.)

Distances: Rt. 86 to junction with Haystack Mt. Trail, 2.40 mi.; to junction with Whiteface Inn Trail, 3.61 mi.; to summit of McKenzie Mt., 5.24 mi. (8.43 km.). Ascent, 2240 ft. (680 m.). Elevation, 3861 ft. (1177 m.).

NORTHVILLE-LAKE PLACID TRAIL FROM AVERYVILLE RD. TO DUCK HOLE

This is the most northerly section of the 130-mi. Northville-Lake Placid Trail, which starts near Northville close to the southern boundary of the Adirondack Park. The Adirondack Mt. Club has published a separate guidebook covering the entire trail for those interested in traversing this classic route. This partial description is included here for those interested in access to the remote areas at the headwaters of the Cold River. (Two other sections of the N-P Trail, from Long Lake to Shattuck Clearing, and from Shattuck Clearing to Duck Hole, are included in the Southern Section.)

The start is on Averyville Rd. near Lake Placid. From the

junction of Rtes. 73 and 86 in Lake Placid, proceed 0.2 mi. E on Rt. 73 and turn S on Averyville Rd., which crosses Old Military Rd. at 1.0 mi., where there is a large DEC sign marking the official terminus of the Northville-Placid Trail. Continuing straight ahead on Averyville Road, the trailhead is another 1.2 mi. on the L, just before a bridge over the Chubb River. There is a small turnout on the L, and additional parking at the top of the hill beyond the bridge on the R.

Leaving the road (0 mi.) and marked with blue DEC disks, the trail begins following an old road along the R bank of the Chubb River, but veers L away from the river at 0.1 mi. and soon arrives at the trail register. From the register the trail climbs at a steady, gradual grade until 0.5 mi., where it levels out and continues with short ups and downs. A dim fisherman's trail from Bear Cub Rd. to the Chubb River crosses the trail at 1.3 mi., and the trail begins crossing an extensive spruce swamp at 2.2 mi. At 2.4 mi. an unmarked trail diverges L, with the end of the spruce swamp coming at 2.5 mi. The trail crosses a large brook on a good bridge at 3.3 mi. and continues on to join an old tote road at 3.7 mi., where it swings L and begins a gradual climb to a beaver pond on the R at 4.1 mi. From here there is a view of a new slide on the W side of Street Mt. which came down as a result of the earthquake of October 7, 1983.

The trail, now on the flat, passes to the E of the beaver pond, with another unmarked trail diverging R at 4.4 mi. Bearing L, the trail crosses a large brook at 4.8 mi., and crosses two more brooks before descending slightly to a bridge over the Chubb River at 6.1 mi. On the far side of the bridge the trail joins the original route from Averyville. Turning L and proceeding up the L bank of the Chubb River, the trail reaches a junction with a side trail leading L to Wanika Falls Lean-to at 6.7 mi. This trail climbs steeply and crosses the Chubb River on a bridge just above a small falls to reach the lean-to on the R bank 0.1 mi. from the main trail. The actual Wanika Falls are about 100 yds. above the lean-to.

From the junction with the side trail to Wanika Falls, the N-P Trail climbs steeply at first and then more easily to a height of land at 7.0 mi. and begins descending. Crossing several brooks as it descends, the trail levels out past a brook at 7.6 mi. and continues with easy ups and downs to Moose Pond Lean-to at 8.3 mi. This is a picturesque spot to camp, with wild and rugged views of the Sawtooth Range across the pond.

Past the lean-to, the trail descends to the L bank of Moose Creek at 8.5 mi., but soon leaves the brook and crosses a beaver dam at 8.8 mi. The trail now continues to parallel Moose Creek but remains some distance back from it. At 9.7 mi. the trail begins to climb away from Moose Creek and reaches a small height of land at 10.2 mi., after which it descends into the valley of Roaring Brook. At 10.5 mi. there is a short steep pitch up followed by a more moderate descent to the R bank of Roaring Brook at 10.6 mi. The trail now continues along the brook to a junction at 11.7 mi. (Trail L with red markers crosses Roaring Brook and leads to Indian Pass and Upper Works at Tahawus via the Preston Ponds; see Southern Section.) Continuing straight ahead at this junction and now marked with both red and blue markers, the trail proceeds with several easy ups and downs to a large open area leading down to the bridge and dam at Duck Hole at 12.2 mi.

Here there are two lean-tos and plenty of tent sites. One lean-to is just before the bridge and dam, and the other is in the woods on a point of land 100 yds. E of the dam. A ranger station at the W edge of the clearing was removed in December of 1977 in order to bring the area into compliance with wilderness use guidelines. A blue trail crosses the dam and leads to Bradley Pond and the trailhead at Tahawus. The N-P Trail heads W along an old truck trail which connects with a trail heading to Ward Brook and the trailhead at

Coreys. See Southern Section for descriptions of all these trails.

Distances: Parking area on Averyville Rd. to Wanika Falls, 6.7 mi.; to Moose Pond Lean-to, 8.3 mi.; to junction with Preston Ponds Trail, 11.7 mi.; to Duck Hole, 12.2 mi. (19.6 km.).

SCARFACE MT.

Due to the construction of a federal prison, the former access to Scarface has been closed, but in the fall of 1981 the DEC completed a new approach to this peak. This new route adds nearly a mile to the old route, but it is easy walking and the unique views from this seldom visited summit still make this trip worthwhile.

The present trail starts 0.1 mi. down Ray Brook Rd. from Rt. 86 directly across from DEC Region 5 Headquarters. A large sign marks the start, and there is a small parking lot off the road. From the parking lot (0 mi.), the trail goes through a pine forest, crosses the now abandoned railroad tracks, and comes to an elaborate bridge over Ray Brook at 0.51 mi. Climbing the opposite bank on a series of steps, the trail continues on the flat to a clearing at 0.69 mi. and then gradually ascends to a higher plateau and clearing with a large rock in its center. Just beyond this point, at 1.51 mi., the trail joins a road which was the original route. Note this turn well for the return trip.

Turning L, the trail descends slightly along this road and then turns sharp L off the road at 1.71 mi. Continuing mostly on the level, the trail reaches a brook at 2.06 mi. Following up the R bank, the trail crosses the brook at 2.16 mi. and soon veers away as the grade steepens. After several alternating steep and easy pitches, the trail comes close to the top of a col on the ridge leading W from Scarface, and then at 3.00 mi. begins a steep climb to the first ledge at 3.09 mi. From this ledge Saranac Lake and surrounding lakes are visible, and a better view is possible by bushwhacking R at this point. The trail continues up the ridge at an easy grade, going in and out of scrub until it ends at 3.35 mi. at a large bare area facing S. There is a 180-degree vista from here, encompassing the Seward and Sawtooth Ranges plus Ampersand and many lakes. Although there may be some markers visible, there is no trail beyond this point to the viewless summit of Scarface.

Distances: Parking lot on Ray Brook Rd. to junction with old route, 1.51 mi.; to ledge near summit of Scarface, 3.35 mi. (5.39 km.). Ascent from parking lot, 1480 ft. (451 m.). Elevation, 3088 ft. (941 m.).

BAKER MT.

This little mountain offers some of the best views of lakes and mountains for the amount of effort involved. From its partially wooded summit, lookouts provide views of Moose and McKenzie Mts. to the E, many of the high peaks to the SE and S, and many lakes to the SW and W.

The start is at the N end of Moody Pond just N of the village of Saranac Lake. Coming into Saranac Lake on Rt. 86 from Lake Placid, turn R at the traffic islands with a branch of the Bank of Lake Placid on the corner. Cross the railroad tracks and immediately turn L on a dirt road which recrosses the tracks and becomes paved again. At the top of a hill, turn R on E Pine St., which crosses a bridge over the railroad tracks and leads to the end of the pond. E Pine St. can also be reached by turning off Rt. 3 just N of the village onto Pine St. There are no signs or markers at the start, but the trail can be followed easily as described below.

Leaving the road (0 mi.), the trail starts up an old road and immediately bears R and up to a higher road. Following this road, the trail turns sharp R at 0.07 mi. on to another road. At 0.11 the trail bears L away from the road at the entrance to a small old quarry and climbs along the R edge of the quarry. At 0.14 mi. the trail bears R and begins climbing, passing a yellow boundary line at 0.23 mi. Leveling off briefly at 0.39 mi., the trail soon begins climbing a ridge through a beautiful maple forest to the first ledge at 0.64 mi. Now climbing through a predominantly red pine forest, the trail splits shortly above the first ledge, with the L route slightly easier and less eroded. The two routes rejoin at 0.80 mi. on a large ledge just below the actual summit at 0.87 mi.

Distance: Moody Pond to summit of Baker Mt., 0.87 mi. (1.40 km.). Ascent, 900 ft. (274 m.). Elevation, 2452 ft. (747 m.).

AMPERSAND MT.

The view from the totally bald summit of this former fire tower peak is one of the best in the Adirondacks. Sitting on the boundary between the mountains and the lake country, Ampersand offers the best of both views. The name for the peak apparently comes from Ampersand Creek, which was so named because it twisted and turned so much that it resembled the ampersand symbol, "&." The start is on Rt. 3, 8.1 mi. W of Saranac Lake and 7.3 mi. E of the junction of Rtes. 3 and 30 E of Tupper Lake. There is a large turnout on the N side of the road which is also the parking area for the 0.5 mi. trail leading down to Middle Saranac Lake and Ampersand Beach — a nice spot to swim after the climb.

Leaving the S side of the highway (0 mi.) at a small DEC sign, the trail, marked with red DEC disks and yellow paint blazes, proceeds past a locked gate on the level on an old jeep road. This section of the trail has been well maintained and is very easy walking as it gently rises and falls through a beautiful mature forest. At 0.77 mi. the trail crosses a long wet section on an extensive series of bridges and at 1.24 mi. begins a steady climb to the site of the former observer's cabin, which is reached at 1.65 mi.

Turning sharp R, the trail follows up the L bank of a small brook at easy to moderate grades, but at 1.90 mi. it steepens and becomes quite eroded in spite of obvious recent efforts to stabilize it. This rather unpleasant section of trail ends at 2.40 mi., as the grade eases just before the crest of the ridge. The trail now swings L and climbs easily up to a large split boulder on the R at 2.54 mi. Just beyond, the trail reaches a height of land and descends slightly before turning sharp R and climbing onto the open rocks. From here, the trail is profusely marked with yellow paint blazes to the summit at 2.71 mi.

The site of the former fire tower is just beyond and slightly below the true summit. There is a tablet on a rock face near this spot to the memory of Walter Channing Rice, 1852-1924, the "Hermit of Ampersand, who kept Vigil from this Peak, 1915-1923." The summit used to be wooded, but Verplanck Colvin in his survey had the trees removed from this essential survey station. Erosion set in and washed all the soil away, and now nothing remains but the bare rock.

Distances: Route 3 to site of observer's cabin, 1.64 mi.; to summit of Ampersand, 2.71 mi. (4.36 km.). Ascent from highway, 1775 ft. (541 m.). Elevation, 3352 ft. (1022 m.).

EASTERN SECTION

This section is comprised mainly of the hikes included in both the Cascade-Keene-Hurricane and Boquet Valley regions in previous editions of this guidebook. This region now stretches from Poke-o-Moonshine Mt. at the N end, to trails around North Hudson at the S end. The area is characterized by lower rocky peaks with young second growth forests and many views from numerous ledges. Included in this region are the entire Jay and Hurricane Primitive Areas as well as most of the Giant Wilderness Area.

The Cascade Mt., Pitchoff Mt. and Owls Head Trails are now included in the Northern Section, but information on trailless hiking in the Jay Range and other mountains N of Hurricane has been added to this section. Also added is a trail to Round Pond near North Hudson, as well as information on approaches to Northway access points to the Dix Wilderness Area.

With its proximity to the Champlain Valley, this area was the first to be visited by white men, and the natural route along the Boquet and Schroon Rivers, now followed by Rt. 9, was important as early as the Revolutionary War. This area was also the first part of the Adirondacks to be settled, and many of the now seemingly remote areas were once productive farms that existed for many generations. The higher hillsides have nearly all been lumbered or burned, which means there is little virgin timber to appreciate, but the multitude of views makes this an interesting area to explore.

The following are some of the best hikes the area has to offer:

SHORT HIKES:

Poke-o-Moonshine Mt. — 2.36 mi. round trip. This popular fire tower peak offers tremendous views of lakes and mountains for just over 1 mi. of climbing.

The Crows — 3.50 mi. round trip. These two rocky peaks offer numerous views with a complete loop finishing with a pleasant walk down a dirt road. Many shorter variations are also possible.

MODERATE HIKES:

Hurricane Mt. from Rt. 9N — 5.28 mi., round trip. Excellent views with not too much strenuous climbing.

Bald Peak — 7.72 mi., round trip. A spectacular hike finishing with a long, open ridge leading to an unparalleled view of the Champlain Valley. See description for East Trail to Giant and Rocky Peak Ridge.

HARD HIKE:

Giant from the East via Rocky Peak Ridge with descent via Giant Ridge Trail — 10.98 mi., point to point. The outstanding hike in the Adirondacks, with more than 5 mi. of open walking. With over 4800 vertical feet of climbing, this hike is for experienced hikers only, but the rewards are commensurate with the effort. See descriptions for East Trail to Giant via Rocky Peak Ridge and Giant from Chapel Pond via Ridge Trail (see St. Huberts Section).

TRAIL DESCRIBED	TOTAL MILES	PAGE
Hurricane Mt. from Rt. 9N	2.64	192
Hurricane Mt. from the East (Route 9N near Elizabethtown)	1.50	192

HURRICANE MT.

There are three approaches to this popular rocky summit, with the trail from Rt. 9N being the most popular. Hurricane offers one of the most commanding views of any of the lesser peaks, and because of this it was an important survey station for Verplanck Colvin during his Adirondack survey. For many years there was an active fire tower on this peak, but the tower has recently been abandoned and may be removed altogether in the near future. The view encompasses much of the length of Lake Champlain and the Green Mountains in Vermont as well as many of the high peaks. There are also plenty of blueberries starting in early August.

HURRICANE FROM RT. 9N

This trail leaves the N side of Rt. 9N at the height of land 3.6 mi. E of the junction of Rtes. 9N and 73 between Keene and Keene Valley and 6.8 mi. W of the junction of Rtes. 9N and 9 at the S end of the village of Elizabethtown. Marked with red DEC disks, the trail leaves the highway (0 mi.), following a tote road at first up steeply but soon leveling off and becoming a foot path at 0.30 mi. The trail now continues nearly on the level through mostly thick conifers as it crosses a series of four small brooks. Crossing the last one at 1.10 mi., the trail heads into hardwood forest and begins to climb steadily. The first of several steep pitches begins at 1.70 mi., and the trail alternates between steep and easy climbing to the crest of the ridge and the junction with the ADK trail from Keene at 2.48 mi. Turning R, the trail soon climbs up over the summit rocks and reaches the summit at 2.64 mi.

Distance: Route 9N to summit of Hurricane, 2.64 mi. (4.25 km.). Ascent from highway, 2000 ft. (610 m.). Elevation, 3694 ft. (1126 m.).

HURRICANE MT. FROM THE EAST

This approach was the one used by the DEC in manning the fire tower when it was active. The last 1.2 mi. of road on this approach have not been maintained regularly, and this section was impassable for several years in the aftermath of a December, 1979 cloudburst. As of 1984, the road was passable by ordinary vehicles all the way to the former observer's cabin, but new washouts were again threatening to close the road. The trail is very steep from the observer's cabin, which makes it less popular than its shorter distance might indicate.

The start is at the end of a road which branches R off Rt. 9N 2.2

mi. from the junction of Rtes. 9N and 9 at the S end of the Village of Elizabethtown. The dirt road goes R just before a bridge and climbs steadily to a gate at 2.7 mi., where it narrows. Continuing on and then swinging L at 3.1 mi., the road soon enters state land with a small parking area on the R at 3.4 mi. Parking here is advisable since the road steepens after this point with a greater chance of washouts, and spots to turn around are very few.

Leaving this parking lot (0 mi.), proceed up the road to the observer's camp at the end of the road at 0.51 mi. Past the observer's camp, the trail drops down a few yards to a stream, with a lean-to on the R just past the stream. From here the trail begins climbing moderately, but after crossing another stream at 0.70 mi. it climbs steeply with only a few breathers until it emerges on the rocks just before reaching the summit at 1.50 mi.

Distances: Parking area to observer's cabin, 0.51 mi.; to summit of Hurricane, 1.50 mi. (2.41 km.). Ascent from parking area, 1500 ft. (450 m.). Elevation, 3694 ft. (1126 m.).

HURRICANE FROM KEENE

Commonly known as the North Trail to Hurricane, this is the longest approach to Hurricane but the grades are moderate throughout. There is also an attractive and little used lean-to just over a mile from the end of the road, which makes this approach a wonderful first camping trip for young families. The trail is marked with ADK markers and maintained by the Hurricane Chapter of ADK.

The start is at the end of a dirt road now posted as O'Toole Rd. off East Hill Rd. above Keene. From just S of the center of the hamlet of Keene proceed E 2.3 mi. up a long hill. Just past the Mountain House bear L on O'Toole Rd. where East Hill Rd. makes a sharp R turn. This point can also be reached by following

Hurricane Rd. approximately 4.0 mi. from Rt. 9N. Proceed up the dirt road 1.2 mi. to Crow Clearing, where cars may be parked. Leaving the R side of the clearing (0 mi.), the Hurricane Trail passes a gate, crosses a small brook, and crosses a second stream at 0.38 mi. Continuing mostly on the level, the trail reaches Gulf Brook Lean-to at 1.09 mi., where an ADK trail bears L to Lost Pond (see below).

Turning sharp R in front of the lean-to, the Hurricane Trail crosses Gulf Brook and begins a gradual to moderate ascent. At 1.18 mi. the trail crosses a small brook, which it recrosses several more times before finally ending up on the R bank at 1.88 mi. Veering L, the trail now climbs at a steady, moderate grade through a beautiful birch forest to the junction with the trail from Rt. 9N at 2.82 mi. Continuing straight ahead, the trail soon reaches the summit rocks and then the summit at 2.98 mi.

Distances: Crow Clearing to Gulf Brook Lean-to, 1.09 mi.; to summit of Hurricane, 2.98 mi. (4.78 km.). Ascent from Crow Clearing, 1600 ft. (490 m.). Elevation, 3694 ft. (1126 m.).

LOST POND

The trail to this hidden little body of water branches L from the North Trail to Hurricane at Gulf Brook Lean-to, 1.09 mi. from Crow Clearing (see above). Bearing L at the lean-to (0 mi.), the trail, with ADK markers, follows near the R bank of Gulf Brook until it turns sharp L and up at 0.25 mi. The trail climbs steadily with a few switchbacks until it levels off about 300 yds. before reaching the end of Lost Pond at 0.74 mi. The trail continues around the W shore of the pond to the Walter Biesemeyer Memorial Lean-to at 1.05 mi.

An unmarked trail continues past the lean-to approximately 0.25 mi. to the summit of Weston Mt., also known as Rocky Spar Peak.

The view from this rocky summit ranges from Hurricane to Marcy to Whiteface, with only the NE blocked by some low trees. From the summit there used to be a trail that continued on along Nun-da-ga-o Ridge, but all traces of this end of the trail are now lost (see below).

Distances: Crow Clearing to Gulf Brook Lean-to, 1.09 mi.; to Biesemeyer Lean-to on Lost Pond, 2.13 mi. (3.43 km.).

THE CROWS

These two rocky pinnacles which dominate the landscape at the top of East Hill have long been favorites of local hikers. They offer a variety of views from their many ledges, including 28 major peaks from Big Crow. Big Crow can also be ascended separately in 0.73 mi. if one drives to Crow Clearing (see above for description of Hurricane from Keene). Some care is needed in following this trail both going up and down, as it makes many sharp turns winding through the many ledges.

The start is 2.0 mi. above Keene on East Hill Rd. or 0.23 mi. W of the Mountain House. There are no signs at the start, but there is an ADK trail marker on a large maple next to the road. The first part of this trail is on private land and hikers must be very careful to stay on the trail until reaching state land, and of course not camp or build fires on this private land.

Leaving the road (0 mi.), the trail climbs first at an easy grade through an overgrown field. After several steeper pitches interspersed with easier climbing, the trail passes a rock face on the L at 0.40 mi., followed quickly by a climb to the first view. After a short easy stretch, the trail again climbs steeply to a ledge with better views at 0.56 mi. Now mostly on bare rock, the trail continues to climb to the W summit of Little Crow and soon on to the E and true summit at 0.94 mi. Elevation, 2450 ft. (747 m.).

The trail now descends gradually to the col between the two Crows at 1.10 mi. Climbing at first on a traverse, the trail soon swings R and climbs to the summit of Big Crow at 1.35 mi., elevation, 2800 ft. (853 m.). Continuing on the flat across the summit, the trail begins descending steadily at 1.41 mi. and reaches a junction at 1.55 mi. (Unmaintained trail L leads to Nun-da-ga-o Ridge; see below.) Continuing to descend after this junction, the trail levels off at 1.80 mi. and reaches Grow Clearing at 2.08 mi. From here it is 1.19 mi. down the road to the Mountain House and another 0.23 mi. to the starting point.

Distances: Road to Little Crow, 0.94 mi.; to Big Crow, 1.35 mi.; to Crow Clearing, 2.08 mi.; round trip 3.50 mi. (5.63 km.).

TRAILLESS PEAKS NORTH OF HURRICANE

Stretching for nearly 15 mi. N of Hurricane through the Hurricane and Jay Mt. Primitive Areas is an interesting series of peaks, none of which have trails — except for Poke-o-Moonshine Mt., whose trail is described separately below. Although none of these peaks have trails, many have outstanding views. There are numerous old roads into the area, and the forests are generally open second growth — making for generally easy traveling. What follows are some brief descriptions of what is available in this area, and some hints on how to approach these peaks. Beyond this, hikers must rely on map and compass to find their way. Hikers must also be aware that many of the approaches to these peaks are on private land. There appears to be little land on the described ways to these peaks that is actually "posted," but land can change hands or current owners can become more protective. Please respect any posted property; and while traveling on unposted private land, do not do anything that might cause the owner to want to post his property.

Nun-da-ga-o Ridge — Also known on the USGS maps as the Soda Range, this ridge curves E from Big Crow, reaching a height of just over 3000 ft. It was once nearly completely open with a few short wooded sections and an attractive route marked by cairns led all the way to Weston Mt. at the end of the ridge and then down to Lost Pond (see above). There are still a number of open ledges on this ridge, but the trail between them becomes very obscure after the first two ledges, approximately 0.5 mi. from the Big Crow Trail. By the end of the ridge and the ascent of Weston Mt., there is only an occasional trail marker on a tree with no trace of a trail, leaving one to guess even which side of the tree the trail once went. Nun-da-ga-o Ridge is, however, an interesting bushwhack with plenty of blueberries.

Peak 3373 — Also labeled as "Ausable No. 4," this peak has some interesting wide ledges giving excellent views to the S and E. The best approach is from the Lost Pond Trail (see above) where that trail turns sharp L 0.25 mi. above Gulf Brook Lean-to. Continue straight ahead through an old lumber clearing and slowly slab upwards to the top of this broad ridge, which is then followed to its N end. There are several other ledges to be found along the way as well.

THE JAY RANGE

Reaching a height of 3600 feet with many bald summits, these peaks, though officially trailless, are popular enough to have a fairly well-defined path to the top of their bare ridge. The easiest approach is from the "T" intersection at the upper end of the Glen Rd., also called Styles Brook Rd., on the W side of the range. An old tote road leads out of the upper end of the field at this intersection, leading to Merriam Swamp. From the left side of the swamp a well-defined trail leads straight up to the top of the open ridge. From there it is mostly open to the summit of ***Jay***.

Saddleback Mt. at 3615 ft. is more of a challenge but no less rewarding. One can approach it from the height of land to the S on the road between Upper Jay and Lewis, along the ridge from Jay, or from the same approach as for Slip Mt. (see below).

Slip Mt. also presents a challenge with the best approach being from the E on West Hill Rd. leading out of Lewis. Just before the road crosses Spruce Mill Brook, turn R and hike up a private driveway bearing L until the driveway reaches Derby Brook, which is followed to a flat area beneath the summit of Slip. Slip Mt. can also be climbed via its long NE ridge from the end of Seventy Rd. Both **Seventy Mt.** and **Bald Peak** on this ridge offer views, and there are several other views along the ridge, including a spectacular view of Slip's steep E face.

Farther to the N **Death Mt.** has an open summit and can be approached from the end of Seventy Rd. One can also continue on to the summit of Jay along the obvious ridge.

To the E, the prominent rocky little bump known as **Mt. Fay** is a rewarding short climb with views of the Boquet River Valley. Approach Mt. Fay from the end of Seventy Rd.

To the N of the old road connecting Seventy Rd. in Lewis with the Lincoln Hill Rd. leading up from Jay is 2930-ft. **Bluff Mt.** with a prominent cliff on its S side. One can scramble up the steep S face from the height of land on the Jay-Lewis Road, or take the easier SW shoulder from just W of the height of land.

The peaks to the N of Bluff Mt. are generally lower and seem to have greater access problems, but worth exploring are some other peaks including **Baldface Mt.** just N of Poke-o-Moonshine Mt., which is approached from Rt. 9 near Butternut Pond. Be aware that there is another jeep road about 0.25 mi. to the E of the one shown on the current maps. And lastly, **Flagstaff Mt.,** topped by USGS survey station Fordway, at the far NE end of the area, is a good

30-minute jaunt up from the gravel road along the R bank of the Ausable River. The views of Lake Champlain and some of the surrounding farmland are well worth the effort.

Clearly, the only limit to hiking in the Jay Range is one's own imagination.

POKE-O-MOONSHINE MT.

This fire tower peak is extremely popular because of its tremendous view of Lake Champlain and of the high peaks seen in the distance to the SW. Its unusual name appears to be a combination of two Algonquin Indian words, "Pohqui" and "Moosie," which mean, respectively, "broken" and "smooth." The name then, later corrupted by the early settlers, seems to refer to the smooth rocks of the summit or the prominent slab on the SE side and the broken rocks of the impressive cliff on the E side.

The trail starts at the state campground on Rt. 9, 9.3 mi. N of the junction of the road from Lewis to Exit 32 on the Adirondack Northway and 3.0 mi. S of Exit 33. There is presently a parking fee charged at this state facility (and all similar facilities), and parking on the highway in front of the campground is prohibited. This presents no problem in the off-season, but in-season hikers should either be prepared to pay this fee or to walk a few hundred yards extra from outside the "no parking" zone.

Starting from the S end of the campground (0 mi.), the red-marked trail enters the woods and immediately begins climbing, steeply at times, to the base of a cliff at 0.28 mi. Skirting the cliff on the L, the trail switchbacks R to a good lookout on the R at 0.33 mi. The grade now eases somewhat but remains steady to a saddle S of the summit at 0.82 mi. Here are the remains of the fire observer's cabin with a lean-to approximately 65 yds. to the L.

From this saddle there are two trails leading up to the R. The L

Poke-o-Moonshine Mt.
Base maps are Ausable Forks and Willsboro Bay, both 7.5 by
15 minute metric series maps.

trail is now marked as the official route; it leads up past a lookout
on the L and along a shelf before turning R and up to the summit
plateau. Turning R again, the trail goes through open woods to the
summit and tower at 1.18 mi. (The R trail leading up from the
observer's cabin is the old route, now badly eroded, which leads
past an old spring house and then up steeply through a slot in the
summit cliffs. It joins the current trail 0.09 mi. below the summit.)

Distance: Campground to summit of Poke-o-Moonshine, 1.18
mi. (1.90 km.). Ascent, 1280 ft. (390 m.). Elevation, 2180 ft. (664
m.).

GIANT FROM ROUTE 9N

This is one of the longer approaches to Giant, but it has its
attractions for those who don't like company while approaching a
popular peak like Giant. (See St. Huberts Section for history and
naming of Giant.) This trail from Rt. 9N, also referred to as the
North Trail, offers generally easy grades, an interesting lookout, a
unique geological formation, and a secluded and seldom used
lean-to. The Owl Head Lookout (not the plural form to distinguish
it from the peak above the Cascade Pass Road) is also popular as a
short day trip, with its magnificent view of the E face of Giant as
well as Rocky Peak, Lake Champlain and the Green Mountains.

The trail starts on Rt. 9N at a large DEC sign, 4.5 mi. W of the
junction with Rt. 9 at the S end of the village of Elizabethtown or
5.5 mi. E of the junction of Rtes. 9N and 73 between Keene and
Keene Valley. Off the highway, there is a small parking lot and trail
register on the L of a private gravel road. Park here (0 mi.) and
continue down the road and cross a small bridge in 150 yds.
Immediately after the bridge, the trail (now marked with red
markers) turns sharp L off this road and begins a gradual climb as it
joins and then leaves a relatively new lumber road. Entering state

land at 0.43 mi., the trail continues its gradual climb before leveling out and then reaching Slide Brook at 1.11 mi. There are several possible campsites in this area.

Crossing Slide Brook on a good bridge, the trail climbs steeply up the bank of the brook, swings L and crosses a small tributary brook before beginning a steady easy to moderate climb above the R bank of the small brook. Returning to the brook, the trail crosses it several times as it works up through a small ravine. At the top of the ravine at 1.80 mi., the trail swings sharply R, crosses a few boggy areas, and continues to swing slowly to the R as it climbs at a moderate grade to the top of the ridge at 2.49 mi. Here there is a junction with a side trail leading L and up 0.13 mi. to the summit of Owl Head Lookout. (Climbers ending their trip here should go 0.10 mi. L when returning to the main trail for a spectacular view of the cliffs on the Lookout.)

The trail soon begins to descend through a small open area to a small valley at 2.70 mi., after which it climbs briefly and then descends again before starting up through a very open grove of maples at 3.38 mi. Just beyond this point there is a good view from rocks just off to the L of the trail. There is one more short descent before continuing the climbing to the top of High Bank, a remarkable bank of glacial gravel with only a few birches growing on it, which is reached at 4.14 mi. Continuing on, the trail crosses a dry stream bed at 4.41 mi. At 4.57 mi. there is a view of the slides on Giant 50 ft. on the L.

The grade continues steady and moderate, but begins to slacken at 5.70 mi., just before a junction with a side trail leading 50 yds. L to a lean-to. For some reason, the sign for this lean-to is now placed approximately 200 yds. down the trail from this junction. Past the lean-to the grade eases off as the trail approaches the junction with the ATIS trail from Hopkins at 6.06 mi. (see St. Huberts Section). Turning L, the trail begins climbing steeply out of the col. At 6.24

mi. there is a sharp switchback to the L to negotiate a small cliff band. From here the grade continues steep for a few yards, but slowly eases until it levels off at 6.83 mi. Descending slightly, the trail resumes its climb and arrives at a ledge on the R at 7.20 mi., soon after which the trail levels out and crosses other ledges to the summit at 7.40 mi. (ATIS trail continues over the summit to St. Huberts; see St. Huberts Section.)

Distances: Rt. 9N to Owl Head Lookout, 2.62 mi.; to lean-to, 5.70 mi.; to junction with trail from Hopkins, 6.06 mi.; to summit of Giant, 7.40 mi. (11.91 km.). Ascent from Rt. 9N, 3327 ft. (1014 m.). Elevation, 4427 ft. (1349 m.). Order of height, 12.

EAST TRAIL TO ROCKY PEAK RIDGE AND GIANT

This route up the long E ridge of Rocky Peak Ridge and on to Giant is a very challenging but also very rewarding climb. Nearly half of the trail is in the open, and there are exceptional views at nearly every turn of the trail. Bring plenty of water along on any day, and think twice before attempting this route on a particularly hot day, but on a cool day with fall colors at their height this trail is probably the best hike in all of the Adirondacks. For those with less ambition, two intermediate points, Blueberry Cobbles at 1.97 mi. and Bald Peak at 3.86 mi., are also worthy objectives.

Except for a small stand of first-growth hemlock near the start of the trail, this entire route is through smaller second growth. This is the result of the great fire of 1913, which burned all of Rocky Peak and much of Giant. Nearly all of the views along this route are a direct result of this last great fire in the Adirondacks.

The trail begins at a parking lot on Rt. 9, 4.9 mi. N of the junction with Rt. 73 and 1.3 mi. S of the New Russia Post Office. From the parking lot the trail crosses a nearly grown-up field, begins to climb an old tote road, and comes to the L bank of a small stream at 0.67

mi. Following up the L bank, the trail enters a flat notch at the far end of which it swings L and begins climbing again at a moderate to steep grade. The first view is just off the trail to the R at 1.79 mi.

Continuing up, the trail comes to the first lookout on Blueberry Cobbles on the L at 1.86 mi. and then comes to a junction at 1.97 mi., with a red trail which bypasses the top of Blueberry Cobbles leading R. (In season, there are enough blueberries along this section of trail to make blueberry cobbler for an army.) The yellow trail L leads past many other views of the Boquet Valley and the Dix Range before turning sharp R and down at 2.32 mi. to Mason Notch, where the red bypass trail rejoins it. The trail climbs over the lightly wooded summit of Mason Mt. (2330 ft.) at 2.82 mi. before descending to Hedgehog Notch at the base of Bald Peak. There is an interesting cleft in the rock just to the L of the trail. Now the trail begins to climb steeply over mostly bare rock to the summit of Bald Peak (3060 ft.) at 3.86 mi., where there are good views in all directions.

Turning L and following the ridge W, the trail passes a huge balanced glacial erratic at 4.02 mi. and then begins to descend the R side of the ridge to Dickerson Notch at 4.21 mi. From the notch, the trail begins a long climb to the prominence at the E end of the summit ridge. Unlike most of the trail so far, there are only a few views to serve as excuses to rest, but there is one good ledge on the R as the grade begins to ease off just before reaching the bald summit of Rocky Peak (4060 ft.) at 5.41 mi.

The trail now crosses several minor rocky bumps before descending to the outlet to Mary Louise Pond (also referred to as Lake Marie Louise) at 6.06 mi. Skirting the N side of the pond, the trail now climbs the beautiful open meadows to the summit of Rocky Peak Ridge at 6.66 mi. From here are views in all directions, with the slides on Giant's E face dominating. Total ascent from the parking lot, 4190 ft. (1277 m.). Elevation, 4420 ft. (1347 m.). Order of height, 20.

Bearing NW, the trail descends steadily into the col between Giant and Rocky Peak Ridge at 7.40 mi. and immediately begins to climb steeply, first through an open meadow and then into the woods. Angling R, the trail comes to a junction with a side trail at 7.70 mi. (Trail R leads 60 yds. to a spectacular view of some of the slides on the E face of Giant.) Swinging back to the L after this junction, the trail soon gains the crest of a ridge and follows this up to its junction with the ATIS trail from St. Huberts at 7.91 mi. Turning R, it is an easy hike to the summit of Giant at 8.04 mi.

Distances: Parking lot to Blueberry Cobbles, 1.86 mi.; to Bald Peak, 3.86 mi.; to summit of Rocky Peak Ridge, 6.66 mi.; to summit of Giant Mt., 8.04 mi. (12.92 km.). Total ascent from parking lot, 4810 ft. (1466 m.). Elevation, 4627 ft. (1410 m.). Order of height, 12.

SUNRISE TRAIL TO MT. GILLIGAN

Formerly known as Sunrise Mt., this little peak rises directly above the Boquet River and offers views of Pleasant Valley, Rocky Peak Ridge and the Dixes from the summit and the several lookouts along the way. The trail starts from Rt. 9, 3.6 mi. N of its junction with Rt. 73 and 2.6 mi. S of the New Russia Post Office. A dirt road leads to a bridge over the river, with a fisherman's parking lot just before the bridge. Park here (0 mi.), cross the bridge, and turn L off the road after 150 yds. just before reaching a house on the L. Marked with ADK markers, the trail proceeds on the flat for a few hundred yards before climbing to a higher shelf up to the R and then, after some more flat going, climbs steeply up to the first lookout at .30 mi., with a good view of Dix.

Continuing on, the trail dips briefly and then climbs steadily to another lookout at 0.57 mi. Now the grade is easier along the top of the ridge before it dips down and crosses an old lumber road in a small col at 0.79 mi. Climbing past an interesting overhung rock, the trail reaches a broad open area at 0.86 mi., with good views of Rocky Peak Ridge and the Dix Range. Just after this ledge, the trail joins and briefly follows an old lumber road before branching L and up to the final lookout at 1.12 mi. at the end of the trail. The wooded summit of Mt. Gilligan is about 100 yds. beyond.

Distance: Parking area near Rt. 9 to lookout below summit of Mt. Gilligan, 1.12 mi. (1.80 km.). Ascent, 670 ft. (204 m.). Elevation, 1420 ft. (433 m.).

TRAIL FROM SHARP BRIDGE CAMPSITE TO ROUND POND AND EAST MILL FLOW

This trail is a relatively flat and pleasant walk through some fine woods, giving access to picturesque Round Pond as well as the beautiful and unique open area known as East Mill Flow. This trail was cut out about ten years ago, but has not been well maintained recently. It is still quite passable and one only needs to be careful not to lose it in the alders at a few of the stream crossings.

The start is at Sharp Bridge Campground on Rt. 9, 7.1 mi. N of the village of North Hudson and 2.9 mi. S of Exit 30 on the Adirondack Northway. Parking is at the gravel turnout just outside the gate. From the parking area (0 mi.), the trail goes to the far end of the large, flat field near the Schroon River and then goes along the L bank of the river on an old road. Crossing several small brooks, the trail comes to an old bridge abutment at 0.83 mi. This was apparently the original crossing point used as early as the 1830s both by the predecessor of Rt. 9 and by a road leading W from Port Henry to Tahawus and beyond. Turning sharp L at this point, the trail follows this old road for several miles.

The trail climbs briefly, drops to cross a small brook, and then begins a steady climb to a height of land at 1.53 mi. Dropping down the other side in two short pitches, the trail continues mostly on the level through several magnificent stands of white pine to the R bank of East Mill Brook at 2.69 mi., at the S end of East Mill Flow. Swinging R, the trail drops down and makes a somewhat difficult crossing of the brook before scrambling up the far bank and continuing along the E side of this extensive open swamp. At 3.41 mi. the trail crosses the outlet to Round Pond in a thick clump of alders, turns sharp R, and heads up a gentle grade. At 3.55 mi., just before coming within sight of Round Pond, the trail turns sharp R off the old road and proceeds to the outlet of Round Pond at 3.90 mi. (The old road leads straight ahead to the NW shore of Round Pond with a good campsite located across the pond on some low rocks.)

From the outlet, the trail climbs S away from the pond and skirts numerous small swampy areas as it crosses a low divide and proceeds down to a junction with an unmarked trail leading L at 4.53 mi. (Trail L leads along E shore of Trout Pond to rough access road.) Continuing R, the trail makes its way along the W shore of Trout Pond and comes to the North Hudson-Moriah Rd. at 5.22 mi. This trailhead is approximately 5.3 mi. from Rt. 9, N of North Hudson, and is not marked by any sign.

Distances: Sharp Bridge Campground to East Mill Flow, 2.69 mi.; to outlet to Round Pond, 3.90 mi.; to North Hudson-Moriah Rd., 5.22 mi. (8.40 km.).

DIX RANGE via NORTH FORK OF THE BOQUET RIVER

The trailless peaks of the Dix Range may be approached via this unmarked hunter's trail. There are several interesting ponds in this area, as well as some nice camping spots. Although the trail is fairly plain, there are no signs or markers, and one should carry a map and compass in the event one loses the trail.

The trail begins on Rt. 73 on the S side of the N Fork of the Boquet River, at a stone bridge approximately 1.5 mi. N of the junction of Rtes. 73 and 9. Leaving the highway (0 mi.), the trail goes up along the R bank of the stream to a crossing point at 0.4 mi. Now heading away from the Boquet, the trail crosses a small stream and returns to a bank high above the river 150 yds. later at 0.7 mi. There is a good swimming hole and picnic spot at the small flume in the river, which can be seen through the trees.

From this swimming hole, the trail climbs high above the river before turning L and down to cross it at 1.2 mi. Heading SW, the trail crosses another large tributary at 1.4 mi., with Lillypad Pond just out of sight to the L of the trail. The trail now climbs easily and then descends to the L bank of the S Fork of the Boquet at 2.3 mi. The trail continues up the L bank, much of the time high above it, passing the "Rock of Gibraltar" on the L at 3.1 mi. and coming to the L bank of a tributary coming down from Dix at 3.3 mi. Not far beyond, the trail ends at the remains of some old hunter's camps. From here there are easy approaches to most all of the Dix Range, as well as several outstanding camping spots in this remote and seldom visited area. (See "Peaks Without Maintained Trails" for more information on climbing beyond this point.)

NORTHWAY ACCESS POINTS TO THE DIX WILDERNESS AREA

With the construction of the Adirondack Northway through this area in the mid 1960s there came a need to provide access across this controlled-access highway, since parking was of course prohibited on the highway itself. There are now three points where one can easily cross the Northway along the ten-mile stretch from North Hudson to Exit 30 near Underwood. These access routes connect with the valleys of Lindsay Brook, West Mill Brook and Walker Brook, and are described briefly below.

Lindsay Brook Access: This route, marked with red markers, starts S of the Schroon River opposite Sharp Bridge Campground (see above). Going up a road for 0.1 mi., the trail turns sharp R and crosses a stream, negotiates a flooded area, and continues on through a pine forest to a culvert under the Northway at 0.9 mi. No trail continues beyond this culvert.

West Mill Brook Access: This route begins 1.6 mi. S of Sharp Bridge Campground or 5.5 mi. N of the village of North Hudson. There is a large wooden signpost (but no sign) at the start of a narrow dirt road which leads down to West Mill Brook at 0.2 mi., where there is a good ford. (Park just before on R at times of high water.) From the ford, the road crosses an extensive open sandy area and reaches a concrete culvert under the Northway at 0.8 mi. At 1.1 mi. there is a parking area just before a gate controls further access along the old road leading along the R bank of West Mill Brook. This road leads approximately 2 mi. farther W before turning S and becoming obscure.

Walker Brook Access: This access is 3.7 mi. S of Sharp Bridge Campground or 3.4 mi. N of North Hudson. Just south of two houses, there is an old green metal signpost at the end of a dirt road. Go down this road for 0.3 mi. and bear R on a poorer road that leads to the L bank of the Schroon River, where cars may be parked. Just upstream is a good wooden foot bridge leading to a good road on the far side, which is followed uphill to a flat area 0.5 mi. from Rt. 9. Bear R just beyond and cross under the Northway through a concrete culvert at 0.7 mi. Walker Brook is approximately 0.2 mi. beyond, with an old road leading up its L bank giving access to Camels Hump, Niagara and Nipple Top Mts.

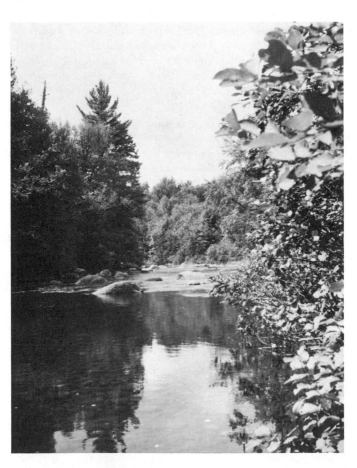

Cold River from Ouluska Lean-to
Photo by Tom Dunn

SOUTHERN
SECTION

This region stretches across the southern edge of the High Peaks Wilderness Area and a small portion of the Dix Wilderness Area. With the exception of the well-traveled trails leading to Marcy and Dix, much of this area is remote and seldom visited. There are outstanding opportunities for solitude, and one must be willing to backpack to reach all of the terrain within the region's boundaries.

The following descriptions are the ones formerly found in the Elk Lake and Sanford Lake Regions of previous editions of this guidebook; sections of the Northville-Placid Trail from Long Lake to Duck Hole have also been incorporated into this section. Some of the trails stretching across the great distances near the Cold River and in the Santanoni Preserve have been measured with several different devices, including an odometer on a bicycle, giving distances only to the nearest tenth of a mile. For consistency, the distances on all trails in this section are expressed to the nearest tenth, but this should pose no problem over the much greater distances found in this area.

Except for Goodnow Mt., there are no short hikes in this area, and very few moderate hikes; but there are great possibilities for extended backpacking trips beyond the obvious traverse of the Northville-Placid Trail. For the serious and experienced hiker, this area is the place to go to find new challenges.

SHORT HIKE:

Goodnow Mt. — 3.0 mi. round trip. An easy ascent on a good trail leads to a fire tower with expansive views of the high peaks and the equally wild country to the S.

MODERATE HIKES:

Summit Rock in Indian Pass — 8.74 mi. round trip. Except for the final half mile, this is an easy hike to a close-up view of the largest (nearly 1000 ft. high) cliff in the Adirondacks. See description for Indian Pass from Upper Works.

Camp Santanoni on Newcomb Lake — 9.00 mi. round trip. The road to Newcomb Lake has easy grades and leads to an authentic "great camp" on the shore of a beautiful lake.

HARDER HIKES:

Dix Mt. via Hunters Pass with return via Beckhorn — 13.90 mi. round trip. An interesting loop trip on this impressively rugged peak with outstanding views from the summit.

Newcomb Lake, Shattuck Clearing, Duck Hole, Henderson Lake backpacking trip — 35.2 mi. point to point. This 4-5 day trip leads along little-used trails past three attractive lakes with good campsites and also parallels the ruggedly beautiful Cold River for several miles. It requires only a short shuttle between start and finish points. See descriptions for: Road to Newcomb Lake, Foot Trail to Shaw Pond, Moose Pond Horse Trail, Cold River Horse Trail, Shattuck Clearing to Duck Hole via Northville-Placid Trail, and Duck Hole via Henderson Lake.

ELK LAKE AREA

To reach the trails starting from Elk Lake, leave the Adirondack Northway (Interstate 87) at Exit 29 in North Hudson. Then go W 4 mi. on Blue Ridge Rd., following signs for Newcomb. Turn R off Blue Ridge Rd. onto a gravel road marked with a sign for Elk Lake Lodge. At 5.2 mi. on this gravel road there is a parking lot on the R just before the road drops down to Elk Lake. The road beyond here is private and open only to guests at Elk Lake Lodge. In winter, this road is usually plowed only as far as Clear Pond, 3.3 mi. from Blue Ridge Rd.

All of the trails starting from this parking lot cross private land, and hikers should observe the normal courtesies when on private land, which means that there is no camping permitted for 5 mi. along the Elk Lake-Marcy Trail or for 1.88 mi. along the Dix Trail. Hikers should also be aware that the privately maintained trails are not open to the public and that all of these trails are closed to the public during the hunting season. Refer to the map accompanying this guidebook for the exact location of private lands in this area.

ELK LAKE-MARCY TRAIL

This is one of the longer approaches to Marcy and involves an additional climb and descent of about 700 ft. over the Boreas-Colvin Range before actually beginning the ascent of Marcy. Although the section of trail across Marcy Swamp has recently been improved with the addition of a long series of bridges, the upper section of this trail is very rough and wet, having seen little maintenance in recent years; and the one lean-to on the trail, at Panther Gorge, is in very poor condtion. Since much of this trail is on private land, hikers should be aware that no camping is permitted until approximately 6.5 mi., with exception of a small piece of state land at 5.0 mi.

Leaving the DEC signpost across the road from the parking lot (0 mi.), the blue-marked trail climbs through thick woods for a few yards and then descends and crosses a private trail at 0.14 mi. Continuing to descend, the trail crosses The Branch (outlet to Elk Lake) on a suspension bridge at 0.34 mi. and then climbs gently to a lumber road at 0.44 mi. Turning L on the road, the trail crosses Nellie Brook and then takes an immediate R up a steep bank. Quickly leveling off, the trail zig-zags along a series of old overgrown lumber roads and emerges on a wide gravel lumber road at 0.69 mi. Turning R on this road, the trail takes the R fork at 1.05 mi., crosses Nellie Brook a few yards later, and climbs over a ridge.

The trail descends to cross Guideboard Brook at 1.74 mi., and at 1.96 mi. a private trail comes in from the R. Continuing along the lumber road, the trail takes a R fork at 2.21 mi. and then turns L off the road at 2.36 mi. The trail now climbs over a hill and descends to Guideboard Brook at a point just below a beaver dam. Passing the beaver pond on its E side, the trail crosses Guideboard Brook at the head of the pond at 2.77 mi. and follows up a tributary to an old road at 2.83 mi. From here, the trail climbs with a few steep pitches to the top of the pass through the Boreas-Colvin Range at 3.34 mi.

Elevation, 2650 ft. (808 m.). Ascent from Elk Lake, 600 ft. (180 m.).

From this pass, the trail descends moderately, crosses a small brook at 3.45 mi. and continues along a side hill with short ups and downs, followed by a moderate climb to another height of land at 4.26 mi. Elevation, 2590 ft. (789 m.). From here, the trail descends moderately and crosses an old lumber road at 4.61 mi. Continuing down, at 4.75 mi. the trail passes a collapsed building on the R, which is all that is left of a lumber camp. Turning L at this old building, the trail descends to another lumber road at 4.87 mi., which the trail follows for a few yards before turning sharp R and down and entering state land shortly before reaching a junction at 5.00 mi. (Trail R leads along Pinnacle Ridge over Mt. Colvin and Blake Peak to St. Huberts; see St. Huberts Section.)

The Elk Lake-Marcy Trail continues to descend to a junction at 5.16 mi., where it again enters private land. (Trail R and L at this junction is private and closed to the public.) Continuing straight ahead a few yards, the trail crosses the Upper Ausable Lake Inlet on a two-log bridge. (Heading toward Elk Lake, be sure to make a sharp L at the E end of this bridge.) The trail is now on the flat in Marcy Swamp, where a series of new bridges built by the ADK Trail Crew now makes pleasant walking out of this former nightmare section of trail. At 5.54 mi. the trail enters a large open area with a view of Marcy before re-entering the woods and starting to climb at 5.66 mi.

At 6.10 mi. the grade steepens and remains steady to a junction at 6.48 mi. (Trail R is private and closed to the public.) Now on the level, the trail again enters state land at 6.55 mi. and begins climbing the first of several pitches at 6.61 mi. At about 7.00 mi. the trail levels off in a wet area and remains wet and rough much of the way from here to Panther Gorge. At 7.56 mi. the trail crosses a fair-sized brook and then traverses a small bog, with Marcy Brook coming into view on the L at 7.79 mi. Shortly after, the trail turns sharp R away from an old tote road the trail had briefly followed. Soon swinging back L, the trail parallels Marcy Brook to a brook crossing at the confluence of two streams (PBM 3012 ft. on large rock between two brooks) at 8.27 mi.

Continuing on, the trail enters thick woods at 8.66 mi. and reaches Panther Gorge Lean-to at 9.00 mi. There are many campsites behind the lean-to. Just past the lean-to, the trail reaches a junction with the ATIS trail leading R and steeply up to Bartlett Ridge and Haystack (see St. Huberts Section). Turning L, the Elk Lake-Marcy Trail crosses Marcy Brook and bears R and up a steep climb. (Watch carefully for the markers leading to the R, as there are several plain but false trails leading straight up the far bank of the brook.) At 9.11 mi. the trail crosses a small brook and begins a steep climb. After a few more steep pitches, the grade begins to ease off, but the trail remains very rough all the way to Four Corners and the junction with the yellow trail from Lake Colden and Upper Works at 10.18 mi. (Red trail L leads 0.52 mi. to the summit of Skylight; see below.) This junction is the former site of Four Corners Lean-to, but since it is above 4000 ft. no camping is now permitted here.

Turning R with yellow markers, the trail climbs steadily up a rocky, eroded section of trail. At 10.37 mi. there is a boulder on the L which has split away from the mountain, forming a crevice. A few yards through this crevice there is a lookout at Gray Peak and Lake Tear. Swinging R, the trail continues the ascent to a good lookout on the R at 10.61 mi. Reaching timberline soon after, the trail climbs over bare rock to the top of Schofield Cobble at 10.72. This little prominence is named for Josephine Schofield, fiancee of Henry Van Hoevenberg, after whom Mt. Jo near Heart Lake is also named. She thus has the distinction of being the only person after whom two Adirondack peaks have been named, even though she died within a year of her ascent of Marcy and never had a great association with the Adirondacks — except, of course, in the memory of Henry Van Hoevenberg.

After dipping slightly beyond Schofield Cobble, the trail, marked with cairns and yellow paint blazes, begins its final steep ascent to the summit of Marcy at 10.96 mi. See "Mt. Marcy" in Introduction for history and description of the view. At the summit the trail joins the trail from Heart Lake, which also connects with the trails to Johns Brook Lodge and Keene Valley. (See Heart Lake and Keene Valley Sections for descriptions of these trails.)

Distances: Elk Lake parking lot to pass over Boreas-Colvin Range, 3.34 mi.; to Upper Ausable Lake Inlet, 5.21 mi.; to Panther Gorge Lean-to, 9.00 mi.; to junction at Four Corners, 10.18 mi.; to summit of Marcy, 10.96 mi. (17.63 km.). Total ascent from Elk Lake, 4200 ft. (1280 m.). Elevation, 5344 ft. (1629 m.). Order of height, 1.

DIX via HUNTERS PASS

Dix Mt. was named by Ebenezer Emmons in 1837 for John A. Dix, then Secretary of State for Governor Marcy and later governor himself. He also served as U.S. Senator, Secretary of the Treasury, and a Major General in the Civil War. The first ascent was in 1807 by a surveyor named Rykert, who had the task of running a line that now forms the southern boundary of the town of Keene and passes directly over the summit.

There are two trails from Elk Lake, coinciding for the first 4.33 mi. The Hunters Pass Trail is 0.74 mi. longer but has a little less steep climbing and some interesting views from above Hunters Pass.

Leaving the parking lot (0 mi.) with red DEC markers, the trail proceeds mostly on the level, crosses a private trail, and reaches a wide gravel lumber road at 0.51 mi., where the trail turns L. (Hikers returning on this section of trail should watch very carefully for the sharp R turn off the lumber road.) Crossing Little Sally Brook shortly after joining the road, the trail climbs at a gentle grade through some fresh lumbering to a height of land at about 1.00 mi. Now descending, the trail soon reaches the end of the new lumbering and continues a gentle descent with a glimpse of the slides on Macomb at 1.53 mi. The descent ends at Big Sally Brook at 1.61 mi., and the wide road ends shortly afterwards at another brook crossing. From here the trail is quite wet to the yellow-blazed state land boundary at 1.88 mi. Continuing on the flat and crossing two small brooks, the trail crosses the first of several small brooks that are discolored by iron as a result of the great Macomb slide of 1947. (The foot of the slide is just barely visible to the R at this first orange-colored brook.) At 2.25 mi. the trail crosses a larger brook, which is the favored approach to the Macomb slide. (See "Peaks Without Maintained Trails.")

Just past this brook are some possible campsites on both sides of the trail, after which the trail crosses another brook and comes to Slide Brook Lean-to on the L at the edge of a large clearing at 2.32 mi. There has been some question as to which of these two brooks is actually Slide Brook; but in reality both are, as the slide caused Slide Brook to split about 0.2 mi. above the trail.

Swinging L and slightly down through the clearing, the trail crosses a brook at the far edge of the clearing and continues on at easy grades through an open hardwood forest. At 3.10 mi. a small cairn on the R marks the beginning of a route to Hough and South Dix. (See "Peaks Without Maintained Trails.") The Dix Trail continues ascending for a few more yards before swinging L and beginning a steady descent to Lillian Brook Lean-to on the L bank of Lillian Brook at 3.66 mi. Swinging R and crossing the brook, the trail climbs to 3.76 mi. and then descends moderately to steeply to some rough going along a side hill above Dix Pond. Descending to the level of Dix Pond at 4.10 mi., the trail passes through two lumber clearings to a junction at 4.33 mi. (Yellow trail R is the Beckhorn Trail; see below.)

Continuing straight ahead, the trail crosses the East Inlet and begins a steady climb along the R bank of the brook. Eventually pulling away from the brook, the trail crosses a large tributary at 5.49 mi. and continues at a moderate grade with a few steeper pitches to Hunters Pass at 6.12 mi. Crossing to the far side of the boulder-strewn pass, the trail begins a steep to very steep climb up past some overhanging rocks to a short breather at 6.28 mi. The climbing soon resumes to another level stretch and view toward Nipple Top at 6.48 mi. Just beyond, the trail reaches "Balanced Rock" lookout, followed by slightly easier but still steady climbing to a junction at 6.89 mi. (Trail from L with blue markers leads to Round Pond and Rt. 73; see St. Huberts Section.)

Turning R, the climbing continues steady but not quite as steep along the ridge to the summit crest at 7.14 mi. From this point, hikers should use care to remain on the marked trail so as not to damage the fragile alpine vegetation. The going is now nearly level past one rock on the L with a U.S. Coast and Geodetic Survey marker and on to the summit with an old survey bolt at 7.31 mi. This bolt was placed by Verplanck Colvin in 1873 as part of his Adirondack Survey. The view is unobstructed in all directions, with Elk Lake seen to the SW, Lake Champlain and the Green Mts. to the E, and the Great Range to the NW. The trail with yellow DEC disks from the lumber clearing via the Beckhorn continues straight over the summit (see below).

Distances: Elk Lake parking lot to Slide Brook Lean-to, 2.33 mi.; to Lillian Brook Lean-to, 3.66 mi.; to junction with Beckhorn Trail, 4.33 mi.; to Hunters Pass, 6.12 mi.; to Round Pond Trail from Rt. 73, 6.89 mi.; to summit of Dix, 7.31 mi. (11.76 km.). Ascent from Elk Lake, 2800 ft. (853 m.). Elevation, 4875 ft. (1486 m.). Order of height, 6.

DIX via BECKHORN

This trail leads up the steep SW ridge of Dix to a small subsidiary peak known as the Beckhorn, a name conferred by "Old Mountain" Phelps because of its resemblance to the beckiron on a blacksmith's anvil. Take the red-marked Dix Trail to the lumber clearing at 4.33 mi. (see above). Leaving the junction (0 mi.) with yellow markers, the trail soon begins climbing steeply, with one short easier stretch before reaching a small brook at 0.51 mi. Climbing out of the brook, the trail gains the crest of a ridge with some more easy going until the climbing starts again at 0.88 mi. From here the trail climbs at a steady, steep grade, with a few views possible back to Elk Lake, to a slight sag at 1.50 mi., followed by more steep climbing to the open rocks just below the Beckhorn. Now following cairns and paint blazes, the trail passes over the Beckhorn at 2.09 mi., down steeply, and on to the summit at 2.26 mi.

Distances: Elk Lake parking lot to junction at lumber clearing, 4.33 mi.; to summit of Dix, 6.59 mi. (10.60 km.). Ascent from lumber clearing, 2600 ft. (792 m.). Elevation, 4875 ft. (1486 m.). Order of height, 6.

BOREAS MT.

The fire tower on this peak has been abandoned for some time and is presently unsafe to climb, but there are some interesting if limited views of the high peaks from various ledges near the summit. The trail starts on the Elk Lake Rd. (see above), 3.3 mi. N of the Blue Ridge Rd. at the outlet to Clear Pond and just before a gate and a house on the L. There is a small parking lot and DEC sign on the L. From the parking lot (0 mi.) and marked with red DEC disks, the trail descends at easy grades to a bridge over The

Branch at 0.35 mi. Continuing mostly on the level, the trail detours R around a small beaver pond at 0.70 mi. and then begins a longer reroute to the R at 0.82 mi. Crossing a stream at 1.07 mi., the trail climbs easily to a small clearing and lumber road at 1.22 mi., where it rejoins the original route. (Coming down, one must look carefully for this new route, which leaves the lower L corner of the clearing.)

From this clearing, the Boreas Trail goes straight up along a grassy road on the R bank of a small stream. At 1.40 mi., the trail goes sharp L and up steeply to a higher road where it turns R and continues a moderate climb. Bearing R at a junction at 1.65 mi., the trail crosses a stream and continues up the L bank to a crossing to the R bank at 1.92 mi. Resuming the steady climb, the trail detours briefly around an eroded section, bears R, and recrosses the stream at 2.08 mi. before continuing up to a large clearing at 2.47 mi., with the abandoned observer's cabin up and to the L.

Past the old cabin, the trail climbs moderately on an old logging road to a stream crossing at 2.79 mi., after which the grade steepens to the top of the ridge at 3.33 mi. in a small blowdown area. Swinging sharp L, the trail continues steeply to the summit and tower at 3.40 mi., where there are views to the N, E, and W to be found with a little looking around.

Distances: Elk Lake Rd. to old observer's cabin, 2.49 mi.; to summit of Boreas, 3.40 mi. (5.47 km.). Ascent from road, 1925 ft. (587 m.). Elevation, 3776 ft. (1151 m.).

SANFORD LAKE AREA

The trails to Marcy, Lake Colden, Indian Pass and Duck Hole all begin at or near the end of a road that leads from Rt. 28N near Newcomb past the mining operations at Tahawus to the abandoned village of Adirondack, commonly referred to as Upper Works. This area has a long and interesting history, beginning in 1826 when an

Indian guide led a party through Indian Pass to show them a vein of iron ore. For the next thirty years or so this was, in spite of transportation difficulties, a thriving operation which employed up to 400 men. The last expansion of the operation during this early phase was in 1854 and included the building of the great stone furnace, the remains of which can still be seen next to the road. This operation was built up the river from the original development located near the present center of mining operations; hence the name "Upper Works."

By 1858, operations had ceased, only to start again during World War II, when this deposit became a major source for the important metal titanium. Mining by the National Lead Company (now called NL Industries) continued after the war on an expanding basis, with the titanium used as a pigment for paint. In 1965, the entire village of Tahawus was moved to Newcomb to accommodate a new and larger excavation, and the tailings "desert" which the road crosses reached its present size. For various reasons, operations have now virtually ceased; but the property around these trailheads remains in the hands of the National Lead Company. This means that camping is not permitted at Upper Works, and that on some trails one must hike a considerable distance to reach state land where camping is permitted. See the map which accompanies this guidebook for the exact location of private land.

This access road is reached from Rt. 28N, 7.3 mi. N of Aiden Lair or about 5 mi. E of the Town Hall in Newcomb. An alternate approach is from Exit 29 on the Adirondack Northway (Interstate 87) via Blue Ridge Rd. Approximately 20 mi. from Exit 29, Blue Ridge Rd. joins the access road, 1.6 mi. from Rt. 28N.

About 6 mi. from Rt. 28N, the road forks with the main road continuing straight across a bridge over the Hudson to the mine. Turn L here on a narrower road marked with a sign for "Marcy and the High Peaks." At 2.0 mi. from this turn, there is a parking lot on the L for the Bradley Pond Trail to Duck Hole. At 2.8 mi., one passes the large stone furnace on the R; and at 3.0 mi. there is a parking lot on the R for the Hanging Spear Falls approach to Flowed Lands as well as the route to Allen Mt. Shortly beyond are some abandoned buildings, and the parking lot at Upper Works is reached at 3.5 mi.

MT. MARCY AND LAKE COLDEN via CALAMITY BROOK TRAIL

This is the shortest approach to Marcy from the S and it is an attractive route highlighted by the camping areas on Flowed Lands and Lake Colden and the pretty falls and flumes on the Opalescent River. For years, many hikers believed for understandable reasons that the name "calamity" was applied to this trail because of its condition, but recently ADK and DEC trail crews have done extensive work on this trail and it is now relatively dry and much more pleasant to hike.

Starting at the Upper Works parking lot (0 mi.) with red and yellow markers, the trail follows a wide road, bearing L at a junction at 0.09 mi. (Road R at this junction is the old route of the Calamity Brook Trail.) The trail then crosses the outlet of Henderson Lake at 0.22 mi. and bears R to avoid a private road leading to the shore of the lake. After a short climb and descent, the trail comes to a junction at 0.36 mi. (Yellow trail continues straight ahead for Indian Pass and Duck Hole; see below.) Turning sharp R on a good trail with red markers, the trail rejoins the old route at 0.73 mi. Now climbing at an easy grade near the R bank of Calamity Brook, the trail crosses the brook on a suspension bridge at 1.29 mi. and continues mostly on the flat around the E side of an extensive wet area. At 1.82 mi. the trail recrosses Calamity Brook and comes to a junction with a blue-marked trail from the Indian

Pass Trail. (End of red markers.)

Turning R, the trail follows the R bank of the brook at a gentle grade, but then pulls away from the brook at 2.12 mi. and begins a steady, moderate climb. Shortly above a switchback to the R at 2.25 mi. the grade begins to ease, and the trail enters state land at 2.40 mi. as the trail continues a gradual climb. At 2.91 mi. the trail swings sharp L away from the old tote road and soon descends a ladder to a bridge over the brook. (At low water one can save a few steps by crossing the brook on the stones.) Crossing the bridge, the trail quickly rejoins the tote road and climbs at a moderate grade until 3.28 mi., where it eases. The trail is now gently rolling, crossing numerous small streams and reaching an open area with many log bridges at 4.08 mi. After a short climb and descent, the trail reaches another open marsh which it skirts on the R side and reaches the N end of Calamity Pond at 4.34 mi.

A side trail leads 20 yds. straight ahead to the Henderson Monument, erected in memory of David Henderson who was accidentally shot and killed (the "calamity") on this spot while scouting for additional water sources to power the blast furnaces at the iron works. His scouting efforts eventually led to the construction of Flowed Lands dam which could at one time divert the entire flow of the Opalescent down Calamity Brook and past the blast furnaces.

Turning sharp R, the Calamity Brook Trail climbs gradually along a very rocky section of trail to a junction at Flowed Lands at 4.66 mi., with the two Calamity Lean-tos up to the R. (Red trail R is the Hanging Spear Falls Trail which leads to several lean-tos on Flowed Lands and eventually back to the road below Upper Works; see below.) As of 1984, the dam at Flowed Lands had been partially breached because it was deemed unsafe. This accounts for the current low water level in the lake. The DEC plans to rebuild the dam, but at a lower level, to bring the water about half way back up to its former height.

Turning sharp L and now with red markers again, the trail crosses the now dry channel by which the Opalescent River was once diverted to Calamity Brook. The trail follows around the NW shore of the lake and at 5.02 mi. begins a climb up behind a rocky promontory before descending again to lake level and crossing Herbert Brook at 5.40 mi. Continuing on with a few short climbs and descents, the trail reaches a junction at the top of the ladder leading to the bridge over Lake Colden Dam at 5.72 mi. (Blue trail straight ahead leads in 300 yds. to two of the six lean-tos in the vicinity, and in 0.46 mi. to Lake Colden Interior Outpost on the NW shore of the lake and then on to Heart Lake. See Heart Lake Section.)

Turning R and down across the dam (still with red markers), the trail comes to a lean-to on the L and several designated camping areas. Another lean-to is located about 200 yds. beyond this first one on the R bank of the Opalescent River; two more lean-tos are located across the river and 0.2 mi. down the L bank toward Flowed Lands. At most water levels one can cross near the Lake Colden dam, but at high water proceed up the Marcy Trail 250 yds. to the suspension bridge over the Opalescent and then back down the L bank. There are also many designated campsites in this area, generally located back away from the river beyond the trails that parallel the river.

Just past the first lean-to the trail comes to a trail register and junction. (Yellow trail L leads along E shore of Lake Colden to Avalanche Pass and Heart Lake; see Heart Lake Section.) Bearing R, the Marcy Trail soon comes to a suspension bridge over the Opalescent and turns sharp L on the far side. Continuing up the L bank at easy grades, the trail passes a waterfall at 6.10 mi. and ascends a ladder at 6.40 mi. to some ledges above a beautiful flume in the Opalescent. The grade eases above the flume and, after crossing a small tributary, the trail joins an old tote road and climbs away from the river at easy to moderate grades. At 7.28 mi. the trail reaches a height of land and descends a moderate grade to the junction with the now-abandoned Twin Brook Trail at 7.39 mi. This is the end of the red markers, and the trail is now marked with yellow DEC disks, the color of the former Twin Brook Trail which led from Twin Brook through the pass between Cliff and Redfield Mts.

From here, the trail bears L and gently down 200 yds. to Uphill Lean-to located on the L bank of Uphill Brook. Past the lean-to, the trail continues down and crosses Uphill Brook on stones near its confluence with the Opalescent River. The trail now follows close to the L bank of the Opalescent at an easy grade to a junction at 7.95 mi. (Blue trail L across Feldspar Brook leads in 100 yds. to Feldspar Lean-to and then on over Lake Arnold Pass to Marcy Dam and Heart Lake; see Heart Lake Section.) Turning R, the Marcy Trail soon begins climbing at a moderate grade, crosses a tributary at 8.05 mi., and begins a steady, steep climb up a rough, eroded section of trail high above the L bank of Feldspar Brook. At about 8.75 mi. the grade begins to moderate and finally becomes level just before reaching the outlet to Lake Tear of the Clouds, the highest pond source of the Hudson River (elevation, 4346 ft.) at 9.19 mi. Across this little body of water, fringed with spruce and balsam, the rocky dome of Mt. Marcy rises in full view.

Bearing R, the trail ascends a few yards to the former site of Lake Tear Lean-to. (Camping is prohibited in this area as it is over 4000 ft. in elevation.) Continuing on, the trail drops back to the lake level and continues mostly on the level through some very wet terrain to Four Corners where it joins the blue trail from Elk Lake at 9.53 mi. (Red trail R leads 0.52 mi. to the summit of Skylight; see below.) As at Lake Tear, no camping is permitted at this former lean-to site as it is above 4000 ft. in elevation.

Turning L and still with yellow markers, the trail climbs steadily up a rocky, eroded section of trail. At 9.72 mi. there is a boulder on the L which has split away from the mountain, forming a crevice. A few yards through this crevice there is a lookout at Gray Peak and Lake Tear. Swinging R, the trail continues the ascent to a good lookout on the R at 9.96 mi. Reaching timberline soon after, the trail climbs over bare rock to the top of Schofield Cobble at 10.07 mi. This little prominence is named for Josephine Schofield, fiancee of Henry Van Hoevenberg, after whom Mt. Jo near Heart Lake is also named. She thus has the distinction of being the only person after whom two Adirondack peaks have been named, even though she died within a year of her ascent of Marcy and never had a great association with the Adirondacks — except in the memory of Henry Van Hoevenberg.

After dipping slightly beyond Schofield Cobble, the trail, marked with cairns and yellow paint blazes, begins its final steep ascent to the summit of Marcy at 10.31 mi. (See "Mt. Marcy" in Introduction for history and description of the view.) At the summit the trail joins the trail from Heart Lake, which also connects with the trails to Johns Brook Lodge and Keene Valley. (See Heart Lake and Keene Valley Sections for descriptions of these trails.)

Distances: Upper Works parking lot to Calamity Lean-tos at Flowed Lands, 4.66 mi.; to junction at Lake Colden dam, 5.72 mi.; to Uphill Lean-to, 7.46 mi.; to junction with Lake Arnold Trail near Feldspar Lean-to, 7.95 mi.; to Four Corners and junction with Elk Lake-Marcy Trail, 9.53 mi.; to summit of Marcy, 10.31 mi. (16.59 km.) Ascent from Upper Works, 3800 ft. (1158 m.). Elevation, 5344 ft. (1629 m.). Order of height, 1.

SKYLIGHT FROM FOUR CORNERS

From Four Corners, the junction of the Elk Lake and Calamity Brook Trails to Marcy, a red-marked trail leads S and up to the open, rounded dome of Mt. Skylight. Leaving the junction (0 mi.), the trail makes a steady climb up a wet, rocky trail to timberline at 0.40 mi. From here the grade is easier through an open alpine meadow with cairns to mark the way to the summit at 0.52 mi. There are outstanding views of the surrounding peaks, with 30 major peaks being discernible. Legend states that if a climber fails to carry a rock from timberline to place on one of the two huge cairns on the summit, it will surely rain.

Distance: Four Corners to summit of Skylight, 0.52 mi. (0.84 km.). Ascent from Four Corners, 578 ft. (176 m.). Elevation, 4926 ft. (1501 m.). Order of height, 4.

FLOWED LANDS via HANGING SPEAR FALLS

This much longer approach to Flowed Lands leads past the beautiful Hanging Spear Falls, one of the highest in the Adirondacks. There is also an attractive lean-to and camping area at Gorge Lean-to, which makes it worthwhile to plan some extra time to make this longer route part of a round trip when backpacking in the area. The start for this route is the former Twin Brook Trail to Marcy, but since that trail has now been abandoned past Twin Brook Lean-to, this is not a practical route to Marcy, being nearly 4 mi. longer than the Calamity Brook Trail. Hikers should also be aware that there is no bridge across the Opalescent River at Flowed Lands, and this crossing can be difficult in high water.

The trail starts at a parking lot on the R side of the road to Upper Works, 3.0 mi. from the junction with the road leading to the mining operations. (See above for complete driving directions.) From the trail register (0 mi.), with yellow markers, the trail follows a road 0.10 mi. to the R bank of the Hudson River where it turns R a few yds. to a suspension bridge. Crossing the bridge, the trail soon rejoins the road and continues on the level to a long bridge over the N end of Lake Jimmy at 0.58 mi. At 0.74 mi. the trail reaches a junction and swings sharp R. (Trail straight ahead with red markers leads to Mt. Adams; see below.)

The trail now crosses a small stream and several small wet areas and comes to a gravel road at 1.22 mi. Turning sharp R onto the road, the trail turns sharp L and down on another road at 1.40 mi. and swings R again in another 100 yds. Now a footpath again, the trail soon comes to the shore of Lake Sally with occasional views across the lake at the N edge of the tailings "desert." After a last view of the lake at 1.88 mi. the trail heads SE over a low divide and comes to the Opalescent River at 2.62 mi. Swinging L, the trail follows near the R bank of the river to an open area and gravel road leading R across the river at 3.66 mi. (This road was formerly the popular approach to Allen Mt., but the private property across the river is now closed to public hiking and the present route starts at Twin Brook Lean-to. See "Peaks Without Maintained Trails.")

The yellow trail continues to follow a gravel road along the R bank of the river until the trail bears R off the road and almost immediately crosses a suspension bridge over the Opalescent River at 3.82 mi. At the far side of the bridge the trail turns L and climbs at an easy grade along an old tote road, sometimes leaving the old road to avoid washouts or blowdown areas. Hiking this trail in either direction, one must remain alert in this section for sharp changes of direction; but it is otherwise very easy walking as the trail crosses a brook at 4.21 mi. and Lower Twin Brook at 5.05 mi. on the broken remains of an old lumber bridge. At 5.30 mi. the trail reaches Twin Brook Lean-to, where the Twin Brook Trail to Marcy formerly branched R.

Continuing to the L and now with red markers, the trail soon crosses Upper Twin Brook, bears L along the edge of a large lumber clearing, and ascends gradually to a gravel lumber road coming in from the R at 5.48 mi. Continuing to ascend gradually on this road to a crest at 5.73 mi., the trail descends and soon branches R from the lumber road, coming to a yellow post marking the boundary of state land at 5.93 mi. The trail is now level through a beautiful maple forest and comes to a side trail (not well marked) at 6.32 mi. leading L 50 yds. to Gorge Lean-to. Past this junction the trail crosses a high water course of the Opalescent River and comes to the rocky bank of the river at 6.42 mi. Following up the L bank, the trail detours R briefly to avoid a washout, but soon rejoins the old tote road and climbs away from the river at easy to moderate grades.

At 7.50 mi. the trail crosses a brook and begins to climb more steeply along a side hill near the gorge. Shortly after this stream crossing there is a side trail L (which rejoins the old road 70 yds. further on) leading to several views of Hanging Spear Falls. At a certain volume of water, the falls are divided by a rock which gives the appearance of a "hanging spearhead." The trail continues its steep climb, passing another lookout on the L at 7.56 mi. and reaching easier going soon after. The trail now follows the L bank of the river at easy grades to the breached dam at Flowed Lands at 8.05 mi. See Calamity Brook Trail description (above) for history and current status of this dam. (From the dam, a yellow-marked side trail leads R 0.55 mi. to Livingston Point Lean-to. With the current low water levels it is also relatively easy to continue along the open shore of Flowed Lands to the lean-tos at Lake Colden, but this route is not marked and will likely have thick alders growing in it in relatively few years.)

Turning L at the dam, the trail crosses the river on stones below the dam and comes to a side trail at the far side which leads L and up 50 yds. to Griffin Lean-to. The main trail climbs up away from the shore and after several ups and downs comes to a side trail R at 8.33 mi. leading to Flowed Lands Lean-to, which has one of the prettiest locations of any lean-to in the Adirondacks. Continuing past this junction, the trail climbs over one more knoll and descends to a junction at the shore of the lake near the Calamity Lean-tos at 8.51 mi. (Blue trail from L is the Calamity Brook Trail leading to Upper Works. Red markers continue straight ahead to Lake Colden and Mt. Marcy. See above.)

Distances: Parking lot to Twin Brook Lean-to, 5.30 mi.; to Gorge Lean-to, 6.32 mi.; to Hanging Spear Falls, 7.55 mi.; to Flowed Lands Dam, 8.05 mi.; to junction with Calamity Brook Trail, 8.51 mi. (13.69 km.).

MT. ADAMS

The fire tower on this peak has been abandoned for many years and is currently unsafe to climb. There are practically no views from this summit without the tower, making this a less than attractive climb. The DEC has continued to mark the trail to this summit and it is still relatively easy to follow, although it has not received much recent maintenance. The Mt. Adams Trail diverges L from the Hanging Spear Falls Trail to Flowed Lands (see above) 0.75 mi. from the parking lot and is marked with red markers. It ascends at first by easy grades past the old observer's cabin and then at moderate to finally very steep grades to the summit, 2.38 mi. from the parking lot, having ascended 1800 ft.

INDIAN PASS FROM UPPER WORKS

This trail leads to Summit Rock in Indian Pass, where it connects with the trail from Heart Lake. The view of Wallface's huge cliff from Summit Rock is one of the most impressive views in the Adirondacks, and is a good objective for a day hike or as a point to be included in a backpacking trip.

The trail starts at the Upper Works parking lot (see above for driving directions) with yellow markers and coincides with the red-marked Calamity Brook Trail at the start. From the trail register (0 mi.) the trail follows a wide gravel road, bearing L at a side road at 0.09 mi. and continuing on to a bridge over the outlet to Henderson Lake at 0.22 mi. Bearing R at the end of this bridge, the trail climbs slightly and continues to a junction at 0.36 mi. (Red trail R is the Calamity Brook Trail; see above.) Continuing straight ahead, the gravel road ends at 0.47 mi. and the trail bears R and begins a gradual climb to a crest at 0.77 mi., after which it descends. After some more ups and downs on this old jeep road, the trail bears R while the road heads straight ahead to a ford, and soon comes to a junction at 1.54 mi. (End of the yellow markers. Red trail L leads to Duck Hole; see below.)

Continuing straight ahead with red markers, the Indian Pass Trail enters state land at 1.66 mi., with Henderson Lean-to on the L near Indian Pass Brook just beyond. Passing behind the lean-to, the trail comes to an old lumber clearing at 1.96 mi., with a trail junction a few yds. beyond at the far end of the clearing. (Blue trail going straight is the crossover trail to the Calamity Brook Trail; see below.) Turning L, the Indian Pass Trail crosses the brook and proceeds at easy grades to Wallface Lean-to at 2.68 mi. near the R bank of Indian Pass Brook.

Still pretty much on the level, the trail veers away from the brook; just before reaching a large rock on the R at 2.86 mi., there is a view of Wallface ahead. After crossing three smaller brooks, the trail crosses the outlet to Wallface Ponds at 3.19 mi., beyond which the trail crosses several high water courses of the brook on some wet ground. At 3.47 mi. the trail approaches the R bank of Indian Pass Brook and follows it to a crossing at 3.86 mi., where there is another view of Wallface up the brook. The grade soon becomes steep as it

winds among large boulders and ledges. After a short downgrade at
4.13 mi. the trail again climbs steeply, with a ladder necessary at one
point, until it reaches a side trail leading L a few yds. to Summit
Rock at 4.37 mi. This is not the actual summit of the pass, but has
by far the best view and is the usual destination coming from either
direction. The actual height of land is another 0.46 mi. beyond, and
the trail continues 6.00 mi. more to Heart Lake (see Heart Lake
Section).

Distances: Upper Works to junction with Duck Hole Trail, 1.54
mi.; to Henderson Lean-to, 1.70 mi.; to junction with crossover to
Calamity Brook Trail, 2.01 mi.; to Wallface Lean-to, 2.68 mi.; to
Summit Rock, 4.37 mi. (7.03 km.). Ascent from Upper Works, 870
ft. (265 m.). Elevation, 2660 ft. (810 m.).

INDIAN PASS-CALAMITY BROOK CROSSOVER

This trail leads through a pass at the end of the MacIntyre Range
to connect the Indian Pass and Calamity Brook Trails. Its
construction dates back to a time when the Tahawus Club
controlled the area near Upper Works and would not permit hikers
to pass through. An alternate route was thus needed to allow hikers
to travel between Duck Hole and Lake Colden. With the current
trail layout, however, this crossover trail saves only a miniscule 0.03
mi. between these two points and involves some rough, wet trail
— complicated by recent beaver activity — plus 500 ft. of additional climbing. Hikers approaching from Indian Pass do save
almost a mile, but the trail is now infrequently used.

From the junction, 2.01 mi. from Upper Works on the Indian
Pass Trail (0 mi.), the grade is easy at first, but soon becomes
steeper as the trail follows a brook, crossing and recrossing it
several times before climbing more steeply to the top of the pass at
0.88 mi., having gained 500 ft. from the Indian Pass Trail.

Descending, the trail skirts a meadow at 1.00 mi. and follows down a brook, crossing it several times and reaching a beaver swamp at 1.68 mi. After some tough going around the R side of the swamp, the trail crosses the swamp at 1.83 mi. and follows a soggy tote road to the L of the brook and finally reaches dry ground at 1.97 mi. The trail reaches the junction with the Calamity Brook Trail at 2.14 mi.

Distance: Indian Pass Trail to Calamity Brook Trail, 2.14 mi. (3.44 km.).

DUCK HOLE via HENDERSON LAKE

This is the easiest route to Duck Hole and involves relatively little climbing compared to the route via Bradley Pond. The trail begins at Upper Works (see above for driving directions) and follows the Indian Pass Trail to the junction at 1.54 mi. Leaving the junction (0 mi.), the trail immediately crosses Indian Pass Brook on a good log bridge and turns L, but soon swings R and away from the brook. At 0.28 mi. the trail crosses a beaver pond via an old dam and a log, but this arrangement appears temporary (as of 1984) and in the future could require a detour to the R.

Past the beaver pond, the trail is mostly level to a junction at 0.60 mi. with a trail leading L and down to a private dock on Henderson Lake. Swinging R, the trail crosses a long series of bridges over a wet area and reaches a brook which it crosses at 0.68 mi. Recrossing the brook at 0.77 mi., the trail veers away and approaches the R bank of another brook, which it follows up past some interesting cascades at 0.86 mi. Just beyond, the trail skirts a beaver pond on its L side and continues on to a brook crossing at 1.33 mi. Recrossing this brook twice more, the trail begins a moderate climb which levels off at 1.84 mi. Descending slightly, the trail is now mostly level through an almost imperceptible divide between the St. Lawrence and Hudson watersheds, having gained only 370 ft. (113 m.) from Henderson Lake.

Dropping slightly after the pass, the trail comes to a junction in the middle of a series of bridges over some wet areas. (Trail straight aheads leads to a private dock on the Preston Ponds.) Turning sharp R, the trail soon begins climbing along the outlet to Hunter Pond, crossing it at 2.36 mi. The trail continues up the L bank, reaches Hunter Pond at 2.65 mi., crosses the outlet, and skirts the pond to the N before climbing a short steep pitch to the top of a pass at 2.81 mi. Starting down, the trail skirts a beaver pond on its R side at 2.98 mi. and joins an old lumber road just past the pond. The trail now descends a wet and eroded section of lumber road to the remains of Piche's lumber camp at 3.20 mi.

After the camp, the trail crosses to the R side of the brook and continues descending at easy grades before veering away from the brook and descending more steeply over old corduroys with Lower Preston Pond visible through trees to the L. Crossing a small swamp at 4.00 mi., the trail climbs easily to a boundary line, enters state land at 4.19 mi. and, after another descent and climb to a height of land, descends to the NE shore of Duck Hole at 4.43 mi. Turning N and after several more short, steep ups and downs, the trail reaches the L bank of Roaring Brook, which it crosses on stones to a junction with the Northville-Placid Trail on the far bank at 4.86 mi. There is no bridge, and this crossing could be difficult in times of high water. (Blue trail R leads 11.7 mi. to junction with Averyville Rd. near Lake Placid; see Northern Section.)

Turning L and now with red and blue markers, the trail proceeds with several easy ups and down to a large open area leading down to the bridge and dam at Duck Hole at 5.34 mi. There are two lean-tos at Duck Hole, and plenty of tent sites. One lean-to is just before the bridge and dam, and the other is in the woods on a point of land 100 yds. E of the dam. A ranger station at the W edge of the clearing was removed in December of 1977 in order to bring the area in to compliance with wilderness use guidelines. A blue trail crosses the dam and leads to Bradley Pond and the trailhead at Tahawus (see below). The N-P Trail heads W along an old truck trail which connects with a trail heading to Ward Brook and the trailhead at Coreys (see below).

Distances: Trail junction S of Henderson Lean-to near bridge over Indian Pass Trail to E end of Preston Ponds, 2.26 mi.; to junction with N-P Trail at Roaring Brook, 4.86 mi.; to Duck Hole, 5.34 mi. (8.59 km.). (Distance from Upper Works, 6.88 mi. or 11.07 km.).

DUCK HOLE via BRADLEY POND

This trail leads to Duck Hole through the pass between the Santanoni Range and Henderson Mt. and gives access to the routes up to trailless Santanoni, Panther and Couchsachraga Peaks. The first 4.28 mi. of this trail is on private land, where no camping is permitted, and the previously used routes to the trailless Santanonis that left this trail before it reached state land are now closed. (See "Peaks Without Maintained Trails" for more information on the currently acceptable climbing routes to these peaks.)

The trail begins at a parking lot on the L side of the road to Upper Works, 2.00 mi. N of the bridge to the mining operations. (See above for complete driving directions.) There is a large parking lot 100 yds. back from the road. From the trail register (0 mi.), the trail follows a good gravel road with blue markers at gentle grades. At 1.14 mi. it crosses the outlet to Harkness Lake, where there is a great view of Wallface Mt. The trail now climbs over a small rise, drops down, and begins a longer climb which eases just before the trail makes a sharp R turn off the road at 1.84 mi.

The trail now descends along the R bank of a brook, crosses the brook on a good bridge, and continues on the flat through a grassy clearing with plenty of raspberries. At the far end of the clearing, the trail swings L and crosses Santanoni Brook at 2.05 mi. on an elaborate bridge with a series of log steps up the far bank. At the top of the bank, the trail swings L onto an old tote road and begins ascending at easy to moderate grades up the valley.

At 2.35 mi. the trail encounters some recent lumber roads which cross and recross the trail for about 300 yds., after which the trail continues a steady, moderate climb to a series of beautiful cascades on the L at 3.35 mi. At 3.51 mi. the trail passes the abandoned Santanoni Trail on the L (now closed to the public) and continues to a crest at 3.65 mi. After a short descent, the trail crosses a wet area on a series of good bridges, but beyond here the trail is almost unremittingly wet until well past Santanoni Lean-to. At 4.25 mi. the trail enters state land and the current legal route to the Santanonis diverges L across a beaver dam. Continuing on, the trail reaches Santanoni Lean-to (still posted as Bradley Pond) at 4.42 mi. There are some designated campsites up behind the lean-to. This is the top of the pass, 2950 ft. (900 m.), 1110 ft. (338 m.) above the trailhead.

Past the lean-to the trail begins to descend. It is often difficult to distinguish the trail and the brook for the first part of the descent until at 4.84 mi. the trail crosses a larger stream, swings to the R and then back L to recross the stream, and then continues down to a crossing of the L fork of the main stream at 5.08 mi. Turning R on relatively flat ground, the trail crosses the main brook but returns to the L bank at 5.60 mi. Still mostly on the flat, the trail detours to the L to avoid some recent beaver and blowdown activity and crosses a beaver dam at 6.03 mi.

The trail wanders through more blowdown areas and climbs above the swamp where there are views of Panther to the SW. At 6.55 mi. the trail returns to the L bank of the stream. From here it is mostly very enjoyable walking along the picturesque stream. At 7.07 mi. the trail crosses again to the R bank and continues on the level to a corner of private land at 7.77 mi., where it turns L and crosses the brook for the final time and climbs over a small ridge to the SW shore of Duck Hole at 7.93 mi. Skirting the pond, the trail crosses a rock crib dike at 8.00 mi. and soon comes to the dam with the lean-to and trail junction just beyond at 8.22 mi. Here the trail meets the Northville-Placid Trail, marked here with blue and red markers, which leads R to Averyville Rd. near Lake Placid (see Northern Section), with a connection to the trail from Upper Works (see above). To the L, the N-P Trail leads to Shattuck Clearing and Long Lake with a connection to the trail to Ward Brook and Coreys. (See below.)

Distances: Parking lot to Santanoni Lean-to, 4.42 mi.; to Duck Hole, 8.22 mi. (13.23 km.).

DUCK HOLE FROM COREYS via WARD BROOK TRUCK TRAIL

This is the western access to Duck Hole and the High Peaks Region and also offers the easiest access to the routes up the Seward Range. The start is on a road which leaves Rt. 3 12.7 mi. W of the traffic light in Saranac Lake and 2.7 mi. E of the junction of Rtes. 3 and 30 E of Tupper Lake. This road is marked with a large DEC sign for "High Peaks via Duck Hole." It is paved through the little settlement of Coreys, but turns to gravel at about 1.5 mi., crosses Stony Creek at 2.5 mi., and continues to a parking area on the R, 5.8 mi. from Rt. 3. As the signs indicate, the road enters a private preserve shortly beyond the parking lot, and this is as far as the public may travel. From this parking lot, both a foot trail and a horse trail depart for the Ward Brook Truck Trail and Duck Hole. The horse trail is not described here because it exactly parallels the hiking trail, is considerably wetter, and is generally unsuited for hiking.

Leaving the trail register (0 mi.) with red markers, the foot trail bears L and crosses a swamp on some good bridges and climbs a bank to higher ground at 0.60 mi., where an old trail comes in from the R. Now mostly on the level and soon joining the posted property line of the Ampersand Club, the trail comes to the Calkins Brook Truck Trail at 1.23 mi. (Road L is blocked by a gate at the boundary of private land. Road R leads to Calkins Brook and Shattuck Clearing; see below.)

Continuing past the road and still mostly level, the trail crosses several brooks and passes within sight of Blueberry Pond on the L at 2.25 mi. At 3.38 mi. the trail beings a descent to a large brook, crosses it at 3.49 mi., and at 4.54 mi. comes to Blueberry Lean-to on the R. Just beyond the lean-to, the trail joins the Ward Brook Truck Trail coming in from the L from the private Ampersand Club. (Hikers heading towards Coreys must be sure to make this sharp L turn off the truck trail.)

Turning R on the road, the trail passes the junction with the horse trail at 4.70 mi. and then crosses three fair-sized brooks before reaching Ward Brook Lean-to at 5.35 mi. (The first of these brooks is the favored approach to Seward. See "Peaks Without Maintained Trails.") The first brook beyond Ward Brook Lean-to is the favored approach to Seymour; after this brook the trail climbs easily to a crest before dipping down a bit to two lean-tos and a horse barn at 6.08 mi.

Climbing again at easy to moderate grades, the trail reaches its highest point at 7.00 mi. and descends in several stages to an open swamp at 8.04 mi. before climbing over another hill and dropping down to a junction with the Northville-Placid Trail at 8.67 mi. (Blue trail R leads to Shattuck Clearing and Long Lake; see below.) Continuing on with red and blue markers, the trail comes to the two Cold River Lean-tos (Nos. 1 and 2) at 9.07 mi. Just past the lean-tos, the trail crosses Moose Creek just above its confluence with the Cold River, climbs the far bank, and then follows along the R bank of the Cold River to a junction at 9.44 mi. (Horse trail R fords the Cold River and continues down the E side of the river to Shattuck Clearing with a connection to the Santanoni Preserve and Newcomb; see below.)

Past this junction, the trail climbs over a low ridge and arrives at the trail junction and former site of the ranger station at 10.31 mi. Blue trail R crosses the dam and leads to Bradley Pond and the road below Upper Works (see above). Trail bearing L with blue and red markers is the continuation of the N-P Trail leading to Lake Placid (see Northern Section) and with a connection to a trail leading to Henderson Lake and Upper Works (see above). There are two lean-tos and several good campsites at Duck Hole. One lean-to is located by the dam and the other is 100 yds. E of the dam on a beautiful wooded point.

Distances: Parking area to Blueberry Lean-to, 4.54 mi.; to Ward Brook Lean-to, 5.35 mi.; to Northville-Placid Trail, 8.67 mi.; to Cold River Lean-tos, 9.07 mi.; to Duck Hole, 10.31 mi. (16.59 km.).

SHATTUCK CLEARING FROM COREYS
via CALKINS BROOK TRUCK TRAIL

This is the shortest access to Shattuck Clearing and the Cold River from the W. It follows valleys to the W of the Seward Range at generally easy grades. For much of its distance it parallels Calkins Brook which is, however, frequently referred to as Calkins "Creek." Since all maps show this stream as "Brook," this designation is used throughout for consistency. Except for the first 1.2 mi., this entire route is on gravel roads which are also part of the Cold River Horse Trail system.

The trail begins at the same parking lot, on the road from Coreys, where the Ward Brook approach to Duck Hole begins. (See above for driving directions.) From the trail register at the parking lot (0 mi.), this trail coincides with the trail to Duck Hole for 1.2 mi. to the junction with the Calkins Brook Truck Trail. Turning R, the road climbs at an easy grade to a junction with the horse trail at 1.4 mi. (Trail R leads back to the parking lot. Trail L leads to Ward Brook Truck Trail.) Continuing straight ahead, the Calkins Brook Truck Trail continues climbing at easy grades to a height of land at 2.1 mi., after which the road dips, climbs again, and then begins a gradual, rolling descent. At 3.4 mi. the road comes to the R bank of Calkins Brook, soon crosses and then recrosses the brook at 3.7 mi., and continues the descent. At 4.2 mi. the road climbs sharply and begins a series of slight ups and downs leading to a junction at 4.9 mi. with the Raquette River Horse Trail, which leads 5.5 mi. to the road to Raquette Falls and the parking lot near the bridge over Stony Creek (see below).

Continuing straight ahead, the road makes a rolling descent to a clearing with the two Calkins Brook Lean-tos and a horse barn at 6.1 mi. Swinging L, the road crosses Calkins Brook and begins to climb past a large sand pit. The grades are easy at first, but increase to moderate before reaching a height of land at 7.0 mi. The road now begins a long, gradual descent through occasional small clearings to a larger clearing at 8.1 mi., with a brief view back toward the Seward Range. At 8.8 mi. the road skirts the R side of a large alder swamp with even better views before crossing Boulder Brook at 8.9 mi. and climbing over a small knoll and down to a junction at 9.6 mi. (Trail L leads 200 yds. to Latham Pond where there are a view of the Sewards and some good campsites, but no longer any lean-to.)

Turning R, the road gently descends through a beautiful grove of pines to a junction on the R bank of the Cold River at 10.4 mi.

(Road L leads up along the R bank of the Cold River to two lean-tos. Cold River #3 is 0.4 mi. from this junction and Cold River #4 is 0.6 mi., at the point where the Northville-Placid Trail crosses the Cold River on a suspension bridge.) Turning R at this junction for 200 yds., the road comes to the site of a former lumber bridge over the Cold River. There is a reasonably easy ford just above, and the road climbs the far bank to the site of the former Shattuck Clearing ranger station at 10.6 mi. Like the station at Duck Hole, this structure was removed in 1977 to bring this area into compliance with wilderness area guidelines.

At Shattuck Clearing is a junction with the blue-marked Northville-Placid Trail. Trail R leads 12.5 mi. to Rt. 28N near Long Lake. Trail L leads 0.7 mi. to the suspension bridge over the Cold River and then on to Duck Hole at 11.9 mi. Trail L also leads to the Cold River Horse Trail, which follows the E bank of the Cold River to Duck Hole and connects with another horse trail leading to Newcomb. (See below for descriptions of all these trails.) The Wolf Pond Truck Trail which also leads L from Shattuck Clearing (and is followed for short distances by both the N-P Trail and the Cold River Horse Trail) leads to Rt. 28N, W of Newcomb; but since it crosses the private lands of the Huntington Forest it is closed to the public for hiking and is not an access route to Shattuck Clearing.

Also to the R from Shattuck Clearing is the Pine Point trail, which branches R from the N-P Trail 0.1 mi. from the clearing. It is somewhat overgrown and difficult to follow as it leads 3.0 mi. down the L bank of the Cold River to a point about 1.0 mi. above the mouth of Calkins Brook. The end of this trail is at the upper limit of canoe navigation on the Cold River.

Distances: Parking lot on Coreys Rd. to junction with Calkins Brook Truck Trail, 1.2 mi.; to junction with Raquette River Horse Trail, 4.9 mi.; to Calkins Brook Lean-tos, 6.1 mi.; to Latham Pond junction, 9.6 mi.; to Shattuck Clearing, 10.6 mi. (17.0 km.).

SHATTUCK CLEARING AND CALKINS BROOK
via RAQUETTE RIVER HORSE TRAIL

This approach to the Calkins Brook Horse Trail is 0.6 mi. longer than the one described above, but for those walking from Coreys or for winter travelers when the road is not plowed beyond Stony Creek this road saves 2.8 mi. The trail begins at a parking area on the R side of Coreys Rd., which leaves Rt. 3 12.7 mi. W of the traffic light in Saranac Lake and 2.7 mi. E of the junction of Rtes. 3 and 30 E of Tupper Lake. This road is paved for about 1.5 mi. through the little settlement of Coreys and then turns to gravel, crosses Stony Creek at 2.5 mi., and comes to the parking lot 2.75 mi. from Rt. 3.

From the trail register (0 mi.), the trail follows a gravel road, avoiding a road R 100 yds. from the register, and continues with easy ups and downs, crossing several brooks. At 1.5 mi., where an obscure lumber road goes R toward the river, the trail goes L and climbs away from the river along a small brook. Crossing the brook at 1.7 mi., the trail levels off and at 2.1 mi. comes to a trail leading R to Hemlock Hill Lean-to. Beyond this, the trail dips down to a junction at 2.2 mi. (Trail R crosses Palmer Brook and leads 2.0 mi. to Raquette Falls; see below.)

The horse trail bears L, follows Palmer Brook, and then bears away from it over a hill. Descending to a swamp, the trail crosses Palmer Brook at 2.7 mi. and climbs over another hill and descends to cross a brook at 3.4 mi. This marks the end of the gravel-based road and the beginning of a very muddy section.

Crossing another brook at 3.5 mi., the trail beings a long climb. At 4.6 mi. the trail crosses a small brook and climbs steeply for about 50 yds., after which the grade eases and the trail reaches the top of a pass at 5.1 mi. After a short level stretch, the trail descends steeply to the junction with the Calkins Brook Truck Trail at 5.5 mi. From here it is 1.2 mi. to the Calkins Brook Lean-tos and 5.7 mi. to Shattuck Clearing.

Distances: Parking lot to junction with Raquette Falls Trail, 2.2 mi.; to junction with Calkins Brook Truck Trail, 5.5 mi.; to Calkins Brook Lean-tos, 6.7 mi.; to Shattuck Clearing, 11.2 mi. (18.0 km.).

RAQUETTE FALLS

This spot on the Raquette River is more often visited by canoeists on the route from Long Lake down the Raquette River, but it is also a worthwhile and relatively easy hike. Besides the series of falls on the Raquette River, there are a DEC Interior Outpost, two lean-tos and many good campsites at Raquette Falls.

The trail starts at the same parking lot as the Raquette River Horse Trail and follows the horse trail for the first 2.2 mi. (see above). Turning R at the junction next to Palmer Brook, the trail crosses the brook, climbs over a knoll, and drops down to the edge of a slough of the Raquette River at 2.8 mi. After several more ups and downs, the trail begins a longer climb at 3.5 mi. and reaches the top of a hill at 3.8 mi. The trail now descends some steep switchbacks to the edge of an old clearing and then continues on the flat to a signpost at 4.2 mi. at the junction with the Raquette Falls canoe carry. Trail R leads a few yds. to the river at the lower end of the carry. Trail L leads just over 1 mi. to the upper end of the carry. The best view of the falls is found by going about 100 yds. up the canoe carry and looking for a vague trail leading R to the bank of the river and up along the top of a small gorge. Just up and to the L of the signpost are the DEC Interior Outpost and a large field with the lean-tos located on the edge of the field.

Distances: Parking lot to junction at Palmer Brook, 2.2 mi.; to Raquette Falls, 4.2 mi. (6.8 km.).

SHATTUCK CLEARING FROM LONG LAKE
via NORTHVILLE-PLACID TRAIL

This approach to Shattuck Clearing is a section of the 132-mi. Northville-Placid Trail running from Northville, near the southern boundary of the Adirondack Park, to Lake Placid. This trail is described in full in a separate guidebook, *Guide to Adirondack Trails: Northville-Placid Trail,* published by the Adirondack Mt. Club. The description below and the description of the section from Shattuck Clearing to Duck Hole are adapted from the 1980 edition, written by Bruce Wadsworth. The trail generally follows the E shore of Long Lake for the first 7.5 mi. but is sometimes forced to detour away from the lake to avoid private property. There are several attractive lean-tos and many campsites on the lake in this section, but hikers should be aware that some of the land is private, in particular a large inholding from 5.6 mi. to 7.5 mi.

The trail begins at a parking lot on a side road leading N from Rt. 28N, 1.5 mi. E of the junction of Rtes. 28N and 30 in Long Lake Village. There is a large DEC sign on the highway. At 0.7 mi. up this side road there is a parking area on the R at the top of a hill, and the trail starts just beyond on the R. Leaving the road (0 mi.) the trail descends to a trail register and continues to descend to the outlet to Polliwog Pond at 0.6 mi. Crossing the brook on a wide board bridge, avoid a trail L at 0.9 mi. and cross another brook at 1.1 mi. Just past this brook, an unmarked trail leads L to the two Catlin Bay Lean-tos. The first is visible from the N-P Trail and the second is reached by continuing to the shore of Long Lake and circling L and over a small rise to the lean-to sitting in a beautiful location above the lake.

Continuing straight through the junction, the N-P Trail proceeds over easy ups and downs and soon enters the High Peaks Wilderness Area. At 2.0 mi. the trail bears L and then back R, coming near

Long Lake and following the shore to a sandy beach and stream at 2.4 mi. Swinging away from the lake, the trail climbs, descends, and climbs again to a height of land 200 ft. above the lake at 3.2 mi. Now descending, the trail crosses a brook at 4.0 mi. and comes within view of a large clearing on the L at 4.1 mi., where there are two privies and several side trails. This is Kelley's Point, and two lean-tos are visible on the lakeshore from the clearing. These are perhaps the most attractive lean-tos on this section of trail, but they are heavily used both by hikers and canoeists.

Passing behind the clearing, the N-P Trail reaches a junction at 4.5 mi. with the red-marked trail leading R to Kempshall Mt. Without the tower, which the DEC removed several years ago, there is virtually no view from the summit and this is no longer a worthwhile side trip. The trail L leads a short distance to the lake. Continuing on, the N-P Trail soon joins a wide tote road, crosses a brook at 5.2 mi. and reaches a junction at 5.4 mi., with a side trail leading to the first of two lean-tos at Rodney Point. There is a spring on the L about half way to the lean-to, and a nice sandy beach on the shore makes this a pleasant place to camp. After a short ascent, a less noticeable trail leads L at 5.5 mi. to the second Rodney Point Lean-to.

Just beyond this junction, the N-P Trail leaves state land and crosses several brooks as well as some private water pipes before coming to a muddy bog which it skirts at 6.7 mi. After crossing a small brook at 7.4 mi., the trail comes to a junction at 7.6 mi., with a side trail leading 0.1 mi. L to the two lean-tos at Plumleys. The first lean-to sits on a grassy knoll with a commanding view of the lake, and the second one is 50 yds. further N along the shore. Both lean-tos are attractive camping spots and are worth the side trip even for a lunch break.

Leading out of Plumleys, there is a maze of side trails and hikers must be careful to look for the blue markers. The N-P Trail joins a good tote road, swinging away from the lake, crossing a small brook at 8.0 mi., and then climbing to a height of land at 8.5 mi. Gradually descending from this crest at 9.3 mi., the trail enters a fine stand of white pine developed after a forest fire and differing from the surrounding forest. Just past this stand of pines, the trail crosses a brook flowing out of an open marsh (or vlei) at 9.9 mi.

At 10.2 mi. the N-P Trail reaches a junction with a faint trail leading R to Round Pond. (Still marked with a DEC sign and red markers, this trail reaches this seldom-visited body of water in 0.9 mi.) Continuing past this junction, the trail reaches a wide vlei with a stream crossing made somewhat difficult by the haphazard collection of boards and logs that serves as a bridge. The trail then passes a large clearing on the R and at 10.5 mi. comes to Pine Brook, which is easily crossed on stones. The trail is now pleasant walking to some beaver activity at 11.3 mi., where it abruptly turns L off the tote road to circumvent the beaver pond. Once past this obstacle, the N-P Trail joins a gravel road at 11.7 mi. and turns R and down.

Just after joining the gravel road, the vague Pine Point Trail, also with blue markers, diverges L (see above), but the N-P Trail continues R and down to a junction at Shattuck Clearing at 11.8 mi. The ranger station formerly on this site was removed by the DEC in 1977 to bring this area into compliance with wilderness area guidelines. The gravel road L from the junction is the Calkins Brook Truck Trail which leads to a ford of the Cold River and on to Coreys in 10.6 mi. (see above). The gravel road R is the continuation of the N-P Trail to Duck Hole as well as the Cold River Horse Trail (see below). The Wolf Pond Truck Trail which also leads R from Shattuck Clearing (and is followed for short distances by both the N-P Trail and the Cold River Horse Trail) leads to Rt. 28N, W of Newcomb; but since it crosses the private lands of the Huntington Forest it is closed to the public for hiking and is not an access route to Shattuck Clearing.

Distances: Parking lot to Catlin Bay Lean-tos, 1.1 mi.; to Kelley's Point Lean-tos, 4.1 mi.; to first Rodney Point Lean-to, 5.4 mi.; to trail to Plumleys (two lean-tos), 7.6 mi.; to Round Pond trail junction, 10.2 mi.; to Shattuck Clearing, 11.8 mi. (19.0 km.).

DUCK HOLE FROM SHATTUCK CLEARING
via NORTHVILLE-PLACID TRAIL

This section of the N-P Trail generally follows the NE bank of the Cold River to Duck Hole. This is the wildest section of the entire trail, with the trailless Seward and Santanoni Ranges flanking the valley of the Cold River. Leaving the junction at Shattuck Clearing (0 mi.), the N-P Trail bears slightly R on a gravel road to a somewhat obscure L turn off the road at 0.2 mi. There is a small clearing and campsite at this turn. The trail soon crosses a suspension bridge over Moose Creek, with a good view of the Santanoni Range from the bridge. Beyond this bridge, a pleasant trail leads to another suspension bridge over the Cold River at 0.7 mi., from which there is also a good view of the Santanonis. At the far side, the trail comes to a junction with a trail leading L a few yards to Cold River Lean-to #4. Just beyond this junction, the N-P Trail joins a gravel lumber road. (Cold River Lean-to #3 is 0.2 mi. to the L on this road, which continues on to connect with the Calkins Brook Truck Trail and is also an alternative route from Shattuck Clearing.) The N-P Trail turns R on this gravel lumber road, which was constructed in the early 1950s to allow lumbermen to clean up some of the terrific damage left by the 1950 hurricane. This area is now quite open and there are many views of the surrounding peaks for the next several miles.

After one short descent and climb, the trail descends to the Cold River at a large pool, known as Big Eddy, at 2.0 mi. An interesting falls drops into this pool and the water turns gracefully in its eddy. Beyond Big Eddy, the road climbs away from the river, crosses a brook on a bridge at 3.1 mi., and after a short, steep climb the trail turns sharp R and leaves the gravel road at 3.6 mi. The trail descends steeply and crosses two steep gullies before reaching Seward Lean-to at 4.0 mi.

Just above the lean-to, a large outcrop of rock forms a natural dam called Miller's Falls, where one can swim. Just below the falls, a dark gray dike cuts through the lighter-colored anorthosite granite, and several potholes have been carved in the bedrock. Past the lean-to, the trail again climbs a steep bank to an open area above the river at 4.2 mi. and then descends to the river at 4.4 mi. Now following the river closely, the trail crosses a grassy, muddy stretch at 5.3 mi. and at 5.7 mi. a painted tree indicates a nearby benchmark (PBM 1876) located on a boulder 25 ft. E of the trail. Crossing first a smaller brook, the trail crosses Ouluska Brook at 6.1 mi. and reaches Ouluska Lean-to just beyond at 6.2 mi.

Beyond the lean-to, the trail follows the Cold River to a sharp bend in the river where the trail climbs away from the river and an old lumber road enters from the L at 6.6 mi. Almost immediately, however, the trail swings sharp R away from the road and climbs gradually to the top of a knoll which was the site of Noah John Rondeau's "Hermitage." It was on this high, open bluff that Rondeau lived off and on (mostly on) from 1915 to 1950. He built two diminutive cabins and developed a unique life style that has been the subject of a book and numerous articles. He left the woods briefly in 1947 to appear at the New York Sportsman's Show, where he became the feature attraction. Leaving the woods for good during the 1950 hurricane, he continued to appear at other sportsman's shows, dying in Lake Placid in 1967 at the age of 84.

From Rondeau's, the trail turns sharp L and down across a small valley and then descends gradually to the old lumber road. At 7.0

mi. a newer but badly overgrown lumber roads goes R; it was once a connection to a lumber bridge over the Cold River to the Cold River Horse Trail on the SE bank. Continuing straight ahead, the N-P Trail begins climbing, passing a yellow boundary post marking one's passage from Essex to Franklin County, and coming to a large brook which is crossed on stones at 7.5 mi. The trail continues to climb, and an old tote road enters from the L at 7.8 mi. (This overgrown but followable road leads to the old lumber clearing at the base of Emmons and is a possible access to the Sewards. See "Peaks Without Maintained Trails.")

Just past this old road, the trail swings R, levels off, and begins to descend at 8.0 mi., with a pond visible to the L. With one short interruption, the descent continues to a large brook at 8.7 mi. Crossing this brook, the trail climbs briefly and then continues to descend to another large brook at 9.3 mi., with a small clearing on the far side. Heading across the clearing, the trail soon reaches the R bank of the outlet to Mountain Pond, climbs along the bank, and crosses the brook on a bridge at 9.6 mi. Just beyond, the pond is visible to the L and a series of small ups and downs leads to the junction with the Ward Brook Truck Trail at 10.3 mi. (Trail L with red markers leads 8.7 mi. to parking lot at end of Coreys Rd.; see above.)

Turning R and now with red and blue markers, the trail comes to the two Cold River Lean-tos (Nos. 1 and 2) at 10.7 mi. Just past the lean-tos, the trail crosses Moose Creek just above its confluence with the Cold River, climbs the far bank, and then follows along the R bank of the Cold River to a junction at 11.0 mi. (Horse trail R fords the Cold River and continues down the E side of the river to Shattuck Clearing with a connection to the Santanoni Preserve and Newcomb; see below.)

Past this junction, the trail climbs over a low ridge and arrives at the trail junction and former site of the ranger station at 11.9 mi.

Blue trail R crosses the dam and leads to Bradley Pond and the road
below Upper Works (see above). Trail bearing L with blue and red
markers is the continuation of the N-P Trail leading to Lake Placid
(see Northern Section) and with a connection to a trail leading to
Henderson Lake and Upper Works (see above). There are two
lean-tos and several good campsites at Duck Hole. One lean-to is
located by the dam and the other is 100 yds. E of the dam on a
beautiful wooded point.

Distances: Shattuck Clearing to turnoff for Cold River Lean-tos
Nos. 3 & 4, 0.7 mi.; Seward Lean-to, 4.0 mi.; Ouluska Lean-to, 6.2
mi.; Rondeau's Hermitage, 6.7 mi.; junction with Ward Brook
Truck Trail, 10.3 mi.; Cold River Lean-tos Nos. 1 & 2, 10.7 mi.;
Duck Hole, 11.9 mi. (19.1 km.).

COLD RIVER HORSE TRAIL FROM
SHATTUCK CLEARING TO WARD BROOK TRUCK TRAIL

This seldom-used section of the Cold River Horse Trail System
travels through low, rolling terrain SE of the Cold River. For much
of its length, it follows an old gravel lumber road and is delightfully
easy walking through spectacularly remote country where solitude
is practically guaranteed. The final mile leading to the Ward Brook
Truck Trail, however, is unfortunately quite wet and rather
unpleasant to walk, with the additional problem that there is no
bridge over the Cold River at the N end of the trail, and crossing
could be difficult in high water.

From the junction at the former site of the ranger station at
Shattuck Clearing (0 mi.), the horse trail follows the gravel road SE
for 0.8 mi., where it turns L onto another gravel road. (Road
straight ahead is the Wolf Pond Truck Trail, which is closed to the
public where it enters private land just over 1 mi. beyond.) From
this junction, the trail descends at a gentle grade to Moose Pond

Stream at 1.8 mi., with two lean-tos on the far side.

Past the lean-tos, the trail climbs at easy to moderate grades to a junction at 2.6 mi. (Trail straight ahead with blue horse trail markers leads to Moose Pond and Newcomb; see below.) Turning sharp L, the Cold River Horse Trail descends in gradual rolls to an open area at an old gravel pit at 3.5 mi. and passes a pond on the L at 4.7 mi. Continuing along with short ups and downs, there is a good view of the Seward Range at 5.3 mi.; at 6.9 mi., just before crossing a large stream, the trail comes to a junction. (Red trail R is unmaintained foot trail to Newcomb Lake; see below.) Continuing straight ahead, the trail reaches another junction at 7.8 mi. (Abandoned trail L follows an old lumber road to a ford of the Cold River and on to the N-P Trail.)

Swinging R, the trail comes to Northern Lean-tos at 8.2 mi. Shortly beyond these lean-tos, the gravel-based road swings R while the horse trail continues straight ahead and becomes quite wet, remaining so nearly all the way to the crossing of the Cold River at 10.1 mi. and the junction with the Ward Brook Truck Trail just beyond. To the R it is 0.9 mi. to Duck Hole and to the L 0.3 mi. to the Cold River Lean-tos.

Distances: Shattuck Clearing to turnoff from Wolf Pond Truck Trail, 0.8 mi.; to Moose Pond Stream Lean-tos, 1.8 mi.; to junction with Moose Pond Horse Trail, 2.6 mi.; to Northern Lean-tos, 8.2 mi.; to Ward Brook Truck Trail, 10.2 mi. (16.4 km.).

THE SANTANONI PRESERVE

This tract of land was transferred from private ownership to the State of New York in 1972 through the efforts of the Adirondack Conservancy. Most of this land is now part of the High Peaks Wilderness Area and provides a SE approach to the Cold River area. This area has so far received very little use even though it offers some outstanding opportunities for hiking, fishing, horse-back riding, and skiing. The centerpiece of the area is two-mile-long Newcomb Lake, which has two lean-tos and many campsites along its pristine shores.

Remaining from the days of private ownership are two roads leading to Newcomb Lake and Moose Pond, as well as a huge log structure known as Camp Santanoni on the NE shore of Newcomb Lake. The road to Newcomb Lake is still hard packed and suitable for bicycles, and some people have used various wheeled carriers to transport boats to Newcomb Lake via this road. At one time boats were available for rent on Newcomb Lake, but this is no longer the case. No special camping permits are now required, although of course the normal restrictions that apply to camping on any state land still apply.

The trails described below all start from the gatehouse of the Santanoni Preserve, on a road that leaves Rt. 28N 0.3 mi. W of the Town Hall in the village of Newcomb. A small sign for the Santanoni Preserve marks this road which crosses a narrow iron bridge, passes the stone gatehouse on the R and comes to a small parking area on the R at the top of a hill, 0.3 mi. from Rt. 28N.

ROAD TO NEWCOMB LAKE AND CAMP SANTANONI

This wide gravel road leads at easy grades from the gatehouse near Newcomb to Camp Santanoni, a now abandoned "great camp" at the E end of Newcomb Lake. From the trail register (0 mi.), the road is practically level to some old farm buildings at 0.9 mi. Past the farm, the road swings L and up to an open field at 1.1 mi., where one can see the Santanonis. Descending slightly, the road comes to a beautiful moss-covered stone bridge and begins a steady, gradual climb to a junction at 2.2 mi. (Road L leads to Moose Pond and the Cold River Horse Trail; see below.)

Turning R, the grade soon eases and the road begins a gentle descent across a side hill with more beautiful stone work and some glimpses of the Santanonis through the trees. At 3.6 mi. the red-marked trail along the S side of Newcomb Lake branches L (see below), after which the road drops down to a picnic area on the S shore of the lake at 3.9 mi. Swinging R, the road crosses a bridge and then swings back L along the NE side of a narrow channel and on to Camp Santanoni at the E end of Newcomb Lake at 4.5 mi. This immense, rambling log structure plus numerous out-buildings was built by the Pruyn family of Albany, using material cut on the site. It is slated for eventual removal because four-walled structures are not permitted on Forest Preserve lands, but for now it is a sight to behold and well worth the hike just to see it and to picnic on the shore of this lovely lake.

Distances: Trail register near gatehouse to junction with Moose Pond Road, 2.2 mi.; to foot trail along S shore, 3.6 mi.; to picnic area on S shore, 3.9 mi.; to Camp Santanoni, 4.5 mi. (7.2 km.).

FOOT TRAIL FROM NEWCOMB LAKE TO SHAW POND AND COLD RIVER HORSE TRAIL

This trail leads from the road along the S shore of Newcomb Lake, giving access to a lean-to on the lake shore. It then continues NW toward the Cold River. Since its construction in 1976, it has received very little use and even less maintenance beyond the W end of Newcomb Lake. It is now quite obscure in spots, and following it requires great care. The section from Shaw Pond (near Moose Pond) to the Cold River Horse Trail is particularly obscure and, being somewhat redundant due to the nearly parallel Moose Pond Horse Trail, will probably be officially abandoned in the near future. The section from Newcomb Lake to Shaw Pond as described below will probably remain open since it provides a useful connection from the beautiful camping areas on Newcomb Lake to Moose Pond and the Cold River area.

The trail with red markers starts 3.6 mi. up the road to Newcomb Lake (see above). From the road (0 mi.), the trail drops down and soon joins an old road which follows a broad shelf above a swamp. After a steep descent at 0.7 mi. the trail crosses one brook and begins a rolling descent to a second brook crossing at 1.0 mi., with a beaver dam to the L and a large open area to the R. At 1.2 mi. a side trail with blue markers branches R and leads 300 yds. to a lean-to on a beautiful rocky point on the S shore of Newcomb Lake. This is one of the nicest campsites anywhere.

Continuing on the flat, the trail comes to a small ladder leading down to a bridge over the main inlet to the lake at 1.8 mi. Some care is needed to follow the trail through the thick alders beyond the bridge. Climbing the far bank, the trail comes to a junction at 1.9 mi. (Yellow trail R leads along N shore of lake to a lean-to and the end of the road at Camp Santanoni; see below.) Beyond this junction, the trail is flat through a thicket of fir trees next to an extensive open swamp until it swings R and up at 2.6 mi. The trail now follows a series of old roads with several sharp turns which, though marked with a few disks, requires close attention. At 2.8 mi. the trail crosses a large beaver dam and meadow and joins an old, grassy road which slowly swings L around a large swamp.

Taking a sharp R off this road at 3.5 mi., the trail joins another old road, which it follows up and down along a side hill to the L bank of a large stream at 4.1 mi. The trail now swings sharp R without crossing the stream and follows another vague road. At 4.2 mi. the trail joins a slightly better road and goes R and up some steep to moderate grades; the trail leaves the road, becomes a foot path and comes to a crest at 4.5 mi. Continuing to a higher crest at 4.6 mi., the trail now descends, crosses a brook, and comes within sight of Shaw Pond at 5.1 mi. Proceeding along the W shore of the pond, the trail reaches a large beaver dam at the outlet at 5.4 mi.

The marked trail continues across this dam and along the SW slopes of Little Santanoni and Couchsachraga to the Cold River Horse Trail at about 12.5 mi. As stated above, this final section of trail is practically non-existent and will probably soon be officially abandoned. However, an easy bushwhack of less than 0.1 mi. to the L from the end of the beaver dam, along the L edge of the open marsh, leads to the Moose Pond Horse Trail, 0.2 mi. beyond Moose Pond. It is only about 2.5 mi. longer to Northern Lean-tos or the Ward Brook Truck Trail via the Moose Pond and Cold River Horse Trails than by the foot trail, and the walking is far easier. (See below for description of Moose Pond Horse Trail leading to the Cold River Horse Trail.)

Distances: Santanoni Preserve gatehouse to turnoff from road to Newcomb Lake, 3.6 mi.; to turnoff to lean-to, 4.8 mi.; to junction with trail on N shore of Newcomb Lake, 5.5 mi.; to Shaw Pond, 9.0 mi. (14.5 km.).

TRAIL ALONG N SHORE OF NEWCOMB LAKE

This trail leads from Camp Santanoni past several campsites and on to the Ward Pond Brook Lean-to and a junction with the S shore trail leading to Shaw Pond. Starting from Camp Santanoni (0 mi.) at the end of the road to Newcomb Lake (see above), the trail goes past some out-buildings to the E shore of the lake. There are no signs or markers at the start, but the route is obvious next to the shore past a campsite, an old bath house at a small beach, and on to some campsites near the mouth of Sucker Brook at 0.3 mi. From these campsites, the trail swings R and up to an old lumber road where it turns L, crosses Sucker Brook, and now with a few yellow markers climbs to a crest at 0.7 mi. Continuing to follow the lumber road, the trail descends, climbs over another hill and descends to

Santanoni Brook at 1.5 mi. The road ends past this brook, but the
trail continues on the flat to Ward Pond Brook Lean-to on the N
shore of the lake at 1.6 mi. This little-used lean-to is in excellent
condition and is nearly as nice a site as its companion lean-to on the
S shore. Passing behind the lean-to, the trail continues on the flat to
the junction with the S shore trail at 2.3 mi.

Distances: Camp Santanoni to campsites on Sucker Brook, 0.3
mi.; to Ward Pond Brook Lean-to, 1.6 mi.; to junction with S shore
trail, 2.3 mi. (3.7 km.).

MOOSE POND HORSE TRAIL

Following good road for most of its distance, this trail provides
access to some nice campsites on Moose Pond and then connects
with the Cold River Horse Trail System. From the Santanoni
Preserve gatehouse (0 mi.), follow the road to Newcomb Lake to
the junction at 2.2 mi. Turning L, the road is gently rolling until it
begins a steady descent at 3.6 mi. Crossing a brook at the bottom of
the descent, the road swings R and climbs gently to a large clearing
at 4.7 mi. There are some good views as the road climbs up through
this large open area. After some more gently rolling terrain, the
road enters another clearing at 6.0 mi. Turning L, the road climbs a
steady, moderate grade to a height of land and then descends to a
junction near Moose Pond at 6.7 mi. (Road L leads 0.2 mi. to two
campsites on Moose Pond.) Bearing R, the road (now marked with
blue horse trail disks) passes several large open swamps, crosses
Ermine Brook at 8.1 mi., and swings L. The road now goes up and
down along a side hill above the outlet to Moose Pond before
dropping steeply down to Calahan Brook at 10.4 mi. This is the end
of the gravel road.

The trail now climbs moderately to an old lumber road at 10.7
mi., turns sharp R and continues climbing to a better road at 10.9

mi. Again turning sharp R, the trail follows this sometimes muddy road along a gently rolling profile to the junction with the Cold River Horse Trail at 11.8 mi. (Trail straight ahead leads to Moose Pond Stream Lean-tos and Shattuck Clearing. Trail R leads to Northern Lean-tos and Duck Hole.)

Distances: Santanoni Preserve gatehouse to turnoff from road to Newcomb Lake, 2.2 mi.; to Moose Pond, 6.7 mi.; to junction with Cold River Horse Trail, 11.8 mi. (19.0 km.).

GOODNOW MT.

Although not technically in the the High Peaks Region, this fire tower peak is included in this guide because it offers a marvelous view of many of the high peaks. This trail is entirely on the private land of the Huntington Forest, owned by the College of Environmental Science and Forestry in Syracuse. The trail is closed from October 15 to the end of the big game season. Originally constructed as a bridle path, it has been beautifully maintained by the staff of the Huntington Forest. This staff has also continued to maintain the tower (now officially abandoned by the DEC).

The trail starts on Rt. 28N, 3.6 mi. W of the Newcomb Town Hall in the village of Newcomb, and 10.8 mi. E of Long Lake (see map, page 260). A small DEC sign marks the start, with red markers beyond. From the road (0 mi.), the trail starts on the flat past some lumber roads and then moderately up along a phone line. At 0.3 mi. the trail swings R away from the phone line on a gradual grade, and then switchbacks L to rejoin the phone line at the top of a ridge. After descending slightly, the trail soon climbs again, switchbacks L and then R, and arrives at a flat notch at 1.1 mi., with a well and old horse barn just beyond on the R. Climbing gradually to the crest of the ridge, the trail dips and then climbs easily to the tower at the summit at 1.5 mi. There are some views to the E and S without

Goodnow Mt.
Base map is Newcomb quadrangle, 15 min. series, 1954.

climbing the tower, but from the tower one can see 23 major peaks with the Santanoni Range, Algonquin and Marcy particularly prominent.

Distance: Rt. 28N to summit of Goodnow Mt., 1.5 mi. (2.41 km.). Ascent from road, 1040 ft. (317 m.). Elevation, 2685 ft. (818 m.).

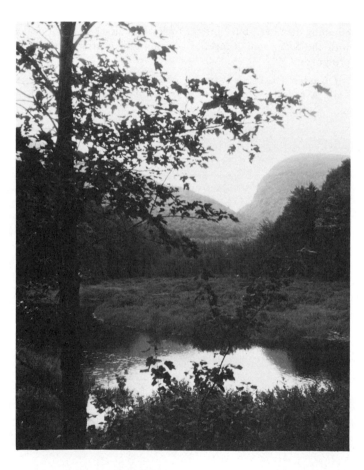

Wallface from Scott Clearing
Photo by Tom Dunn

PEAKS WITHOUT MAINTAINED TRAILS

Of the 46 peaks in the Adirondacks determined to be 4000 feet or more above sea level by the United States Geological Survey at the turn of this century, 20 of them lack trails. Though all of them now possess rough paths beaten out by many climbers, these herd paths are not marked. Because of recent blowdowns and the resulting creation of false herd paths, ascents of these peaks still call for considerable route-finding and tracking skills.

The present interest in trailless climbing dates back to Robert and George Marshall, who in 1924, with their friend and guide Herbert Clark, completed climbing the 46 peaks indicated as over 4000 feet on USGS maps available at that time. Since then, following completed ascents of the same mountains nine years later by Fay Loope, thousands of recreationists have sought out this special outdoor activity. These mountaineers have organized a unique climbing society known as the Adirondack Forty-Sixers. They have their own articles of organization, by-laws, and a distinctive shoulder patch. The Forty-Sixers meet twice a year at places like Adirondak Loj or Johns Brook Lodge, and publish a newsletter known as *Adirondack Peeks.*

The Forty-Sixers also maintain metal canisters on the summits of trailless peaks; inside each canister is a notebook in which each climber should register. Hikers should be careful to close the lid on the canister after they have registered.

In deciding what constituted an individual peak, the Marshalls set an arbitrary rule that it should rise 300 ft. on all sides or be at the end of a ridge at least 0.75 mi. from the nearest peak. Since then, more recent surveys using better equipment and aerial photography have indicated that four of the peaks — Blake, Cliff, Nye and Couchsachraga — are under 4000 ft., and that some peaks fail to qualify if the above rule on separate peaks is strictly applied to the new survey data. The same (1953) survey raised MacNaughton Mountain, originally indicated as being 3976 ft., to the 4000-foot peerage. But the most recent survey, in 1979, which produced the 1:25,000 scale 7.5-by-15 minute metric scale maps, lowered the mountain once again below the 4000-ft. line.

Since the Adirondack Forty-Sixers was founded to bring together those who had climbed the same 46 peaks climbed by the Marshalls and Herb Clark, it has been resolved that the climbing of these same 46 peaks, regardless of their corrected elevations, shall still be considered a prerequisite for membership in that organization. Technically, however, climbers of the 108 four thousand footers in the Northeastern United States are correct in recognizing only 42 peaks in the Adirondacks over 4000 ft.

If you seriously intend to become a Forty-Sixer, write to The Adirondack Forty-Sixers, Adirondack, N.Y. 12808. It is not necessary to belong to the Adirondack Mountain Club (in fact the "46ers" and the ADK are completely separate organizations), but many Forty-Sixers are also members of ADK.

Climbing the peaks without maintained trails calls for leadership by people who are experienced in map reading and use of the compass and who possess a feeling for route-finding in forested mountain terrain. Fog and rain can complicate staying on course, and dealing with injuries and illness is obviously more difficult away from formal trails. Know the location of all trails in the vicinity of a climb. Know your mountain peaks and be able to recognize them from any viewpoint. *Before* you make your trip, learn to read a topographic map and to use a compass. (Magnetic N is about 15′ W of true N in this area.) Carry with you a guidebook, USGS topographic map, compass, flashlight with extra batteries and bulb, first-aid kit, insect repellant, matches and extra food, and clothing designed to keep you as dry and warm as possible in case bad weather sets in and you are forced to spend the night out.

Climbers of these peaks without maintained trails have a special obligation not to climb alone, to sign *in* as well as *out* at all DEC registers on approach trails, and to let other responsible people know of planned climbing routes. Such consideration is due the people who might have to participate in a rescue party.

It has been Adirondack Mountain Club policy, and more recently DEC policy, to favor keeping a considerable number of Adirondack peaks free from the construction of formal trails so that those desiring it may enjoy the adventure of route-finding on their own in less frequented areas. Climbers of these peaks have taken pains to leave the routes, bivouac areas, and summits as free as possible of human presence. This includes refraining from placing any markings such as blazes or surveyor's flagging along the route, as climbers are expected to be able to find their own way back to civilization. To hold erosion to a minimum, climbers are asked to keep to a single herd path wherever possible. Most eroded sections are by now fairly well stabilized. Making new herd paths creates more erosion.

The following are brief, general descriptions of routes on the peaks without trails.

COLD RIVER AREA

Seymour. This peak was named for Horatio Seymour, several times governor of New York. The popular route ascends the first brook 0.10 mi. SE of Ward Brook Lean-to. The most westerly branch leads to an easily ascended slide, above which the going is easy to the top of the ridge. Follow the ridge SW to the summit. Ascent from the SW by way of Ouluska Pass Brook is more difficult because of blowdown. Descent into Ouluska Pass, the col between Seymour and Seward, is complicated because of blowdown and cliffs.

Seward, Donaldson and Emmons. Seward was named for William Henry Seward, who succeeded William L. Marcy as governor. He was one of the founders of the Republican Party and Secretary of State in Lincoln's cabinet. Donaldson, the first Adirondack peak to be named during the 20th century, stands as a monument to Alfred Lee Donaldson, who wrote the first and most complete history of the Adirondacks. The southernmost peak in the Seward Range honors the memory of Ebenezer Emmons, state geologist and leader of the 1837 expedition which made the first ascent of Mt. Marcy, and the man who gave the name "Adirondacks" to this mountain region.

The usual route to Seward begins at the bridge 0.23 mi. SE of the clearing where the red foot trail from Coreys-Axton joins the fire truck trail. This is the third bridge NW of Ward Brook Lean-to. After starting on the E side of the brook, follow traces of old tote roads on the W side to the end of the second growth where blowdown begins. Avoid the ridge to the W. For easier going, climb part way up the ridge to the E, eventually striking the NE ridge of Seward, which leads to the summit. Present herd paths descend to the S flanks of the western Seward ridge, reaching Donaldson more or less on a compass line from Seward's summit. For Emmons from Donaldson, stay on the ridge to the col, then drop to the W to avoid blowdown, returning to the Emmons ridge as soon as practical.

Today, most people reaching Emmons over Seward and Donaldson from the Ward Brook Lean-to area find it easier to return by retracing their steps over the latter two peaks. There are other alternatives. The return through Ouluska Pass is complicated by blowdown. The descent via Calkins Brook has some difficult sections. The return via the Northville-Placid Trail and the Duck Hole Truck Road takes about the same time as returning over Donaldson and Seward, but this route, formerly the usual route chosen, is now more difficult to find because once-open lumber roads are now badly overgrown.

To descend to the Northville-Placid Trail, find a herd path leaving the ridge about 0.25 mi. N of the Emmons summit. This route descends through blowdown into the valley leading SE to a brook from Ouluska Pass (which is located between Seward and Seymour). About 0.25 mi. up Ouluska Brook from its junction with the brook from Emmons, find a large lumber clearing. (A R turn will lead down Ouluska Pass Brook to the Northville-Placid Trail and Ouluska Pass Lean-to on the Cold River about 0.5 mi. S of the Rondeau hermitage site.) From the SE edge of this clearing an overgrown lumber road heads SE and E in about a mile to the Northville-Placid Trail at a point 0.9 mi. NE of the former Noah John Rondeau hermitage.

A more difficult route to the Seward Range is from the W by way of Calkins Brook. This stream is reached from Coreys and Axton by way of the trail to the Ward Brook area and the Calkins Brook Truck Trail. (See Southern Section.) Avoid striking directly for Emmons from the head of the Calkins Brook. It is easier to cross over the summit of Donaldson.

Santanoni. The name of the highest peak W of the Hudson River, and the dominating one in its range, is derived from the name Saint Anthony; it filtered down through the French Canadians to the Abenaki Indians, who adopted their own pronunciation of the word. The traditional approach was a herd path starting 3.41 mi. from the old Tahawus Club road on the trail to Duck Hole via Bradley Pond (see Southern Section); but being on private land, this route is now closed to the public. A legal route, and currently the most used, leaves the above-mentioned trail crossing a beaver dam at about 4.00 mi. from the old Tahawus Club road and about 0.25 mi. S of the Santanoni Lean-to. Following a survey line past the northern end of Bradley Pond, it climbs steeply over rough terrain to state land about a third of the way up Panther

Mountain, beyond which a herd path contours westerly some 0.25 mi. to the brook descending from the Panther-Santanoni ridge. A half mile of rock hopping up the brook leads to a herd path which reaches the above-mentioned ridge about 0.5 mi. south of the summit of Panther at the point where a herd path leads W down a ridge to Couchsachraga. The route to Santanoni leads S along the ridge, a distance of more than a mile.

Panther. The most used route to Panther's attractive summit employs the approach described above for Santanoni. It turns N at the top of the ridge, the distance from this point to Panther's summit being about 0.50 mi.

Couchsachraga. Pronounced "Kook-sa-kra-ga," this term is an ancient Algonquin name for the Adirondacks which means "dismal wilderness." Most people today reach Couchsachraga by way of herd paths leading W down the long ridge from the point 0.5 mi. S of Panther's summit where the route from the trail to Duck Hole via Bradley Pond strikes the ridge. Travel from the Panther-Santanoni ridge to Couchsachraga can take two hours or more. The easiest way back from Couchsachraga to the above-mentioned trail is to return by the same route.

Another approach is from the Cold River area up a stream crossed by the horse trail about 5.50 mi. E of Shattuck Clearing and 4.00 mi. SW of the Northville-Placid Trail NW of Duck Hole. (See Southern Section.) A rarely used trail from the Santanoni Preserve joins the horse trail at this point. Follow up the stream past a beaver swamp and up a grade beyond, avoiding the first tributary from the SW beyond the top of the grade. Following the second tributary's most westerly branch to near the Little Couchsachraga-Couchsachraga col, strike upwards SE to the summit. There are at present no continuous herd paths on the route, which calls for alert route-finding.

MacNaughton. MacNaughton is named after James MacNaughton, grandson of Archibald McIntyre, who headed the original Adirondack Iron Works. Though not officially one of the forty-six peaks, it is the one mountain to be raised to the 4000-ft. status on the 1953 USGS map. The upper reaches of the mountain are almost completely covered with blowdown. Leave the Henderson Lake-Duck Hole Trail at the brook crossing beyond the beaver pond about 0.60 mi. NW of Hunter Pond. (See Southern Section.) Follow the SE side of the brook valley nearly to the summit ridge. Climb N over two summits to the register on the third and NW summit. All three summits are about the same height, the middle one having a good view.

Two other routes to MacNaughton are popular. One is from the Wallface Ponds on a compass line generally SW; the other is from Indian Pass following the outlet to the Wallface Ponds, bearing generally NW from the flat swampy area above the steeper descent of the outlet. There are no plain herd paths on MacNaughton. Cripplebrush is thick and blowdowns are numerous.

HEART LAKE AREA

Table Top. The popular routes up Table Top leave Marcy Brook either just above Indian Falls on the Van Hoevenberg Trail to Marcy from Adirondak Loj, or from a point about 0.30 mi. further up the brook. Head E or NE from the starting points to the summit. Detour the summit blowdown (though a herd path of sorts now cuts straight through it) by skirting it to the NW.

Street and Nye. Colvin named the first peak in honor of Alfred Billings Street, New York State Law Librarian and author of the book *The Indian Pass*. The latter peak bears the name of William B. Nye, the well-known North Elba guide, best known for having carried Matilda across the "Hitch-Up Matilda" ford on Avalanche

Lake. Leaving the Indian Pass Trail at the W corner of Heart Lake (see Heart Lake Section), follow the old Nye Ski Trail to Indian Pass Brook. Descend Indian Pass Brook to the first tributary entering from the L (W). Follow the herd paths along this brook into the basin E of, and separated by a ridge from, the summit of Nye. The best herd path as of 1984 leads to a col on the ridge S of this basin. It then turns W, climbs steeply to the ridge top extending NE from Street, follows it toward Street a short distance, and then descends westerly to join the herd path between Street and Nye. Turn N for Nye and S for Street on a herd path descending to an attractive vlei and then reaching Street by staying W of the Street-Nye ridge top.

The easiest routes from Rocky Falls involve flanking the base of Street away from Indian Pass Brook to join the regular herd paths, though Street may also be climbed by various "direct assault" routes above the lean-to.

A beautiful but longer approach to Street and Nye lies up the valley above Wanika Falls, reached from Lake Placid via the Northville-Placid Trail. (See Northern Section.) From Wanika Falls follow the larger, more easterly branch of Wanika Falls Brook (the headwaters of the Chubb River) and stick to the flanks of Nye in the brook's upper reaches.

Esther Mountain. This major peak N of Whiteface has in the past been listed as a peak with a trail in the Lake Placid section of the guidebook. The ski trails once cut to its summit, however, are now so overgrown that they are somewhat difficult to follow — showing that nature "reclaims its own" rapidly when man does not interfere by maintaining trails.

This most northern of the major Adirondack peaks was named for Esther McComb, who in 1839, at the age of 15, became lost while trying to climb Whiteface from the N, and made the first recorded ascent of this mountain instead. A tablet to her memory was placed on the summit in 1939 by the Forty-Sixers.

Take the Wilmington-Whiteface Trail (see Northern Section) to the junction at 3.44 mi. where the latter trail begins to flank the sides of the hump known as Lookout Mountain. Leaving the red-marked trail (0 mi.) where an old illegible sign points NW, a herd path to Esther ascends to the summit of Lookout Mountain at 0.4 mi. where a ski lodge once stood. From here, the route to Esther descends into a col at 0.7 mi. and continues N along the ridge to Esther's summit at 1.3 mi. from the Whiteface Trail.

ELK LAKE AREA

Macomb, South Dix, East Dix, Hough. Macomb honors the memory of Alexander Macomb, who defeated the British in the Battle of Plattsburgh on September 11, 1814. Hough bears the name of one of the early Adirondack conservationists, Franklin B. Hough (pronounced "Huff").

The most popular route up Macomb follows the great slide of 1947. Take the Elk Lake-Dix Trail (see Southern Section) to Slide Brook, divided at this point into two channels some 100 yds. apart, beyond which there is a lean-to. Follow the brook easterly for about 0.60 mi. to the first tributary of significance which comes in from the SE. Ignoring a false herd path and secondary tributary joining the key tributary from the S, follow the key tributary about 0.75 mi. to the first major slide descending from the NE. Above the brook, the going is steep and covered with dangerous loose rock and dirt. Beyond the first pitch, however, it is less steep and the footing improves. The slide leads to the base of the cliffs below the summit of Macomb's South Peak. A fine herd path bypasses these cliffs on the north side, leading to the ridge connecting the South Peak and Macomb's summit. (Be sure to walk a few yds. south to the top of the South Peak for an excellent view.) The summit of Macomb is about 0.50 mi. N over a well-worn herd path.

Macomb may also be climbed by following the main valley of Slide Brook to the ridge N of the summit. A large slide descending to the upper reaches of the brook offers a feasible route half-way up the summit ridge, above which a herd path leads to the ridge top N of the summit.

Another possible route follows the valley of West Mill Brook up from Rt. 9 near North Hudson. (See Eastern Section for description of approaches to West Mill Brook under Northway.)

From Macomb to South Dix, the going is easy, following the height of land and up spectacular open rocks below South Dix's summit. From South Dix to East Dix is likewise an easy walk of about an hour over a good herd path. Going from South Dix to Hough, skirt the blowdown just N of the South Dix summit on its W side and then climb the hogback between South Dix and Hough. There is a bivouac site in the col between the hogback and Hough (with wet-weather water available). From Hough to Dix, continue along the ridge to the Beckhorn of Dix.

Good descent routes to the Elk Lake-Dix Trail lead from the col between Macomb and South Dix, and from the col between the S side of Hough and the hogback. Herd paths lead along Lillian Brook and then follow an old lumber road to the height of land on the Elk Lake-Dix Trail between the Slide and Lillian Brook valleys (0.70 mi. N of Slide Brook Lean-to).

The Dixes may also be climbed from the NE via the North and South Forks of the Boquet River (see Eastern Section). Another very interesting approach to East Dix is from the E via Lindsay Brook. (The route to and under the Northway connecting with the valley of Lindsay Brook is described in the Eastern Section of the guidebook.)

SANFORD LAKE AREA

Marshall (Clinton or Herbert). Colvin named this peak in honor of Governor DeWitt Clinton. He at first attached the name to the peak we now call Iroquois, but later transferred it to the southernmost peak of the MacIntyre Range. ADKers have called it Herbert in honor of Herbert Clark, and the Adirondack Forty-Sixers call it Marshall for Robert Marshall, who died in 1939. The latter name is now officially approved by the New York State Board of Geographic Names, but it is labeled "Clinton" on the 1954 USGS maps. The 1978 USGS "Ampersand Lake" 7.5-by-15 minute metric series sheet, however, does show this peak as "Mt. Marshall."

The lean-tos around Lake Colden and Flowed Lands make good bases for climbing this mountain. The map would suggest that the best route to Marshall is via the yellow DEC trail from Lake Colden to the Indian Pass Trail. Bad blowdown on the small peak between Algonquin Pass and Marshall, however, makes Herbert Brook the best approach to the peak. This brook crosses the red trail 0.74 mi. NE of the Calamity Lean-tos and 0.32 mi. from the Lake Colden dam. An obvious herd path leads up its easterly bank. Follow the brook through the blowdown. Avoid following a tributary entering from the R (going up) about 0.50 mi. up the brook. Open rock slides make the ascent attractive for part of the way. At the head of the brook, near the col one valley SW of Algonquin Pass, head SW for Marshall, staying close to the ridge line.

Another route more practical for a day trip from Heart Lake leaves the yellow Lake Colden-Indian Pass Trail a short distance NW of the height of land in Algonquin Pass between Marshall and Iroquois. Flank the small peak between Algonquin Pass and Marshall on its NW side, avoiding the top of the ridge where there is blowdown. Descend to the col between this peak and Marshall and climb SW to the summit. Herd paths on this route are not continuous.

Gray Peak. This mountain, the highest of the trailless peaks, was named by Colvin for Professor Asa Gray, one of the most noted botanists of his day. Climb from the Sanford Lake-Marcy Trail at the outlet of Lake Tear of the Clouds over a ridge into a valley. The route then heads N to the summit ridge, striking it about 200 yds. W of the summit. Another route leads from the lowest extension of timberline on the westerly side of Marcy, dipping to the S of the ridgeline at times to avoid cliffs, but this route involves as much time as taking the longer route via Lake Tear of the Clouds.

Redfield. This peak was named by Colvin for Professor William C. Redfield, meteorologist and organizer of the first expedition to Marcy. It was Redfield who first described Marcy as the "High Peak of Essex" after a reconnaissance up the Opalescent River above Lake Colden before the first ascent in 1837.

Because blowdowns in 1970 made the approach to Redfield from the Cliff-Redfield col very difficult, the best route to Redfield's summit follows Uphill Brook from Uphill Lean-to (see Southern Section) to a point about 0.25 mi. above a high waterfall on the main stream, where a tributary comes in from the R (S). Follow this tributary and then head straight for the summit to avoid bad blowdown on the NE section of the summit ridge.

Another route to Redfield leads from Lake Tear of the Clouds SW to the summit. Stay below the summit ridge until directly under the top of the mountain. There is no continuous herd path on this route.

Cliff. This self-explanatory name was bestowed by Colvin. Start from the height of land between Cliff and Redfield on the now abandoned Sanford Lake-Marcy Trail (see Southern Section). Head W, in general keeping to the R of the higher cliffs. Reaching the northeastern summit, follow the broad ridge SW about 0.5 mi. to the true summit, which rises steeply beyond the col.

Allen. This mountain was named by Reverend Joseph Twichell for his close friend Rev. Frederick B. Allen, who became Superintendent of the Episcopal City Mission in Boston. The naming took place on a camping trip to the Upper Ausable Lake with Charles Dudley Warner and Dr. Horace Bushnell when they were caught in the great cloudburst of August 20, 1869. This was the same storm that caused the great landslide on Mt. Colden.

The formerly popular approach to Allen from the trail to Marcy via Hanging Spear Falls and Flowed Lands (See Southern Section) over private land has been closed to the public. The most used route now follows a herd path from the Twin Brook Lean-to on the above-mentioned trail. It begins by heading SW to Lower Twin Brook, which it follows along its NW side. In about a mile, the herd path crosses the brook and heads generally SE, contouring to a low pass. Descending the valley SE of the pass past beaver ponds, the route crosses a sizeable brook shortly before crossing Skylight Brook, to join the old route. Continuing NE up the Skylight Brook valley for some 0.70 mi., the herd path turns SE again, following a tributary, the beautiful Allen Brook, past its source to the ridge top a short distance S of the summit. Allow at least 4 hours from the Twin Brook Lean-to.

Climbing Allen from Skylight as well as from the Elk Lake-Marcy Trail involves travel through blowdown and thick second growth without the aid of herd paths.

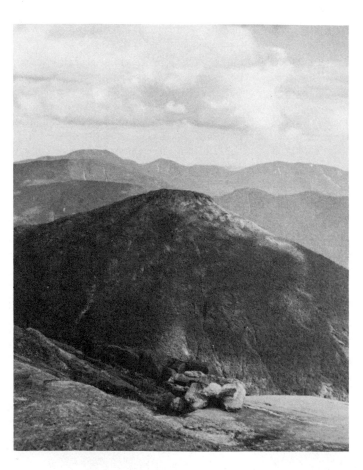

Haystack from Marcy
Photo by H. Hammond

APPENDIX I

GLOSSARY OF TERMS

Bivouac
Camping in the open with improvised shelter or none at all.

Bushwhacking
To make one's way through bushes or undergrowth without the aid of a formal trail.

Cairn
A pile of stones to mark a summit or route.

Chimney
A steep, narrow cleft or gully in the face of a mountain, usually by which it may be ascended.

Cobble
A small stony peak on the side of a mountain.

Col
A pass between two adjacent peaks.

Corduroy
A road, trail or bridge formed by logs laid side by side transversely to facilitate crossing swampy areas.

Couloir
A deep gorge or gully on a hillside.

Cripplebrush
Thick, stunted growth at higher elevations.

Dike
A band of different colored rock, usually with straight, well-defined sides. Formed when igneous rock is intruded into the existing rock. Dikes can manifest themselves either

as gullies if the dike rock is softer (as in the Colden Trap Dike), or as ridges.

Duff   Partly decayed vegetable matter on the forest floor. It can burn easily. Burning duff has started many forest fires.

Lean-to   A three-sided shelter with an over-hanging roof on the open side.

Lumber Road   A crude road constructed for the purpose of hauling logs.

Tote Road   A better road constructed in connection with logging operations and used for hauling supplies to a lumber camp, etc. Often built with corduroy, many of these roads are still evident after 80 years and are often used as the route for present-day trails.

Vlei   A marsh or swampy meadow (pronounced "vly").

APPENDIX II

HIGHEST ONE HUNDRED
ADIRONDACK MOUNTAIN PEAKS

In order to stimulate greater interest in the very substantial outlying mountainous area, a list of the highest 100 mountains in the Adirondacks has been prepared. It is presented with the idea of making hikers aware of the many possibilities for interesting and worthwhile climbs and explorations in all parts of the Adirondack Park. It is not presented with the idea that one should climb them all, or form a club. Forty of the new listings are presently trailless, and some are privately owned, with permission needed to climb.

Heading the list are the original 46 high peaks. These were all originally thought to be at least 4000 ft. high by early surveys, but more recent surveys have lowered several of these peaks. These original 46 peaks are, however, still the peaks recognized by the Adirondack Forty-Sixers as the requirement for membership, and they are the group referred to as the "high" or "major" peaks. The criteria for these original 46 peaks were that each peak be at least 3/4 mi. distant from the nearest higher summit, or that it rise at least 300 vertical feet on all sides. In selecting the additional 54 peaks, the criteria used are a 3/4 mi. distance *and* a 300 ft. rise on all sides.

An asterisk in the roster indicates that there is a footnote; the number of the footnote will correspond to the numbr on the roster. Under "Remarks," a "c" following elevation indicates that the elevation shown is that of the highest contour line. The symbol "Tr" indicates that there is presently a standard, maintained trail to the summit. An extra "T" means that there is a fire tower on the summit. A "P" indicates private ownership.

No.	Name	Elev.	Remarks	Topographical Map and Sector
1	Mt. Marcy	5344	Tr	Mt. Marcy (W)
2	Algonquin Peak	5114	Tr	Mt. Marcy (W)
3	Mt. Haystack	4960	Tr	Mt. Marcy (C)
4	Mt. Skylight	4926	Tr	Mt. Marcy (W)
5	Whiteface Mt.	4867	Tr	Lake Placid (C)
6	Dix Mt.	4857	Tr	Mt. Marcy (SE)
7	Gray Peak	4840c		Mt. Marcy (W)
8	Iroquois Peak	4840c		Mt. Marcy (W)
9	Basin Mt.	4827	Tr	Mt. Marcy (C)
10	Gothics	4736	Tr	Mt. Marcy (C)
11	Mt. Colden	4714	Tr	Mt. Marcy (W)
12	Giant Mt.	4627	Tr	Elizabethtown (W)
13	Nipple Top	4620c	Tr	Mt. Marcy (E)
14	Santanoni Peak	4607		Santanoni (C)
15	Mt. Redfield	4606		Mt. Marcy (W)
16	Wright Peak	4580	Tr	Mt. Marcy (W)
17	Saddleback Mt.	4515	Tr	Mt. Marcy (C)
18	Panther Peak	4442		Santanoni (C)
19	Table Top Mt.	4427		Mt. Marcy (C)
20	Rocky Peak Ridge	4420c	Tr	Elizabethtown (W)
21	Macomb Mt.	4405		Mt. Marcy (SE)
22	Armstrong Mt.	4400c	Tr	Mt. Marcy (C)
23	Hough Peak	4400c		Mt. Marcy (SE)
24	Seward Mt.	4361		Santanoni (W)
25*	Mt. Marshall	4360		Santanoni (E)
26	Allen Mt.	4340c		Mt. Marcy (SE)
27	Big Slide Mt.	4240c	Tr	Mt. Marcy (N)
28	Esther Mt.	4240		Lake Placid (C)
29*	Upper Wolf Jaw Mt.	4185	Tr	Mt. Marcy (C)

30*	Lower Wolf Jaw Mt.	4175	Tr	Mt. Marcy (C)
31	Street Mt.	4166		Santanoni (NE)
32	Phelps Mt.	4161	Tr	Mt. Marcy (W)
33	Mt. Donaldson	4140		Santanoni (W)
34	Seymour Mt.	4120		Santanoni (W)
35*	Sawteeth	4100c	Tr	Mt. Marcy (C)
36	Cascade Mt.	4098	Tr	Mt. Marcy (N)
37	South Dix	4060	Tr	Mt. Marcy (SE)
38	Porter Mt.	4059	Tr.	Mt. Marcy (N)
39	Mt. Colvin	4057	Tr	Mt. Marcy (C)
40	Mt. Emmons	4040		Santanoni (W)
41	Dial Mt.	4020	Tr	Mt. Marcy (E)
42	East Dix	4012		Mt. Marcy (SE)
43*	Blake Peak	3960c	Tr	Mt. Marcy (S)
44	Cliff Mt.	3960c		Mt. Marcy (W)
45	Nye Mt.	3895		Santanoni (NE)
46	Couchsachraga Peak	3820		Santanoni (C)
47	MacNaughton Mt.	4000		Santanoni (E)
48	Green Mt.	3980c		Elizabethtown (NW)
49*	Peak, Unnamed (Lost Pond)	3900c		Santanoni (E)
50*	Moose Mt.	3899		Saranac Lake (E)
51	Snowy Mt.	3899	TrT	Indian Lake (N)
52	Kilburn Mt.	3892		Lake Placid (S)
53*	Sawtooth Mts. (No. 1)	3877		Santanoni (W)
54	Panther Mt.	3865		Indian Lake (N)
55	McKenzie Mt.	3861	Tr	Saranac Lake (E)
56	Blue Ridge	3860c		Indian Lake (W)
57	North River Mt.	3860c		Mt. Marcy (SW)
58	Sentinel Mt.	3838		Lake Placid (S)
59	Lyon Mt.	3830	TrT	Lyon Mt. (N)

60*	Sawtooth Mts. (No. 2)	3820c		Santanoni (N)
61*	Peak, Unnamed (Indian Falls)	3820c		Mt. Marcy (W)
62	Averill Peak	3810		Lyon Mt.
63	Avalanche Mt.	3800c		Mt. Marcy (W)
64	Buell Mt.	3786		Indian Lake (N)
65*	Boreas Mt.	3776	TrT	Mt. Marcy (S)
66	Blue Mt.	3760c	TrT	Blue Mt. (C)
67	Wakely Mt.	3760c	TrT	W. Canada Lakes (NE)
68	Henderson Mt.	3752		Santanoni (C)
69	Lewey Mt.	3742		Indian Lake (W)
70*	Sawtooth Mts. (No. 3)	3700c		Santanoni (N)
71	Wallface Mt.	3700c		Santanoni (E)
72*	Hurricane Mt.	3694	TrT	Elizabethtown (NW)
73	Hoffman Mt.	3693		Schroon Lake (E)
74	Cheney Cobble	3683		Mt. Marcy (SW)
75	Calamity Mt.	3620c		Santanoni (E)
76	Little Moose Mt.	3620c		W. Canada Lakes (NE)
77*	Sunrise Mt.	3614	TrP	Mt. Marcy (SE)
78	Stewart Mt.	3602		Lake Placid (S)
79*	Jay Mts.	3600		Ausable Forks (SW)
80	Pitchoff Mt.	3600c	Tr	Mt. Marcy (N)
81	Saddleback Mt.	3600c		Ausable Forks (SW)
82	Pillsbury Mt.	3597	TrT	W. Canada Lakes (SE)
83	Slide Mt.	3584		Lake Placid (S)
84	Gore Mt.	3583	TrT	Thirteenth Lake (NE)
85	Dun Brook Mt.	3580c		Blue Mt. (E)
86	Noonmark Mt.	3556	Tr	Mt. Marcy (E)
87*	Mt. Adams	3540c	T	Santanoni (E)
88	Fishing Brook Mt.	3540c		Blue Mt. (NE)

89	Little Santanoni Mt.	3500c	Santanoni (SW)
90	Blue Ridge	3497	Blue Mt. (SW)
91*	Peak (Fishing Brook Range)	3480c	Blue Mt. (NE)
92	Puffer Mt.	3472	Thirteenth Lake (W)
93*	Sawtooth Mts. (No. 4)	3460c	Santanoni (N)
94*	Sawtooth Mts. (No. 5)	3460c	Santanoni (N)
95	Wolf Pond Mt.	3460c	Schroon Lake (N)
96	Cellar Mt.	3447	W. Canada Lakes (NE)
97*	Blue Ridge Mt.	3440c	Schroon Lake (NE)
98*	Morgan Mt.	3440c	Lake Placid (N)
99	Blue Ridge	3436	Raquette Lake (SE)
100*	Peak, Unnamed (Brown Pond)	3425	Indian Lake (N)

*25. **Mt. Marshall.** This is shown as Mt. Clinton on the 1953 map. Formerly known as Herbert Mt., Clinton was officially named Mt. Marshall for Robert Marshall in 1942. It is shown as Mt. Marshall on the 1978 "Ampersand Lake" 7.5-by-15 minute metric map.

29 and 30. **The Wolf Jaws.** The map reads Wolfjaw. Since frog leg is two words, it is assumed that wolf jaw is too. Early mountaineers used a single hyphenated word.

35. **Sawteeth.** This mountain was named for the profile of its several summit nubbles, which were said to resemble the teeth of a great saw. Sawtooth as shown on the 1953 map is incorrect but has been corrected on the 1978 "Mt. Marcy" 7.5-by-15 minute metric map.

43. **Blake Peak.** Blake Peak rather than Blake Mt. is the name

in common use.

49. **Peak, Unnamed (Lost Pond).** This mountain is easily located since Lost Pond lies practically on its summit. The coordinates are 44 degrees 10'N x 70 degrees 02'W.

50. **Moose Mt.** (St. Armand Mt. on sign boards.) In spite of signs pointing to trails up this mountain, and several recent maps showing trails, there is no trail. See Northern Section for information on routes up this peak.

53. **Sawtooth Mts.** The Sawtooths comprise a large, completely wild area southeast of Ampersand Mountain. It is a region of many knobs, five of which qualify for the list. These have been numbered from one to five in order of descending altitude. Numbers 4 and 5 are the same height, but No. 4 is much more massive. The highest peak, elevation 3877 ft., is central to the region. The coordinates are 44 degrees 11'N x 70 degrees 07'W.

60. **Sawtooth Mts. (No. 2).** The 3820-ft. twin knobs of this summit mark the N end of a three-step ridge which lies W of the main 3877-ft. peak. The coordinates are 44 degrees 11'N x 74 degrees 08'W.

61. **Peak, Unnamed (Indian Falls).** Lying to the NW of Indian Falls on the trail from Marcy Dam to Mt. Marcy, the coordinates are 44 degrees 08'N x 73 degrees 56'W.

65. **Boreas Mt.** The fire tower has been abandoned for many years, is officially closed, and is of questionable safety.

70. **Sawtooth Mts. (No. 3).** Lying ½ mi. W of the Essex County line, this 3700-ft. peak marks the SE threshold of the Sawtooths. The coordinates are 44 degrees 10'N x 74 degrees 07'W.

72. **Hurricane Mt.** The fire tower has recently been abandoned and may be removed in the near future.

77. **Sunrise Mt.** The trail to this summit is mostly on private land and is closed to the public. One can approach without a trail from the E on public land, or one might try asking permission at Elk Lake Lodge to ascend the trail.

79. **Jay Mts.** The 1953 map shows a 3340-ft. peak W of Grassy Notch for Jay Mt. This is believed to be an error.

87. **Mt. Adams.** The fire tower on this peak has been abandoned for many years, is officially closed, and is of questionable safety. The trail has not been maintained for several years, but is still followable.

91. **Peak (Fishing Brook Range).** This 3480-ft. unnamed peak marks the end of a long ridge leading SW from Fishing Brook Mt., 43 degrees 55′N x 74 degrees 19′W.

93. **Sawtooth Mts. (No. 4).** This 3460-ft. peak at the NW end of the Sawtooths lies about a mile SSE of Beaver Pond. Coordinates, 44 degrees 12′N x 74 degrees 10′W.

94. **Sawtooth Mts. (No. 5).** Also 3460 ft., this summit is found about 1 mi. NE of the pass between Ward Brook and Cold River country. Coordinates, 44 degrees 11′N x 74 degrees 03′W.

97. **Blue Ridge Mt. (Schroon Lake Map).** The 2825 ft. elevation shown for this mountain on the 1953 map is incorrect.

98. **Morgan Mt.** The DEC has recently reopened the trail to Cooper Kiln Pond which passes just to the N of the summit.

100. **Peak, Unnamed (Brown Pond).** This 3425-ft. peak is found about 3½ mi. ENE of Wakely Dam. Brown Pond lies in a slight depression on its westerly slope. The coordinates are 43 degrees 44′N x 74 degrees 25′W.

APPENDIX III

LEAN-TOS IN THE HIGH PEAKS REGION

The following is a listing of all lean-tos within the area covered by this guidebook. They are listed according to the six different sections, with information on USGS map and location.

Shelter	USGS Map	Location
KEENE VALLEY SECTION		
Bear Brook	Mt. Marcy	1 mi. W of Garden on Phelps Trail
Deer Brook	Mt. Marcy	1.5 mi. W of Garden on Phelps Trail
Wm. G. Howard	Mt. Marcy	On Phelps Trail near DEC Interior Outpost
Wolf Jaws	Mt. Marcy	On ADK Range Trail on side of the Wolf Jaws
Orebed Brook	Mt. Marcy	On Range Trail 2 mi. from DEC Interior Outpost
Johns Brook Lodge	Mt. Marcy	On Phelps Trail 1000 ft. W of JBL
Hogback	Mt. Marcy	On Phelps Trail, 1 mi. from JBL
Bushnell Falls No. 1	Mt. Marcy	On Phelps Trail at junction with Hopkins Trail
Bushnell Falls Nos. 2 & 3	Mt. Marcy	On R bank of Johns Brook near Bushnell Falls

| Slant Rock | Mt. Marcy | On Phelps Trail, 1.75 mi. beyond Bushnell Falls |

ST. HUBERTS SECTION

| Boquet River | Mt. Marcy | On Dix Trail, 2.5 mi. below the summit of Dix |

HEART LAKE SECTION

Marcy Dam Nos. 1 to 6	Mt. Marcy	At Marcy Dam, 2.2 mi. from Adirondak Loj
Hudowalski	Mt. Marcy	S shore of pond at Marcy Dam
Phelps	Mt. Marcy	On Van Hoevenberg Trail, 0.65 mi. above Marcy Dam
Kagel	Mt. Marcy	On Marcy Brook near trail to Avalanche Pass
Marcy Brook	Mt. Marcy	On trail to Avalanche Pass
Avalanche Nos. 1 & 2	Mt. Marcy	At junction of Lake Arnold Trail on trail to Avalanche Pass
Beaver Point	Mt. Marcy	On SW side of Lake Colden
Cedar Point	Mt. Marcy	On SW side of Lake Colden
Colden Dam	Mt. Marcy	At S end of Lake Colden near dam at outlet

Winacomac	Mt. Marcy	On R bank of Opalescent River above Lake Colden Outlet
Opalescent Nos. 1 & 2	Mt. Marcy	On L bank of Opalescent River 0.2 mi. below Lake Colden Outlet
Rocky Falls	Mt. Marcy	Off Indian Pass Trail, 2.5 mi. from Heart Lake on L bank of Indian Pass Brook
Scott Clearing	Santanoni	On Indian Pass Trail, 4 mi. from Heart Lake

NORTHERN SECTION

Whiteface Brook	Lake Placid	On Connery Pond Trail, .75 mi. above Whiteface Landing
Whiteface Mt.	Lake Placid	On Wilmington Trail just below junction with highway
Cooper Kiln Pond	Lake Placid	At Cooper Kiln Pond, 2.75 mi. from Franklin Falls Rd.
Taylor Pond Nos. 1 & 2	Lake Placid	SE bay of Taylor Pond
Taylor Pond No. 3	Lake Placid	SW bay of Taylor Pond
Copperas Pond No. 1	Lake Placid	On S shore of Copperas Pond
Copperas Pond No. 2	Lake Placid	On N shore of Copperas Pond

South Notch	Lake Placid	At end of South Notch Trail
Placid	Saranac Lake	On trail to McKenzie Mt.
Wanika Falls	Santanoni	On N-P Trail, 6.5 mi. from Averyville Rd.
Moose Pond	Santanoni	On N-P Trail, 8 mi. from Averyville Rd. and 4 mi. from Duck Hole

EASTERN SECTION

Poke-o-Moonshine	Ausable Forks	At saddle just below summit
Biesemeyer Memorial	Ausable Forks	On Lost Pond
Gulf Brook	Ausable Forks	On N trail to Hurricane, 1 mi. from Crow Clearing
Hurricane Mt.	Elizabethtown	SE side of Hurricane near observer's cabin
Giant	Elizabethtown	On N side of Giant, 1.75 mi. below the summit

SOUTHERN SECTION

Slide Brook	Mt. Marcy	On Dix Trail, 2.5 mi. from Elk Lake
Lillian Brook	Mt. Marcy	On Dix Trail, 3.75 mi. from Elk Lake
Panther Gorge	Mt. Marcy	On Elk Lake-Marcy Trail, 9 mi. from Elk Lake

Calamity Nos. 1 & 2	Mt. Marcy	On Calamity Brook Trail on W side of Flowed Lands
Twin Brook	Mt. Marcy	On Hanging Spear Falls Trail, 5 mi. from Upper Works
Gorge	Mt. Marcy	On Hanging Spear Falls Trail on L bank of Opalescent River
Griffin	Mt. Marcy	At Flowed Lands Dam
Livingston Point	Mt. Marcy	On a point on SE side of Flowed Lands
Flowed Lands	Mt. Marcy	On a point on SW side of Flowed Lands near Hanging Spear Falls Trail
Henderson	Santanoni	On Indian Pass Trail, 1.75 mi. from Upper Works
Wallface	Santanoni	On Indian Pass Trail, 2.75 mi. from Upper Works
Duck Hole Nos. 1 & 2	Santanoni	On NE shore of Duck Hole
Santanoni (Bradley Pond)	Santanoni	On Bradley Pond Trail, 4.5 mi. from Upper Works road
Cold River Nos. 1 & 2	Santanoni	On Ward Brook Truck Trail, 1.25 mi. W of Duck Hole
Number 4 — Nos. 1 & 2	Santanoni	On Ward Brook Truck Trail, 6 mi. from Coreys

Ward Brook	Santanoni	On Ward Brook Truck Trail, 5.25 mi. from Coreys
Blueberry	Santanoni	On trail from Coreys, 1000 ft. W of Ward Brook Truck Trail
Calkins Brook	Long Lake	On Calkins Brook Truck Trail between Coreys and Shattuck Clearing
Raquette Falls	Long Lake	E bank of Raquette River at Raquette Falls Carry
Raquette Falls Nos. 1 & 2	Long Lake	E bank of Raquette River below Raquette Falls
Hemlock Knoll	Long Lake	E bank of Raquette River
Stony Creek	Long Lake	E bank of Raquette River at junction with Stony Creek
Calkins Creek	Long Lake	On Cold River at junction of Calkins Brook
Catlin Bay Nos. 1 & 2	Long Lake	Near N-P Trail on E shore of Long Lake
Kelley's Point Nos. 1 & 2	Long Lake	Near N-P Trail on E shore of Long Lake
Rodney Point Nos. 1 & 2	Long Lake	Near N-P Trail on E shore of Long Lake

Plumleys Nos. 1 & 2	Long Lake	Near N-P Trail on E shore of Long Lake, where N-P Trail leaves the shore of the lake
Cold River Nos. 3 & 4	Long Lake	On R bank of Cold River near Shattuck Clearing where N-P crosses Cold River
Seward	Santanoni	On N-P Trail at Millers Falls on Cold River
Ouluska	Santanoni	On N-P Trail below Rondeau's "Hermitage"
Moose Pond Stream Nos. 1 & 2	Santanoni	On Cold River Horse Trail, 1.5 mi. from Shattuck Clearing
Northern Nos. 1 & 2	Santanoni	On Cold River Horse Trail, 2 mi. S of Ward Brook Truck Trail
Ward Pond Brook	Santanoni	On N shore of Newcomb Lake
Newcomb Lake	Santanoni	On S shore of Newcomb Lake

APPENDIX IV

STATE CAMPGROUNDS
NEAR THE HIGH PEAKS REGION

Public campgrounds have been established by the DEC at many attractive spots throughout the state. Listed below are those campgrounds which might be useful as bases of operations for hiking in the High Peaks Region. A complete listing of all campgrounds is contained in a brochure of New York State Forest Preserve Public Campgrounds titled "Come Back Next Summer." This brochure is available from the DEC, 50 Wolf Rd., Albany, N.Y. 12233.

Below are the campgrounds near the High Peaks Region, listed generally from S to N:

Paradox Lake. Entered from Rt. 74, which meets Rt. 9 2 mi. N of Schroon Lake Village. Hiking trails, boating, fishing. A small campground.

Sharp Bridge. On Rt. 9, 7 mi. N of the village of North Hudson. A fine place to camp, with fishing and swimming in the Schroon River.

Lake Harris. 3 mi. N of Rt. 28N in Newcomb. A good base for hiking in the Santanoni Preserve and Sanford Lake areas.

Lake Eaton. On Rt. 30, 2 mi. W of Long Lake.

Fish Creek and Rollins Pond Campgrounds. On Rt. 30, 12 mi. E of Tupper Lake. Two large campgrounds with good boating and swimming.

Meacham Lake. On Rt. 30, 19 mi. N of Lake Clear Jct.

Buck Pond. Between Rt. 30 and Rt. 3 near Onchiota on Rainbow Lake.

Meadowbrook. On Rt. 86, 4 mi. E of Saranac Lake in Ray Brook. A convenient stopping point in the area.

Wilmington Notch. On Rt. 86, in a picturesque setting 3.5 mi. W of Wilmington on the W Branch of the Ausable River.

Poke-o-Moonshine. On Rt. 9, 12 mi. N of Elizabethtown.

INDEX

Note: Lakes are listed under their names instead of under "Lake."

298

304

OTHER PUBLICATIONS OF
THE ADIRONDACK MOUNTAIN CLUB, INC.
172 Ridge Street
Glens Falls, N.Y. 12801
(518) 793-7737

Guidebooks

ADIRONDACK CANOE WATERS: NORTH FLOW
by Paul Jamieson
> Definitive guide to 700 miles of canoe routes in St. Lawrence and
> Lake Champlain drainage basins

*ADIRONDACK CANOE WATERS: SOUTH AND WEST
FLOW* by Alec Proskine
> Guide to the canoe waters of the Black River Basin, the Mohawk
> Basin, the Upper Hudson Basin and the two major streams of the
> Tug Hill Plateau

AN ADIRONDACK SAMPLER by Bruce Wadsworth
> Fifty day hikes throughout the Adirondack Park; includes
> winter hikes for the snowshoer

AN ADIRONDACK SAMPLER II by Bruce Wadsworth
> Twenty-five backpacking trips throughout the Adirondack Park

GUIDE TO THE EASTERN ADIRONDACKS
by Barbara McMartin
> Hiking trails of the Lake George Region, the Pharaoh Lake
> Wilderness Area, and more

GUIDE TO THE NORTHVILLE-PLACID TRAIL
revised by Bruce Wadsworth
> Detailed description and guide to the 133-mile Northville-Placid
> Trail

ADK PUBLICATIONS

*GUIDE TO THE TRAILS OF THE WEST-CENTRAL
ADIRONDACKS* by Robert J. Redington
   Hiking trails and canoe route from Old Forge area to Blue
   Mountain Lake

NORTHERN ADIRONDACK SKI TOURS by Tony Goodwin
   Thirty selected tours for the novice to expert, from easy jaunts to
   multi-day tours

Natural History

THE ADIRONDACK LANDSCAPE by Jerome Wyckoff
   Complete hiker's guide to common High Peak land formations

TREES OF THE ADIRONDACK HIGH PEAK REGION
by E.H. Ketchledge
   Hiker's identification guide to trees in the Forest Preserve

*ROCK SCENERY OF THE HUDSON HIGHLANDS AND
PALISADES* by Jerome Wyckoff
   Guide to the geology of southern New York State

BIRDLIFE OF THE ADIRONDACK PARK by Bruce Beehler
   Complete text for researcher, includes descriptions of 261 species

How-To

WINTER HIKING AND CAMPING by John Danielsen
   Authoritative basic manual on winter wilderness excursions

General Reading

PEAKS AND PEOPLE OF THE ADIRONDACKS
by Russell Carson
   Geography and lore of the Adirondack High Peaks

ADK PUBLICATIONS

THE ADIRONDACK READER edited by Paul Jamieson
   An anthology of the best writings about the region

TALES FROM THE SHAWANGUNK MOUNTAINS
by Marc B. Fried
   A naturalist's musings, a bushwhacker's guide

Maps

Trails of the Adirondack High Peaks Region
   USGS quads of Marcy, Santanoni, half of Elizabethtown; plus
   7.5′ by 15′ quads of Lake Placid, Wilmington, Lewis and Saranac
   Lake

Old Roads and Open Peaks of the Sacandaga Region
   Portions of USGS quads of Indian Lake, Thirteenth Lake,
   North Creek, Lake Pleasant, Harrisburg, Lake Luzerne

Trails of the West-Central Adirondacks
   Old Forge area to Blue Mountain Lake

Price List available upon request.